BATTLES
OF THE
BIBLE
1400 BC ~ AD 73

BATTLES
OF THE
BIBLE
1400 BC ~ AD 73

FROM AI TO MASADA

MARTIN J. DOUGHERTY   MICHAEL E. HASKEW   PHYLLIS G. JESTICE   ROB S. RICE

METRO BOOKS
NEW YORK

This 2008 edition published by Metro Books,
by arrangement with Amber Books.

Metro Books
122 Fifth Avenue
New York, NY 10011

Editorial and design by
Amber Books Ltd

Project Editor: Michael Spilling
Picture Research: Kate Green
Design: Joe Conneally

ISBN-13: 978-0-7607-9367-1
ISBN-10: 0-7607-9367-0

Printed and bound in Dubai

10 9 8 7 6 5 4 3 2 1

CONTENTS

INTRODUCTION

THE EARLIEST ACCOUNT OF A MILITARY CAMPAIGN THAT HAS SURVIVED ANYWHERE IN THE WORLD TELLS OF AN EGYPTIAN INVASION OF CANAAN IN THE TWENTY-FOURTH CENTURY BC. THIS TERRITORY ON THE EASTERN FRINGE OF THE MEDITERRANEAN WAS DESTINED FOR A LONG, OFTEN BITTERLY FOUGHT HISTORY, A SAGA OF VIOLENCE THAT CONTINUES UP TO THE PRESENT DAY. WHETHER RULED BY CANAANITES, PHILISTINES, ISRAELITES, ASSYRIANS, BABYLONIANS, GREEKS OR ROMANS, THE TERRITORY THAT GEOGRAPHERS TEND TO CALL 'PALESTINE' IN IMITATION OF THE ROMANS WAS NOT IN ITSELF PARTICULARLY RICH OR POPULOUS. ITS LOCATION, HOWEVER, GUARANTEED THAT PALESTINE WOULD BE A TEMPTING PRIZE FOR A WIDE ARRAY OF WOULD-BE CONQUERORS.

The prototypical armoured fighting vehicle. This Egyptian two-man chariot dates from the thirteenth century BC. Egyptian chariots tended to be lighter, faster and less stable than their Hittite counterparts.

Palestine forms the main land bridge between Eurasia and Africa, and also controls access to the Mediterranean from Mesopotamia. At the same time, geography hindered the people of the region from forming a state strong enough to confront the empires of the ancient world, making the history of the region a litany of repeated conquest and resistance to foreign rule.

When the region of Palestine first appears in historical records, its occupants were a Semitic people, the Canaanites (also known as Phoenicians), who formed a number of independent city-states. Palestine was well suited to such fragmented political formations, thanks to its great geographical diversity. The region has an enormous range in altitude, from Mount Hermon, which stands 2774m (9100ft) above sea level, to the Dead Sea, which lies 389m (1275ft) below it. The land is broken up into different climatic spheres, with a coastal plain, a belt of hill country,

the deep rift of the Jordan Valley (which runs north–south, dividing Palestine in two), and the plateau of Transjordan. The early Canaanite towns mostly occupied the coastal plain.

To the south of Canaan lay Egypt, to its east Mitanni and to the north the Hittites. All three large states wanted to control the Palestinian land bridge, as did the Hyksos, a more mysterious Semitic people who conquered northern Egypt in the eighteenth century BC. The Canaanite city-states were able to maintain a tenuous independence only because of their skill at playing off the rivalries between the great empires. In the process, they adopted new military technologies.

For example, the Hyksos introduced the war chariot to the region in the eighteenth century BC, along with the composite bow and perhaps also the sickle 'sword'. The sickle sword was, in fact, more closely akin to the axe than the sword, but was a great improvement over traditional war axes, since haft and blade were cast together as a

single piece and thus could not come apart in battle. For the next millennium, the war chariot provided the elite striking force of armies in the region, usually employed tactically as a mobile fighting platform from which archers could shoot.

After driving the Hyksos invaders from their land, the Egyptian pharaohs of the New Kingdom launched a much more aggressive policy toward Palestine, determined to hold the region as a buffer zone to prevent future invasion. This brought the Egyptians into direct conflict with the Hittites, who were expanding southward at the same time. The first battle account that provides enough detail to reconstruct the chain of events was fought in Palestine between Egypt and the Hittites, the Battle of Kadesh in 1274 BC.

ARRIVAL OF THE HEBREWS

The biblical history of Palestine begins in the thirteenth century BC, when most scholars agree that the Hebrews, a nomadic people ethnically and linguistically akin to the Canaanites, began to occupy the region.

The territory that they infiltrated was in deep disarray at the time. Most of the Canaanite cities had been overrun and destroyed by the Sea Peoples, seaborne marauders who disrupted the entire eastern Mediterranean world in the thirteenth century BC.

The Sea Peoples had also brought down the mighty Hittite Empire of Anatolia and severely weakened Egypt. Some of the Sea Peoples eventually settled on the southern coast of Palestine, where they were known as Philistines. They did not, however, penetrate far inland. Consequently, a power vacuum existed at the time of the Hebrew occupation.

The Hebrew settlement of Palestine, as narrated in the biblical book of Joshua, leaves much to be desired as an account of military action – detailed military descriptions were not of central interest to the author. Between the biblical account and modern archaeology, though, it is possible to reconstruct the broad lines of the process. It is clear that the Hebrews did not have a sophisticated fighting force. The

Warfare as described in the Bible almost always had an ideological element, since the Israelites' enemies were polytheists, as shown in this twelfth-century BC Egyptian painting of Ramses III worshiping his gods.

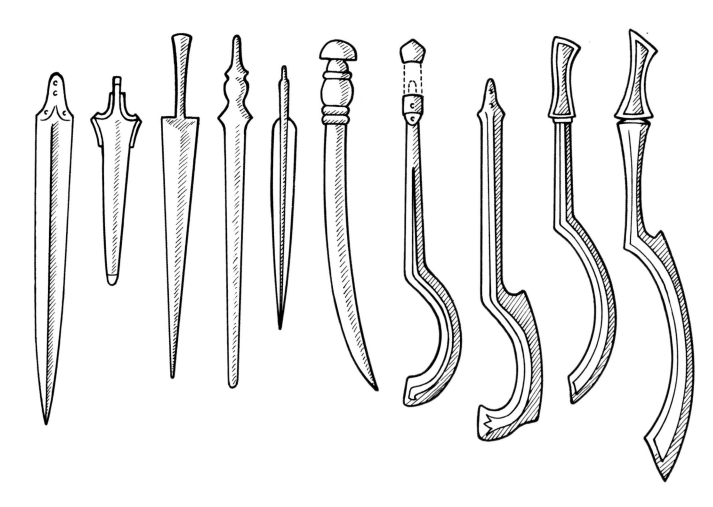

A selection of Bronze Age and early Iron Age cutting weapons used in the ancient Near East, ranging from early sickle swords on the right to more advanced long daggers on the left.

warriors did not have chariot forces, and appear to have relied on slings rather than more sophisticated bows for distance fighting. They were, however, skilled at the ruses of war, taking advantage of topography to lessen the advantage of their more numerous and better-organized enemies. For instance, at the Battle of Megiddo the Israelites faced a Canaanite force, commanded by Sisera, which included a substantial chariot squadron. The Israelite commander Barak occupied the hilly ground where the chariots could not advance, descending on the chariots in a surprise attack only at a time of heavy rain, when the chariots got bogged down.

The Hebrews' greatest disadvantage in their efforts to establish themselves in Palestine was that they did not understand siege warfare – and Canaan was a land of walled cities. They certainly took some Canaanite fortifications, such as Jericho, although historians have debated for generations about what military realities might lie behind the biblical account of processions around the city until 'the walls came a-tumblin' down'. In general,

however, the fortified Canaanite cities were not conquered for up to 300 years, the Hebrews settling instead in the sparsely populated highlands.

It is also clear that early Israelite warfare was a vicious process, with little pity for defeated enemies. Modern readers who are shocked by tales of Assyrian atrocities would do well to remember that the Israelites, too, frequently slew captive men, women and children, as occurred when Joshua's army took Jericho.

THE PHILISTINE MENACE
The Philistine city-states along the south coast were a greater challenge and threat. Philistine military technology was advanced, and included the first true slashing sword (the Naue Type II), which had rendered the Sea Peoples so deadly throughout the eastern Mediterranean. By the time they came into active conflict with the Hebrew hill-men, the Philistines had weapons made of iron. Philistines apparently even made common use of metal armour consisting of vertical strips, which provided basic protection from bronze

weapons. By contrast, Israelite equipment was very simple: daggers, swords, armour and even bows were rare in that period. David's legendary confrontation with the gigantic Goliath, armed only with a sling, may not be far from the reality of early Israelite forces. The early armies, under the Judges (who exercised a loose, prophetic authority over the Israelite tribes), consisted of the personal war bands of leaders, along with tribal levies.

By about 1020 BC, the Hebrews were in such danger of being overrun by the Philistines that the hitherto independent tribes united under a single war leader, Saul. Saul began a large-scale military reorganization, continued by his successors, which abruptly militarized and modernized the new state of Israel. The new king built up an army of some 3000 men, the first

steps towards the creation of a professional fighting force in the new state. Saul and his son Jonathan enjoyed some success against the Philistines, but their military organization could still not match the Philistines in battle; Saul's military career ended abruptly at the Battle of Mount Gilboa, at which he was defeated and killed along with three of his sons. His body and that of his son Jonathan were hung from the town wall as an eloquent demonstration of what the Philistines thought of their Israelite enemies.

Saul's successor, King David (c.1002–c.970 BC), built on his predecessor's successes and his own experience as the leader of a bandit force to make Israel into a thoroughly militarized state. The Bible is firm in crediting David with the creation of the first Israelite army to be competitive

The Negev Desert on the Israel/Egypt frontier still gives a good impression of the challenges that faced chariot warriors in parts of ancient Israel. The rugged terrain of the Negev also limited invasion from the south.

David's victory over Goliath has come to symbolize the victory of the 'little man' over a better-armed and stronger foe, as in this fifteenth-century bronze relief by Lorenzo Ghiberti.

among the more ancient political units that operated on the Near Eastern stage. This development was essentially a matter of state organization: the state of Israel became complex enough to be able to collect men, arm them and pay them. David's army included large numbers of mercenaries, who brought a new military discipline and expertise to the land. The infantry was apparently armed with spears and javelins, and swords also became common, at least for the elites. The composite bow was perhaps introduced as early as David's reign, although archaeologists have discovered lead shot from much later periods, suggesting that the sling also remained a popular weapon. Defensive armour – helmets, shields, and even bronze or iron scale armour – also came into use.

Using this new force as the nucleus for a military establishment that also included local levies, David began a rapid expansion of his small state, doubtless using the profits

of each conquest to continue his military reorganization. One of David's major coups was the conquest of Jerusalem, a strongly fortified and inaccessible upland town that became his capital.

David's broad strategy was apparently to plan his military campaigns in concentric rings from Jerusalem. He succeeded in defeating the Philistine city-states of the coast. To the southeast, he conquered the land of Edom, placing it under direct Israelite rule.

In all, David extended the borders of Israel to the greatest extent the state ever enjoyed, taking advantage of disorder in the surrounding states. The biblical accounts relate that, by the end of his reign, David had even created a chariot force – a sign that the state was now prepared to compete militarily with the much older and more established states of the region. David's son Solomon (c.970–931 BC) consolidated his father's conquests. He is credited with building up a series of fortifications and a chariot corps. By the end of Solomon's reign, however, the people of Israel apparently deeply resented the constant royal demands for money and manpower for the army and building projects.

HISTORY AND THE BIBLE

In recent decades, historians have debated many points in the history of early Israel, including the military rise of the Davidic kingdom. On one side of the controversy, scholars such as Mordechai Gichon have argued that the Bible is basically accurate in its accounts of early Israelite warfare. Their argument is based above all on the geographical and tactical specificity of the biblical record: such accurate accounts, they say, could not have been made up at a much later date.

Other historians and archaeologists, however, have pointed to the evidence that the Old Testament accounts were written centuries after the events they describe, and question the ability of folk memory to pass down accurate accounts for so long by word of mouth. Even more tellingly, archaeologists have found very little trace of David and Solomon's supposedly great kingdom. They have suggested that David was little more than a guerrilla leader in the hill country, who later acquired the status of folk-hero.

In general, however, the biblical account of Israel's military rise is not implausible, even if one accepts the possibility of some exaggeration. The books of Joshua and Judges may have telescoped events, but certainly display warfare at a very simple level, as the Israelites gradually moved from the hill country to engage the Canaanites and Philistines of the coastal plain. Greater military sophistication would not have been possible before the creation of a state that was only likely to coalesce under a threat like that of the Philistines.

We have non-biblical confirmation that King David existed, thanks to a later Assyrian inscription that refers to a Judean king 'of the house of David'. It may be true that the biblical account has credited David and Solomon with some of the accomplishments of their descendants, but the mere creation and survival of the Israelite state was accomplishment enough, carried out as it was so rapidly and under such pressure.

THE DIVIDED MONARCHY

The extremely rapid organization of the state of Israel and its essentially artificial nature can be seen in the fact that, after the death of Solomon in 931 BC, the state rapidly broke apart. Solomon's son Rehoboam became king of the southern region of Judah. When he went north to

This map shows the wars of King David (c.1002–970 BC), including the subjugation of the Negev, the conquest of Jerusalem, the war against Moab and the subjugation of Edom. David successfully established Israel as a force in the region, extending its borders to a greater extent than any leader before or since.

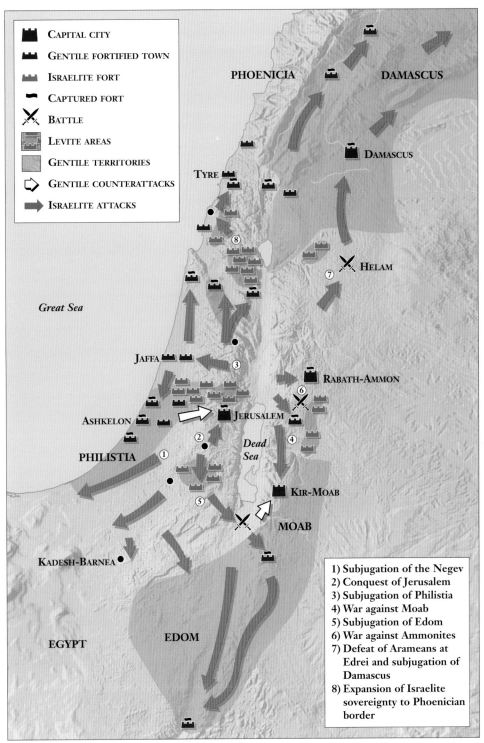

- CAPITAL CITY
- GENTILE FORTIFIED TOWN
- ISRAELITE FORT
- CAPTURED FORT
- BATTLE
- LEVITE AREAS
- GENTILE TERRITORIES
- GENTILE COUNTERATTACKS
- ISRAELITE ATTACKS

PHOENICIA
DAMASCUS
DAMASCUS
TYRE
Great Sea
Helam
JAFFA
RABATH-AMMON
ASHKELON
JERUSALEM
PHILISTIA
Dead Sea
KIR-MOAB
MOAB
KADESH-BARNEA
EGYPT
EDOM

1) Subjugation of the Negev
2) Conquest of Jerusalem
3) Subjugation of Philistia
4) War against Moab
5) Subjugation of Edom
6) War against Ammonites
7) Defeat of Arameans at Edrei and subjugation of Damascus
8) Expansion of Israelite sovereignty to Phoenician border

INTRODUCTION

The united kingdom of Israel reached its height under King Solomon, who built the great Temple in Jerusalem and consolidated his father's conquests. This image is a Victorian impression of what Solomon and his Temple would have looked like.

claim the rest of his inheritance, though, the northern leaders refused to accept him – unless he stopped demanding so much money and labour from the people. Rehoboam refused to make such concessions, the rebel leader Jeroboam organized resistance, and the north broke away to form a separate state of Israel. The stronger and more populous Israel in the north and tiny Judah in the south both continued as monarchies. Both peoples worshipped the same God. But the two states fought each other continuously, the king of neither region ever succeeding in reuniting the divided monarchy.

The northern kingdom of Israel was the stronger of the two states militarily. King

Omri (c.883–872 BC) founded a new capital at Samaria, a strategic site that he fortified heavily. Radiating out from Samaria, Omri created an additional series of fortifications. Such fortified places were key to maintaining independence among the intense rivalries of the Middle East. The Syrians did, in fact, besiege Samaria in the late ninth century BC. They could not break into the city, however, so they settled down to starve the Samaritans into submission. Eventually the Syrians gave up, but by the time they withdrew, the defenders had been driven to cannibalism.

Judah, too, continued to develop militarily, rapidly coming to resemble other small kingdoms of the region. Shortly after the division of the monarchy, Pharaoh Shishak of Egypt invaded. His attack was launched mostly against the northern state of Israel, but King Rehoboam (c.928–911 BC) apparently regarded the attack as a warning and began construction of his own major defensive network. According to 2 Chronicles, he was responsible for building 15 fortified cities, including the formidable Lachish, which guarded the approaches to Jerusalem.

Both Israel and Judah could usually hold their own against their small neighbouring states, although warfare with Damascus and Edom was a frequent occurrence. King Omri was strong enough to arrange a prestigious marriage alliance with one of the Phoenician states of the coast, marrying his son Ahab to Jezebel of Tyre. And Ahab himself was clearly a power in the Middle East. An inscription from the mid-ninth century BC tells us that he could muster 2000 war chariots. Besides the three men needed to operate each chariot, Ahab also had a force of 10,000 infantry at his command. Such a military muster made King Ahab the strongest member of the military coalition described in the inscription – a coalition that was created in an effort to stem the rising aggression of the Assyrian Empire.

THE ASSYRIAN MENACE

The Assyrians were the dominant military power of the Middle East from the creation of the Neo-Assyrian Empire in 911 BC until the destruction of their state in 612 BC. No state in world history, even ancient Sparta, has ever been so completely dominated by warfare. Assyria was devoted to an ideology of war, in which conquests fuelled further military organization and provinces were harshly exploited to provide the manpower and materiel of war. The Assyrian glorification of war can still be seen on the reliefs from Assyrian royal palaces, which depict warfare in all its forms, from the training of armies to the sack of cities and the brutal execution of captives. Incidentally, these reliefs are among historians' best sources for the history of ancient warfare in the biblical lands.

It did not take the Assyrian kings long to turn their eyes towards Palestine. After all, important trade routes passed through Palestine, and the road to Assyria's greatest rival, Egypt, also passed through Palestine. The nature of Assyria's relationship with the nearer Jewish state, Israel, remained ambiguous for a time, however. Shalmaneser III (858–824 BC) began a conquest west of the Euphrates in 852 BC. The bronze gates of Balawat show the Assyrian troops of the time, including chariots with three-man crews, cavalry and infantry (some wearing heavy armour). Shalmaneser's first assault was deterred, however, by a coalition of small states led by Ahab of Israel. When Jehu usurped the throne of Israel, however, he recognized an opportunity and allied with the Assyrians rather than join the coalitions formed against them in 849, 848, and 845 BC.

Successive kings of Israel played complicated and perilous diplomatic games to retain their independence in the face of Assyria's overwhelming power. They also continued to fortify their land – in particular, replacing old-fashioned casemate walls (hollow masonry squares filled in with earth or rubble) with stronger walls of solid stone construction. The rulers of Judah, too, increased their fortifications in the eighth century, against a variety of threats that included Egyptians, Assyrians and their Israelite neighbours.

King Uzziah of Judah (c.786–758 BC) launched a thorough reorganization of the military, which included supplying armaments for the army and ordering improvements in the defences of Jerusalem, his capital. Hezekiah (726–697 BC) went even further, commissioning the excavation of a 518m (1700ft) tunnel that guaranteed secure access to the city's main water supply.

The Assyrian kings could muster field armies of about 50,000 men, an overwhelming force when launched against small states like Israel and Judah. The only possible response to invasion was a defensive one: to retreat behind a city's walls and hope that the enemy would fail to break in. The Assyrians, however, had become masters at the art of siege warfare. Their armies included large contingents of archers and an engineering corps that could break

Assyrian archers, shown in this relief (c. 700 BC) carrying simple bows. Assyrians also used compound bows and are often depicted in siege scenes wearing heavy armour.

West Bank, Israel, in 1991, showing the remains of
ancient Tel-Sabastia and the modern Israeli settlement
of Shavi Shomron in Samaria, as modern Israelis still
designate this territory that belonged in ancient times to
the northern state of Israel, with its capital at Samaria.

into most cities in this land of fortified places. Among their arsenal were special shield-bearers for archers, whose powerful compound bows could easily bring down defenders at the top of a city's wall, as well as more elaborate weapons, such as covered rams and impressive siege towers.

At first, the Assyrian kings were willing to accept the kings of Israel as vassals, but soon the Assyrian kings learned not to trust protestations of loyalty. King Tiglath-Pileser III (745–727 BC) was content to teach rebels a lesson; his successors Shalmaneser V (727–721 BC) and Sargon II

who would be helpful in the Assyrian war effort. Further large-scale deportation followed another Israelite revolt in 720 BC, and Israel ceased to exist as a state.

Sargon II's successor, Sennacherib (704–681 BC), encountered the same difficulties with the southern state of Judah. Kings swore to accept Assyrian overlordship, only to rebel when the opportunity arose. Sennacherib launched a massive invasion in 701 BC to punish the rebels. Although he enjoyed considerable success, taking a large number of Judean fortresses, including Lachish, he had to break short his siege of Jerusalem and return home – perhaps in response to a military threat, although the biblical account suggests a sudden epidemic in his camp. Judah survived, at least nominally, as an independent state until the Babylonian conquest of 586 BC, at which time many Judeans were deported to points far inland, to discourage future rebellion.

PROVINCIAL STATUS

Babylon succeeded Assyria as the great power of the Middle East, but its era of glory was short. Less than 50 years after Babylon's conquest and destruction of

Sennacherib, king of Assyria, seated on his throne. This illustration is copied from the Nineveh reliefs (now in the British Museum) commemorating Sennacherib's victory over the Judaeans at Lachish. The modern copyist has restored the king's head, which was defaced in antiquity, probably shortly after Sennacherib's murder.

(721–705 BC) brought the northern kingdom of Israel to an end, a process that culminated in a three-year siege of Samaria. When the northern capital was captured in 721 BC, Sargon ordered a massive deportation of anyone likely to stir up trouble in the future, as well as craftsmen

INTRODUCTION

This bas-relief from the Arch of Titus in Rome shows Titus' soldiers marching in the triumphal procession that celebrated Titus' suppression of the first Jewish Revolt. They are carrying treasures looted from the Temple of Jerusalem, including the great seven-branch candlestick that stood in the inner sanctuary.

Jerusalem, the Persian Cyrus the Great (559–530 BC) seized Palestine along with the rest of the Babylonian Empire. Cyrus allowed the Judean 'captives' and their descendants to return to their homeland and even to rebuild the Temple in Jerusalem. The region remained subject to a Persian-appointed governor, however, and continued in its status as a quiet backwater for some time. Cyrus's son Cambyses conquered Egypt, but no battles of the campaign were fought in Palestine.

The region changed hands yet again with the invasion of the Macedonian Alexander the Great (356–323 BC). Alexander's initial goal was the liberation of the ethnically Greek coastal city-states of Asia Minor. He soon became convinced, though, that the Persian Empire itself was a

prize within his grasp. Taking advantage of Persian King Darius III's slowness to confront him, Alexander marched down the eastern Mediterranean coast securing the Persian naval bases, most notably the old Phoenician city of Tyre, which held out for seven months against Alexander's siege. For the most part, the provincial towns of Palestine surrendered without a fight. In the confused fighting that followed Alexander's death, the region ended up in the hands of Alexander's General Seleucus, founder of the massive Seleucid Empire – but General Ptolemy, the new Hellenistic ruler of Egypt, also claimed the area.

The two Hellenistic successor states fought no fewer than six 'Syrian Wars' in the period between 274 and 168 BC, during which time Palestine often changed hands.

Much of the fighting was waged at sea for control of the Greek islands, but there were also significant battles fought for control of the coastal towns of Tyre, Sidon and Gaza, and some poorly documented campaigns further inland. The ultimate victor was the Seleucid Empire.

THE MACCABEAN REVOLT

By the time the Syrian Wars came to an end, the Seleucid Empire (an artificial construct in the first place) was coming apart at the seams, with provinces breaking away both in the east and in the west. It was perhaps to inculcate a greater sense of cultural unity that Antiochus IV Epiphanes (175–164 BC) made the decision to force all his subjects to worship the gods of Greece. This naturally led to protests from the Jewish population of Palestine, to which Antiochus responded by desecrating the Temple in Jerusalem and imposing harsh penalties on those who failed to sacrifice to the gods and even on parents who circumcised their sons. Rebellion broke out in 167 BC, led by the Jewish priest Mattathias and his five sons, most notably Judas Maccabeus (whose nickname might mean 'the hammer').

The Maccabees knew that they could not hope to win by conventional military means. The Seleucids employed highly trained professional armies with substantial elephant and cavalry corps in addition to an infantry that fought in a phalanx formation, with ranks of 6m (20ft) spears.

And so, like the first Israelites, Judas Maccabeus and his brothers turned to guerrilla tactics, taking advantage of Palestine's broken terrain to fight a war of surprise attack and military ruses. Although Judas himself was eventually slain in battle against a vastly superior Seleucid army, his brothers continued what had become a full-scale war for independence. In time, they created an independent state under the Hasmonean Dynasty, which survived until 37 BC.

THE ROMAN SETTLEMENT

Hasmonean Judea remained a small and unimportant state, dominated by an imposing neighbour – Rome. As early as 168 BC, a Roman emissary humiliated Antiochus IV in no uncertain terms by ordering him out of Egypt (which he had invaded). Roman interference in Near Eastern affairs became ever more obtrusive, and the Hasmonean kings of Judea soon found themselves client kings of Rome.

However, royal authority became little more than a legal fiction in 63 BC, when the Roman general Pompey the Great (106–48 BC) took a role in the Hasmonean civil war raging at the time. He captured Jerusalem after a two-month siege, imposed tribute, and even desecrated the Temple by entering the Holy of Holies as a sightseer.

Internal divisions remained, and in 37 BC the Romans deposed the last Hasmonean ruler in favour of Herod the Great. Two generations later, Palestine was divided into provinces and placed under the authority of Roman procurators, fairly unimportant officials who seemed appropriate for such a backwater.

The Jews did not take kindly to Roman rule. They rebelled a number of times in the first and second centuries AD, including the Great Revolt of AD 66–73, the Kitos War of AD 115–117, and Bar Kokhba's Revolt (AD 132–135). By the end, Roman forces were everywhere triumphant, despite the Jews' spirited defence at places such as Jerusalem and Masada. The Temple and Jerusalem itself were laid waste, and much of the Jewish population was dispersed throughout the Mediterranean world and the Middle East.

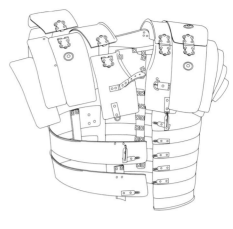

Roman legionaries of the first century BC and first century AD wore lorica segmentata *body armour. The metal plates were held together by hooks and riveted leather straps to create a flexible and effective infantry armour.*

The Macedonian hoplite is considered one of the best ancient infantry soldiers. Carrying a much longer spear than his Greek predecessors, the Macedonian phalanx proved to be effective against all types of armies until the advent of the Roman legions in the the second century BC.

CONQUEST OF AI
C.1400 BC

WITHIN THE RUINS OF A LONG-DESTROYED CITY, THE TRIBES OF ISRAEL MET THEIR FIRST REVERSE AT THE HANDS OF A SMALL AND RESOLUTE BAND OF DEFENDERS. ISRAELITE LEADERSHIP, HOWEVER, PROVED ADEQUATE TO THE UNEXPECTED CHALLENGE.

WHY DID IT HAPPEN?

WHO The wandering tribes of Israel, led by Moses' successor Joshua, moved further into the 'promised land' of the Covenant, encountering unexpectedly strong resistance from a Canaanite outpost among ancient ruins.

WHAT Joshua's scouts provided him with an overoptimistic report that prompted the Israelites to attack. They encountered fierce resistance.

WHERE Ai, 'the ruin', was a thorn in the Israelites' side, lying between Jericho and the newly allied town of Gibeon.

WHEN c.1400 BC, 40 years after the Exodus.

WHY Ai allowed the hostile occupants of Canaan to monitor and interdict the movements of the arriving Israelites. As an isolated outpost, it looked, temptingly to the Israelites, like an easy victory.

OUTCOME The defenders of the garrison were initially successful in driving back the Israelite attackers and so became overconfident. Joshua, through clever military tactics, drew them out and overwhelmingly crushed them.

A good leader – and Joshua was one – knows the importance of maintaining momentum in any undertaking. Jericho lay in ruins. By pressing their advantage, the Israelites stood a chance of being something more than an isolated people in a strange and hostile land. They would have to seize and hold territory, ideally in an area that the Hittites or a resurgent Egypt would find too difficult and expensive to invade.

Forty years in the wilderness had hardened the surviving males of military age into superb and dedicated light infantry, but had provided little by way of the technology

Ruin, re-ruined: archaeologists have excavated the site of Ai, the name itself meaning 'the ruin'. Thirteen hundred years before the site had been an impressive hill fortress, and abandoned. In Joshua's time, there were new fortifications – and new defenders.

necessary for armoured infantry combat or large, set-piece siege actions. The mountainous highlands in the inner countryside favoured the kind of army the Israelites could muster, so Joshua led his people towards the centre of their 'promised land' and their military objective.

The inhabitants of the region were well aware of the fall of Jericho and of the new, aggressive people in their midst. The rulers of the local Hittites, Amorites, Perizzites, Hivites and Jebusites began to form a defensive coalition, while the rulers of the four cities of Gibeon considered an alliance with the destroyers of Jericho.

The city of Bethel, whose rulers had joined the anti-Israelite coalition, was close to the path of Joshua's advance. Modern military tactical analysis, the biblical narrative and archaeological evidence all suggest that it was the occupants of Bethel who fortified the ruins at Ai (Ha-Ai in Hebrew, meaning 'The Ruin') as a defensive outpost against the impending assault.

Some 1300 years before Joshua, the site of Ai had been an imposing mountain stronghold. Enough of the original structure remained to allow Bethel to establish an effective garrison and strong points at minimal cost. Its resources would already have been severely stretched as it rushed to prepare its own defences. Within the ancient ruins, it is likely that as many as 240 defenders, including women and children, awaited the Israelites' advance.

JOSHUA PREPARES

Joshua's preparations for the advance show that he had learned from Moses, whose spies had found Jericho and detected its vulnerabilities. Joshua dispatched a reconnaissance party up the mountain trails to the vicinity of Ai. Its report was optimistic: 'Let not all the people go up, but rather send some two or three thousand men go up and attack Ai, for they are but a few.'

Joshua understood that every offensive operation has the effect of weakening the invading force. It was, therefore, vital to maintain military strength by the most economical use of soldiery. Accordingly, based on the intelligence received, he dispatched two or three elephs – a unit of 1000 men at ideal strength.

Joshua had every reason to believe that the garrison at Ai was fully aware of Jericho's fate. As Bethel itself was not far away, it was therefore not unreasonable to expect a retreat, if not outright surrender. An easy victory here would be good for the future course of the campaign, and Joshua saw no reason to lead the attack personally.

(The result, however, bears comparison with another resolute and much-celebrated defence against seemingly overwhelming numbers that was to occur many years later: the British defence of Rorke's Drift against 3000 Zulus in 1879. Even the numbers involved on the opposing sides are similar.)

The outcome of the first Israelite assault was the first setback of Joshua's campaign. The biblical account tells of a frontal assault repulsed, leaving 36 Hebrew dead. One factor accounting for the Israelites' failure is the steep march they faced from the plain of Jericho, after which

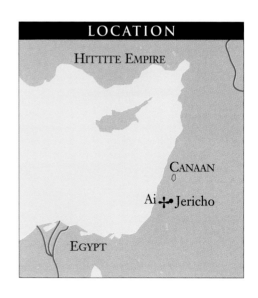

LOCATION

The defences at Ai blocked the advance of Joshua and the Israelites into the mountain valleys, where cities and less-defended opponents awaited their arrival and made their preparations.

HOW AN AXE WAS MADE IN 1500 BC

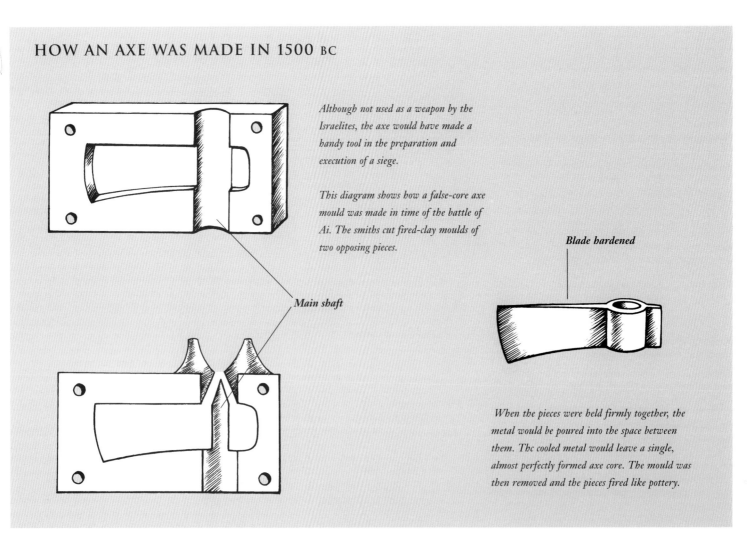

Although not used as a weapon by the Israelites, the axe would have made a handy tool in the preparation and execution of a siege.

This diagram shows how a false-core axe mould was made in time of the battle of Ai. The smiths cut fired-clay moulds of two opposing pieces.

Blade hardened

Main shaft

When the pieces were held firmly together, the metal would be poured into the space between them. The cooled metal would leave a single, almost perfectly formed axe core. The mould was then removed and the pieces fired like pottery.

Opposite: The Hand of God or an earthquake had toppled the decrepit walls of Jericho at the crossing of the Jordan. Ai's defenders sheltered in new, improvised defences and posed a tactical problem that Joshua's first effort failed to solve.

THE OPPOSED FORCES

CANAANITES (estimated)
First day: 200 defenders
Second day: 12,000 reinforcements
Total: 12,200

ISRAELITES (estimated)
First day: 2–3000 light infantry
Second day: 8000 reinforcements
Total: 10–11,000

they were exhausted. Meanwhile, the defenders were fresh, well protected against spears by the height of the ancient ruins and able to fire on their attackers with great power and range.

As to what happened next, battles in modern history show remarkable parallels. German siege artillery utterly demolished the fixed fortifications of Verdun in 1916 and yet found the Kaiser's army utterly balked by ferocious French resistance among the shattered skeletons of the fortresses. The Allied advance in Italy in 1944 found itself stalled for a costly five months when the ruins of the Abbey at Monte Cassino, levelled by Allied bombers, proved more formidable defences than the actual monastery itself.

A CRISIS OF FAITH

The Israelites had been sustained by a belief in God's promise of victory and land in Canaan. Indeed, Joshua put his entire male population through the ritual of circumcision after crossing the Jordan into

Canaan, and the onslaught on Jericho had all the characteristics of religious warfare. Their faith had emboldened the Israelites in their ferocious attack upon the Canaanites. Yet it now seemed that God's promise had been broken, and 'the hearts of the people melted, and became as water' [Joshua 7:5].

Time and again in the Bible, the Israelites' failures or reverses are interpreted as a divine punishment for their sins. Joshua therefore immediately set about determining and exorcising the cause of God's wrath. He speedily located it in the person and family of Achan ben Carmi, who had taken for himself a sizeable portion of the booty from Jericho – treasure that should rightly have been dedicated to God. Achan ben Carmi's punishment was swift and merciless.

With God's wrath thus appeased, Joshua reassured his people that the second assault upon Ai would succeed, and that he himself would lead it. The Bible recounts that God renewed his promise of

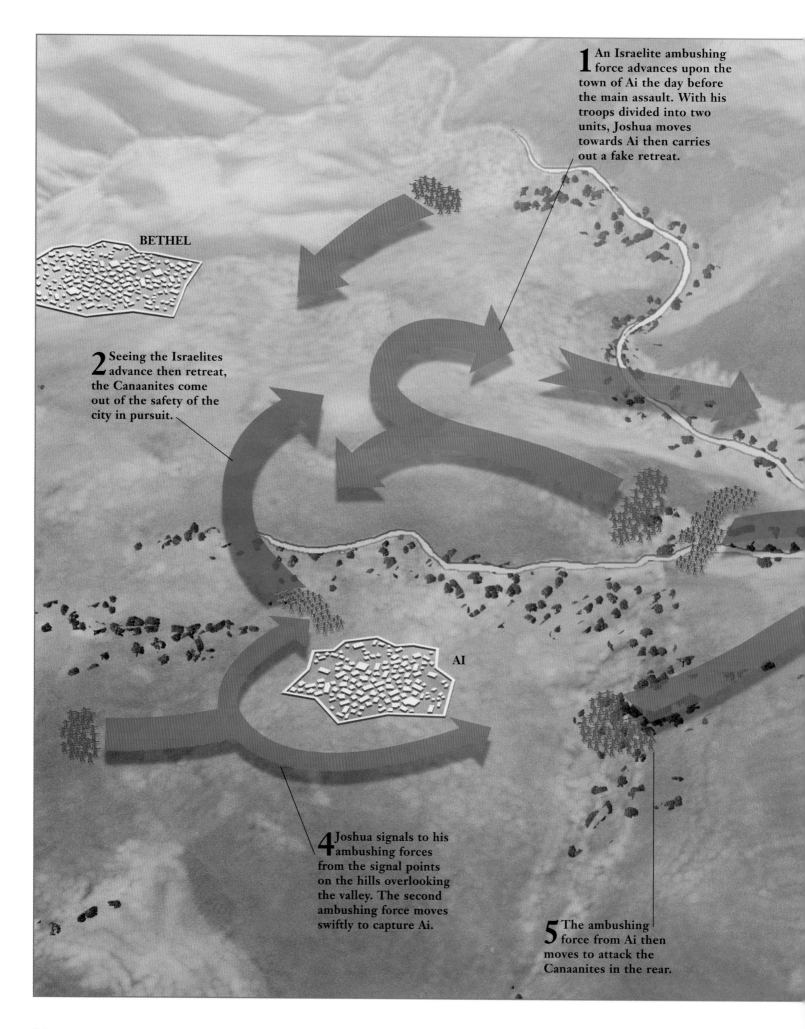

1 An Israelite ambushing force advances upon the town of Ai the day before the main assault. With his troops divided into two units, Joshua moves towards Ai then carries out a fake retreat.

BETHEL

2 Seeing the Israelites advance then retreat, the Canaanites come out of the safety of the city in pursuit.

AI

4 Joshua signals to his ambushing forces from the signal points on the hills overlooking the valley. The second ambushing force moves swiftly to capture Ai.

5 The ambushing force from Ai then moves to attack the Canaanites in the rear.

CONQUEST OF AI

C.1400 BC

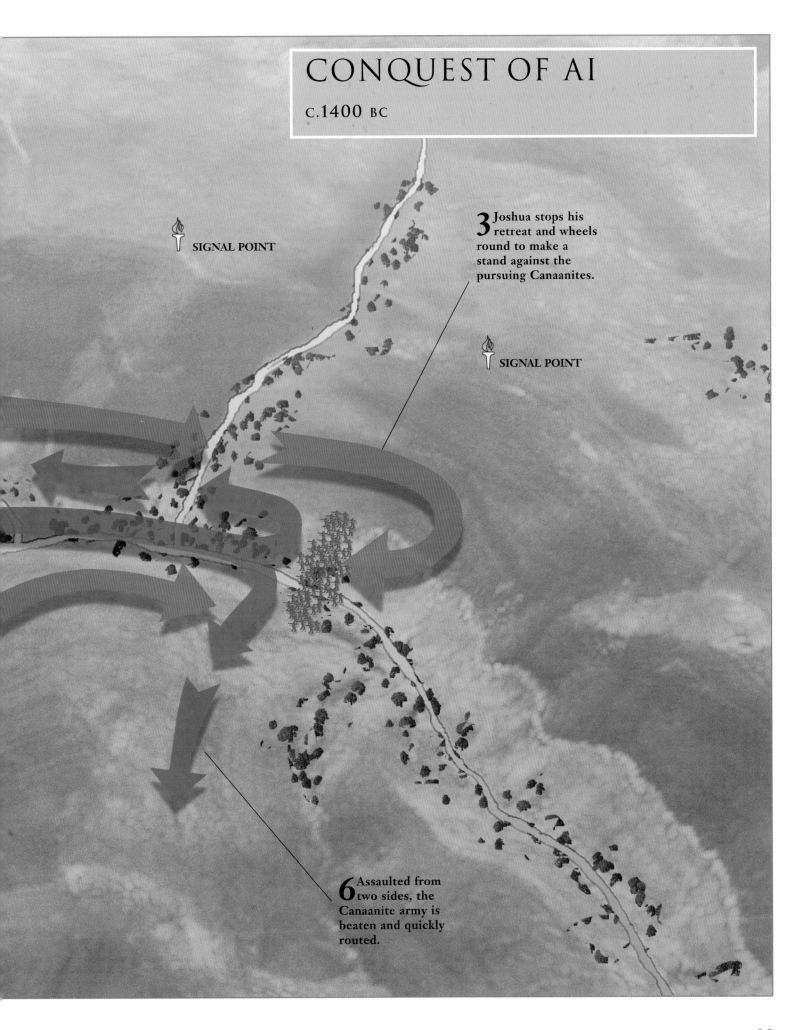

SIGNAL POINT

3 Joshua stops his retreat and wheels round to make a stand against the pursuing Canaanites.

SIGNAL POINT

6 Assaulted from two sides, the Canaanite army is beaten and quickly routed.

CONQUEST OF AI

Right: The last hope in a crisis, the walls of a city were the final barrier to the spears and swords of a merciless enemy. Ai's walls were already in ruins, providing shelter and concealment to the Canaanites who repulsed the first Israelite onslaught.

Below: Joshua proved himself an inspired choice as Moses' successor. Misled by optimistic scouts, he rallied his disheartened people and produced a stratagem that lured Ai's defenders into a fatal ambush.

victory. Like Jericho before it, Ai was to be left a ruin and its spoils dedicated to the God of Israel.

DIVIDE AND CONQUER

It is a reasonable assumption that the garrison at Ai was reinforced following its initial triumph, since it has long been military practice to reinforce success and retreat from defeat. The inhabitants of Bethel may well have chosen to defend their city at a proven strong point, rather than

from within the city itself. According to the Bible, all the defenders of both Ai and Bethel were on the field that day. Meanwhile, Joshua's plans for a second assault were more sophisticated than simply attempting to overrun a few weary defenders by sheer weight of numbers.

The Israelites had several advantages: an obedience to their leader (reinforced by the punishment doled out to Achan ben Carmi), a common ethnicity and the shared experience enjoyed by their troops. Thus

Joshua and the Judges were frequently able to win unlikely victories. Confident that their orders would always be carried out, they were able to divide their forces into independent but effective units. Though it is an axiom that commanders should not divide their forces in the face of strong resistance, the risks and prospects of success do tend to correspond for an aggressive, and lucky, general.

The night before the main assault, Joshua dispatched a handpicked force of

30 elafim to go on a night march, with orders to lie under cover across the road from Bethel until the main assault had drawn at least some of Ai's defenders out from the safety of their defences. Then they would either take the city from behind or delay any further reinforcement from the enemy's rear.

Joshua himself moved his forces nearer to the city and camped in a position where his men would not be exhausted by another long climb.

CONQUEST OF AI

Ever the prudent commander, he made his own defence against a night assault by ensuring that a ravine lay between the main body of his forces and the enemy.

OVERCONFIDENCE

Joshua was careful not to give the defenders of Ai any reason to expect anything more than another frontal attack. With his own march timed to appear before the city at daybreak, Joshua ordered a further five elafim of infantry from his own forces to move in the direction of the forces already lying in wait, ready to support the main assault from the rear or to thin out any

Moses had led the Children of Israel to the promised land of Canaan, but the actual conquest of Canaan would take the combination of planning, energy and adaptability that Joshua exhibited in a string of successful battles.

lingering defenders with a diversionary second attack upon their perimeter.

The following morning, when the 'king' of Ai saw Joshua and his main force moving up the slope towards the gates of his garrison, he decided to sally forth with the bulk of his garrison and disrupt the Israelite attack, taking advantage of the sloping ground of the mountainside to add impetus to the charge and shock of his onslaught. In modern military parlance, this is known as a 'spoiling attack'. After all, he had every reason to suspect that an army that had run once, would run again. If Ai had been reinforced, there might have been more troops in the sally than could have been profitably employed within the perimeter.

The biblical narrative makes it quite clear that Joshua had planned for precisely this contingency, and his faith in all three of his forces was fully justified. As the defenders of the garrison of Ai rushed down upon the Israelites, they retreated in a semblance of bad order. The discipline the defenders had so far maintained now collapsed into disorder as they rushed confidently forward to inflict the greatest number of casualties on their fleeing, 'vulnerable' enemy.

A CITY FALLS

'And Joshua stretched out the javelin that was within his hand towards the city' (Joshua 7:19). Whether Joshua's supporting forces now saw a flag depend from the shaft or the gleam from the tip of a javelin, they swung into action.

With the perimeter utterly or even partially abandoned by the garrison, the Israelites could now employ the sort of basic tactics that allow even light infantry to seize a defended position. Two men, or just one strong man, can raise another upon a shield, a usefully a flat platform for scaling a wall. Upon the wall itself, the defender's advantages of height fade quickly, while the roofs of houses, blockhouses, or any other sort of structures provide a relatively easy means of entrance with much less resistance than the defensive walls.

On Joshua's orders, the Israelites set fires throughout Ai as the two attacking forces advanced into the city, slaughtering everything and everyone in their path.

'And he hanged the King of Ai until the evening.' Neither besieged nor besiegers offer quarter in this illuminated page from the Book of Joshua. Shaken by the Israelite success, the Gibeonites offer alliance in the panel below.

Under a cloud of smoke, the attackers used their spears to open holes in the mud walls and then move from room to room, house to house, objective to objective until they had crushed all resistance in the town.

HAMMER AND ANVIL

The flame and smoke behind them alerted the garrison defenders to the peril that had befallen them. Joshua, however, was by no means done with the defenders of Ai and Bethel. All three strands of the Israelite army now converged on the Canaanites. It was too late for the commander of the garrison defenders to restore any sort of order, and he was soon captured and hanged from a nearby tree, his corpse later thrown into the wreckage.

By the time the Israelites had concluded their long day's slaughter, all that remained of the garrison were cattle and plunder. According to the biblical account, 12,000 men and women were slain. There is no specific reference to the fall of Bethel itself, but with its defenders dead in the remnants of Ai, its fall was inevitable. Further cities would be taken, armies defeated and alliances concluded – as the children of Israel secured themselves firmly in the 'promised land'.

WATERS OF MEROM
c.1400 BC

AFTER THE DEATH OF MOSES, THE HEBREW PEOPLE WANDERED NORTHWARDS, SOMETIMES COMING UNDER ATTACK FROM THE INHABITANTS OF THE LANDS THEY PASSED THROUGH. UNDER THE LEADERSHIP OF JOSHUA, THE HEBREWS WERE ABLE TO DEFEAT THE NORTHERN CANAANITES IN A FIERCE BATTLE.

WHY DID IT HAPPEN?

WHO A Hebrew army under Joshua, opposed by an alliance of Canaanites.

WHAT The Hebrews attacked while their enemies were preparing for battle.

WHERE The valley of the Waters of Merom in Galilee.

WHEN Around 1400 BC.

WHY The Hebrews were at the time a nomadic people seeking a new home.

OUTCOME The Hebrews defeated the Canaanites and took their land.

Canaan (modern-day Palestine) had been a battleground for centuries when the Hebrews arrived. Fertile and welcoming, the region was desirable as a homeland, and supported a number of relatively powerful states.

Canaan had at times been a possession of Egypt. From the time of the foundation of the Eighteenth Dynasty around 1550 BC, Egyptian forces had campaigned in Canaan. First, they pursued the defeated Hyksos into Palestine and then drove onwards, adding these lands to Egypt's empire.

Canaan was the land of the chariot, and it was from the native peoples of Canaan that the Egyptians learned to use light chariots in battle. The revolutionary combination of the chariot and the composite bow gave Egypt a decisive advantage in combat, and in just a few years

(1507–1494 BC) Tuthmosis I had driven his enemies all the way to the River Euphrates.

However, Egypt's influence in Canaan waxed and waned over the centuries. At times the Pharaohs maintained tight control, and at others they were forced to campaign against rebel princes in the region. The problem was that while it was easy enough to launch a campaign of conquest, maintaining effective control over such distances required greater resources than were available.

Consequently, Canaan was an area that repeatedly slipped beyond the control of Egypt until some energetic Pharaoh reconquered it for a time. In 1457 BC, Tuthmosis III (d.1426 BC) launched just such a campaign, crushing an alliance of Canaanite princes who had decided they no longer wished to be Egyptian vassals.

This detail of a relief from the Tomb of Paheri of the 18th Dynasty shows contemporary soldiers. An archer and an infantryman armed with a mace are evident. Their clothing is very uniform.

Tuthmosis's campaign was the pinnacle of Egyptian military greatness, and his victory at Megiddo is the first properly recorded battle in history. He expanded the boundaries of Egypt once more to the Euphrates after a great chariot battle smashed the alliance led by the King of Kadesh.

The Egyptians then found themselves in conflict with the Kingdom of Mitanni, located in Upper Mesopotamia. The Mitanni had backed the Kadesh rebellion and were also at the peak of their power. Conflict between the two over who would rule Syria continued until about 1410 BC, when a peace treaty was finally agreed.

Meanwhile, the Hittites, long-time rivals of both Egypt and Mitanni, were recovering from a long period of weakness caused by internal troubles. As they began to make their presence felt, the Kingdom of Mitanni turned its attention to dealing with the Hittite problem while Egypt looked to its own affairs. Control over Canaan once more relaxed.

CANAANITES AND AMORITES

Many different peoples occupied Canaan, some of whom are confusingly referred to by different names at various times. Those living in the west, near the sea, are generally given the title of Canaanites, while those residing further to the east, in the mountains and around them, are sometimes referred to as Amorites. However, these are not accurate cultural or racial labels. 'Amorite' is, in fact, an Akkadian word meaning 'Westerner', and it was applied to a number of states located in the eastern part of the region.

The Amorite and Canaanite peoples were, in any case, subject, to a great deal of cultural and linguistic mixing, and it is therefore difficult to establish exactly which region was controlled by whom at any one time. What is clear is that these cultures operated with a late Bronze Age level of technology, lagging slightly behind other regions, mainly due to the frequent disruptions caused by Egyptian armies travelling to put down rebellions and reconquer troubled regions.

The peoples of Canaan were able to build impressive cities with deep wells and stout walls, though the sharp divide between the stone-built homes of the rich and the hovels of the lower classes suggested by the archaeological evidence shows that wealth was not universal. The usual political organization was the city-state, with each city tending to its own small area of influence and owing allegiance to Egypt through its prince or city-king.

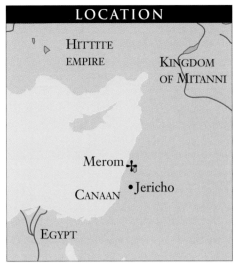

LOCATION

The land of Canaan lay on the route taken by several Egyptian armies marching to put down rebellions or fight foreign armies in Assyria or the Hittite kingdom. The land suffered every time an army passed through.

CANAANITE CHARIOT
The chariot was invented in the land of Canaan, whose flat plains were ideal for mobile warfare. The horses of the period were too small and weak for a true cavalry role, but they could pull a wheeled vehicle at some speed. From this mobile platform, the crew could fight with bows, javelins or hand weapons. Chariots from this period were lightweight and fragile compared to the heavy chariots of the Assyrians some 800 years later. Chariots provided both strategic and tactical variation, allowing the Canaanites to bring combat power to bear anywhere on the battlefield and retreat from disadvantageous situations. Chariot troops not only functioned like later cavalry, they also enjoyed the elite status often accorded to mounted troops in later times.

29

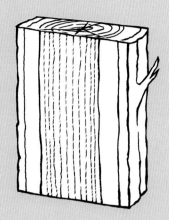
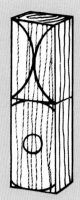

1 This diagram shows the process by which early, solid chariot wheels were made from the trunk of a tree.

2 A plank is cut from the centre of log. The plank is then halved.

3 One half forms the middle plank of the wheel. The other half is further divided to form the two remaining sections.

4 The three pieces of wood are held together by two cross braces to form a complete wheel.

The number of city-states had been on the increase for many years, mainly in the plains regions. However, each city-state stood alone rather than as part of a powerful state. When Egypt was strong, it could protect its vassals. But in 1400 BC, Egypt's control of the region was again slipping and the city-states were vulnerable to whatever new power entered the region – in this case, the Hebrews moving up from the south. In Canaan they found an abundance of good land, weakly held – a perfect opportunity to establish a new home.

ENTER THE HEBREWS

The Hebrews had wandered for many years after their escape from slavery in Egypt. As they headed north into Canaan, they must have known that, although Egypt's control of the region was loose, they were still in lands claimed by their old overlords, whose reach was long. On the other hand, according to their beliefs, Yahweh had promised them these lands.

That said, the Hebrews began the worship of Yaweh only in the latter stages of their wanderings. The name appears nowhere in writings before the Exodus and their arrival in the Promised Land, while Moses is recorded as having received the covenant and law at Mount Sinai on the journey from Egypt.

The worship of Yaweh was incompatible with the religions of Canaan, where the

THE OPPOSED FORCES

EGYPTIANS (estimated)
Chariots:	2000
Infantry:	18,000
Total:	**20,000**

HITTITES (estimated)
Chariots:	3000
Infantry:	20,000
Total:	**23,000**

Tuthmosis's campaign was the pinnacle of Egyptian military greatness, and his victory at Megiddo is the first properly recorded battle in history. He expanded the boundaries of Egypt once more to the Euphrates after a great chariot battle smashed the alliance led by the King of Kadesh.

The Egyptians then found themselves in conflict with the Kingdom of Mitanni, located in Upper Mesopotamia. The Mitanni had backed the Kadesh rebellion and were also at the peak of their power. Conflict between the two over who would rule Syria continued until about 1410 BC, when a peace treaty was finally agreed.

Meanwhile, the Hittites, long-time rivals of both Egypt and Mitanni, were recovering from a long period of weakness caused by internal troubles. As they began to make their presence felt, the Kingdom of Mitanni turned its attention to dealing with the Hittite problem while Egypt looked to its own affairs. Control over Canaan once more relaxed.

CANAANITES AND AMORITES

Many different peoples occupied Canaan, some of whom are confusingly referred to by different names at various times. Those living in the west, near the sea, are generally given the title of Canaanites, while those residing further to the east, in the mountains and around them, are sometimes referred to as Amorites. However, these are not accurate cultural or racial labels. 'Amorite' is, in fact, an Akkadian word meaning 'Westerner', and it was applied to a number of states located in the eastern part of the region.

The Amorite and Canaanite peoples were, in any case, subject, to a great deal of cultural and linguistic mixing, and it is therefore difficult to establish exactly which region was controlled by whom at any one time. What is clear is that these cultures operated with a late Bronze Age level of technology, lagging slightly behind other regions, mainly due to the frequent disruptions caused by Egyptian armies travelling to put down rebellions and reconquer troubled regions.

The peoples of Canaan were able to build impressive cities with deep wells and stout walls, though the sharp divide between the stone-built homes of the rich and the hovels of the lower classes suggested by the archaeological evidence shows that wealth was not universal. The usual political organization was the city-state, with each city tending to its own small area of influence and owing allegiance to Egypt through its prince or city-king.

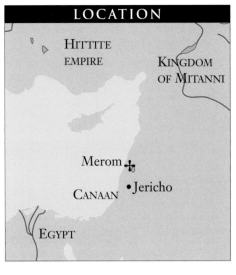

LOCATION

HITTITE EMPIRE

KINGDOM OF MITANNI

Merom

CANAAN • Jericho

EGYPT

The land of Canaan lay on the route taken by several Egyptian armies marching to put down rebellions or fight foreign armies in Assyria or the Hittite kingdom. The land suffered every time an army passed through.

CANAANITE CHARIOT
The chariot was invented in the land of Canaan, whose flat plains were ideal for mobile warfare. The horses of the period were too small and weak for a true cavalry role, but they could pull a wheeled vehicle at some speed. From this mobile platform, the crew could fight with bows, javelins or hand weapons. Chariots from this period were lightweight and fragile compared to the heavy chariots of the Assyrians some 800 years later. Chariots provided both strategic and tactical variation, allowing the Canaanites to bring combat power to bear anywhere on the battlefield and retreat from disadvantageous situations. Chariot troops not only functioned like later cavalry, they also enjoyed the elite status often accorded to mounted troops in later times.

1 *This diagram shows the process by which early, solid chariot wheels were made from the trunk of a tree.*

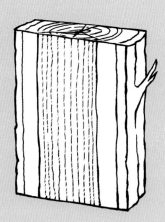

2 *A plank is cut from the centre of log. The plank is then halved.*

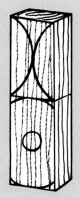

3 *One half forms the middle plank of the wheel. The other half is further divided to form the two remaining sections.*

4 *The three pieces of wood are held together by two cross braces to form a complete wheel.*

The number of city-states had been on the increase for many years, mainly in the plains regions. However, each city-state stood alone rather than as part of a powerful state. When Egypt was strong, it could protect its vassals. But in 1400 BC, Egypt's control of the region was again slipping and the city-states were vulnerable to whatever new power entered the region – in this case, the Hebrews moving up from the south. In Canaan they found an abundance of good land, weakly held – a perfect opportunity to establish a new home.

ENTER THE HEBREWS

The Hebrews had wandered for many years after their escape from slavery in Egypt. As they headed north into Canaan, they must have known that, although Egypt's control of the region was loose, they were still in lands claimed by their old overlords, whose reach was long. On the other hand, according to their beliefs, Yahweh had promised them these lands.

That said, the Hebrews began the worship of Yaweh only in the latter stages of their wanderings. The name appears nowhere in writings before the Exodus and their arrival in the Promised Land, while Moses is recorded as having received the covenant and law at Mount Sinai on the journey from Egypt.

The worship of Yaweh was incompatible with the religions of Canaan, where the

THE OPPOSED FORCES

EGYPTIANS (estimated)

Chariots:	2000
Infantry:	18,000
Total:	**20,000**

HITTITES (estimated)

Chariots:	3000
Infantry:	20,000
Total:	**23,000**

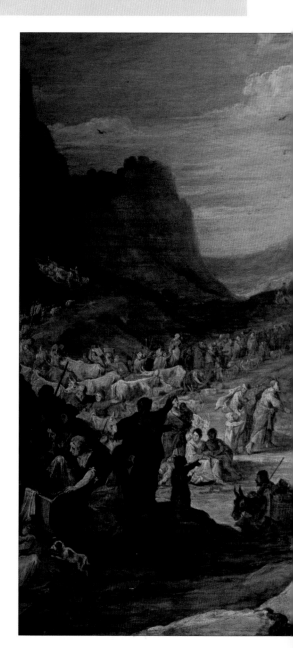

most important god was Ba'al, although the relatively inactive El was head of the pantheon. Canaanite deities included female fertility goddesses, who doubled as war-goddesses at times. Orgiastic practices, which were common, were bound to incur Yahweh's disapproval.

Thus, religious differences were added to the already lengthy list of reasons why the Hebrews were likely to clash with the Canaanites.

With the death of Moses, the leadership of the Hebrews fell upon Joshua, who led his people northwards into Canaan. Conflict was inevitable, and the Hebrews defeated several city-states in succession.

The exact nature of the conquest of what became Israel is difficult to determine. Some sources suggest a swift, deliberate and well-planned campaign, while others tell of a series of gradual expansions, often by individual clans. The truth is probably somewhere in between.

Warfare in that time was often extremely brutal. It was not uncommon for the defenders of a city to be put to the sword and sometimes for the city to be razed to the ground. There are records of the Hebrews making war in this manner, so it is possible that each conquest brought about a hurried alliance of nearby city-states, fearful that they were next in line for this treatment.

Once these new allies attacked the Hebrews, they had to be destroyed for the safety of the Hebrew people to be assured, and this in turn provoked other cities to march against the invaders. Thus the conquest of Israel was in part a matter of self-fulfilling prophecy.

THE HEBREW CONQUEST

The Hebrew conquest of Israel was not total. Some areas were not absorbed until much later. The Hebrews were probably relatively few in number, and could not conquer a huge area. Literal translations of documents from the time claim that they could muster as many as 600,000 men under arms, but this is a vast exaggeration. There is simply no way that the several million people required to support them could have fended for themselves on the march. In any case, a host numbering so many might not have needed to flee from Egypt – they could probably have overrun it instead.

If the vast numbers quoted by some sources are viewed in the same light as documents claiming that the Egyptians were opposed by several million enemy soldiers at Megiddo, it is likely that the Hebrews had only a few thousand people in all, and a smaller number of fighting-men. Little wonder, then, that they were unable to capture either the Plain of Esdraelon (as Tuthmosis III had done after the battle of Megiddo some 50 years earlier) or the coastal plain.

Nevertheless, the Hebrews battled their way northwards, conquering some cities and making alliances with others. They absorbed the Gibeonite confederacy in this way and gained in power as time went on. Other groups were likewise incorporated into the growing Hebrew nation. These included nomads and dispossessed peoples who had been encountered wandering in the wilderness and converted to Yawehism, along with groups that entered what was to become Israel, while the Hebrews were engaged in conquering it.

Some towns and villages, tiring of their existing overlords and intrigued by the religious fervour of the Hebrew patriarchs, threw in their lot with the newcomers

Painted by H. Jordaens III in 1624, this depiction of the Exodus shows the Hebrews escaping from Egypt through the Red Sea. After escaping immediate destruction, the Hebrews were faced with the problem of finding or making a new home.

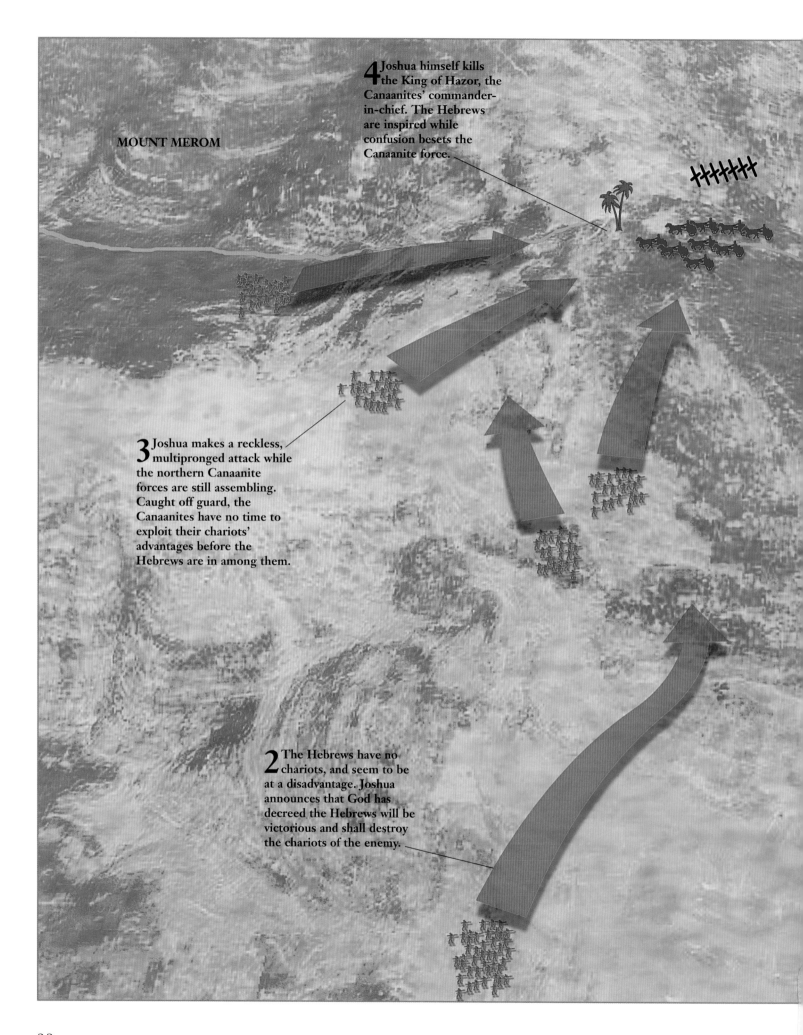

MOUNT MEROM

4 Joshua himself kills the King of Hazor, the Canaanites' commander-in-chief. The Hebrews are inspired while confusion besets the Canaanite force.

3 Joshua makes a reckless, multipronged attack while the northern Canaanite forces are still assembling. Caught off guard, the Canaanites have no time to exploit their chariots' advantages before the Hebrews are in among them.

2 The Hebrews have no chariots, and seem to be at a disadvantage. Joshua announces that God has decreed the Hebrews will be victorious and shall destroy the chariots of the enemy.

1 Worried by the advance of the Hebrews into Canaan, an alliance is formed against them. Several tribes and cities send troops to muster near the Waters of Merom.

CANAANITE DEFENCES

WATERS OF MEROM

5 With no coherent command structure, the Canaanites are unable to respond effectively. Some alliance contingents are overwhelmed and routed while others break and flee without being attacked.

WATERS OF MEROM

1400 BC

WATERS OF MEROM

A fouteenth-century statuette of the god Baal in a golden head-dress that shows Egyptian influences. Baal was widely worshipped in Canaan and the Hebrews did not approve of many practices followed by his worshippers.

that resembled a siege train, could gain access to the walled cities. Once past the walls, they had a fighting chance.

THE NORTHERN ALLIANCE

The city-states of northern Canaan were afraid of the encroaching Hebrews, who seemed quite capable of burning any city that did not join them and agree to worship their gods. The answer was to form an alliance and destroy the invaders, and the northern Canaanites set about doing just that. The alliance consisted of several city-kings, including Jabin of Hazor and Jobab of Madon. Contingents came from many states and tribes, representing Hittites, Jebusites, Perizzites, Amorites, Hivites and Canaanites. They assembled a great host at the valley of the Waters of Merom, including large numbers of infantry and, significantly, chariots.

The Hebrews had no chariots, which meant that the enemy had significant advantages in terms of manoeuvrability and, if they chose to use it, reconnaissance capability. However, the alliance was probably not very well organized, since it was made up of contingents from large numbers of leaders who were, at least in theory, equals.

ON THE EVE OF BATTLE

The force ranged against the Hebrews was daunting. Not only did the enemy have numerical superiority, but they also had better technology. However, the Hebrews were no longer an ill-armed mob. They had taken many cities and would have gained experience in war as well as the chance to arm themselves from their fallen foes. Their foot soldiers would have been equipped as well as those of the enemy, and probably with exactly the same equipment.

The Hebrews also had other advantages. They were developing a 'habit of victory', which, coupled with their fervent religious belief in a promise from Yaweh, tremendously strengthened morale. Indeed, the Old Testament records God speaking to Joshua and telling him not to be afraid of the enemy, for tomorrow they would be delivered slain before Israel; the Hebrews would hamstring the enemy horses and destroy their chariots with fire.

readily and freely, becoming part of the Hebrew culture and eventually merging into the general population of Israel.

It is also possible that there were Hebrews already living in the region when Joshua and his followers arrived. This would, to some extent, explain how the Hebrews could conquer a region inhabited by many times their numbers, and by people who knew how to build fortified towns. With some 'inside' assistance, the poorly armed Hebrews, who possessed nothing

A depiction in relief of a Hittite chariot. The crew are armed with bow and spear, and the axle is located at the rear, which was found to be the best position.

Whatever its provenance, it was a decent enough plan, and Joshua decided to take the initiative. Outnumbered and facing a superior foe, he would level the odds with aggression and daring.

BATTLE AT THE WATERS OF MEROM

As was the way with feudal hosts brought together without a clear command structure, the Canaanite force was still getting organized when Joshua's warriors attacked. The Old Testament speaks of an ambush, but a surprise attack – perhaps after an approach march made under cover of darkness – is more probable. This extraordinarily daring strategy paid off: the Canaanites were caught unprepared and could offer no coherent resistance.

The Hebrews fell on their foes suddenly and with great ferocity, with Joshua fighting at their head. He entered into personal combat with the King of Hazor, killing him with a sword. This was too much for the Canaanites, who broke and were scattered. The Hebrews pursued them wherever they tried to flee. The Old Testament speaks of the Hebrews attacking their enemies until they 'left none of them remaining'.

In the course of their pursuit, the Hebrews were very thorough, as Moses had instructed them to be in the past. They did as commanded, hamstringing horses and burning chariots rather than taking them for their own use.

Joshua then led his people to Hazor and burned it to the ground as an example to others. The population were put to the sword, as were the people of the other cities that had allied with Hazor, though these were not burned. Instead, the Hebrews greatly enriched themselves by taking as spoils of war their livestock and goods.

WATERS OF MEROM

Hebrew leaders are often ascribed supernatural powers given by God. Here Joshua commands the sun and moon to come to his aid during the defence of the allied city of Gideon.

AFTERMATH

The Hebrews were now in control of most of Canaan, including the Jordan plain, the mountains of Israel and the Valley of Lebanon. However, they still needed to complete their dominance, so one by one the city-states that still resisted were broken and their kings put to death. Only those that made alliance with the Hebrews and accepted their rule were spared.

Ruthless, perhaps, but all this was justified to Joshua – it was God's will as given to him by Moses, and the enemy were heathens whose religion was an affront to Yaweh. Just as importantly, this way of making war was more or less the norm for the time – clemency and respect for non-combatants were extremely rare in that period of history. It is perhaps telling that the modern English phrase 'do unto others as you would have done unto you' is slightly different in old Hebrew. It reads 'do unto others as they would do unto you', which has somewhat different connotations.

The Hebrews had recently escaped slavery, had been harried and attacked on their march, and faced utter annihilation at the hands of their foes should they lose. Their conquest might have been vigorous, thorough and extremely brutal but, in the final analysis, they were simply doing to others what would be done to them if they failed.

Opposite: The book of Joshua describes the Hebrew victory over the Amorites as a total catastrophe for the latter. This engraving, by Gustave Doré (1832–1883), illustrates the totality of the disaster.

VICTORY OVER SISERA
1240 BC

THE LOOSELY ORGANIZED ISRAELITE TRIBES WERE INCAPABLE OF CONCERTED ACTION WITHOUT A CHARISMATIC LEADER TO UNITE THEM. THE APPEARANCE OF THE JUDGES WAS A RESPONSE TO THE NEED FOR SUCH LEADERS IN A TIME WHEN THE ISRAELITES WOULD NOT ACCEPT A KING.

WHY DID IT HAPPEN?

WHO An Israelite army under Great Judge Deborah and General Barak, opposed by Canaanites commanded by General Sisera.

WHAT Wet ground rendered the Canaanite chariots impotent just before the armies clashed.

WHERE Near Mount Tabor, Israel.

WHEN 1240 BC.

WHY Great Judge Deborah rallied the Israelites to free their people from Canaanite oppression.

OUTCOME The Canaanites were routed and broken as a military power.

After the conquest of Canaan, there was a period of adjustment and development for the Israelites. They had been wanderers and now had a home. It is obvious from their early settlements that many of the skills of settled people, in terms of construction and metalworking in particular, were lacking. The tribes had taken much from their conquered foes in the time of Joshua and were now beginning to develop the necessary expertise to make things for themselves.

A number of important technical advances were made. One was the use of baked lime plaster to line water cisterns, which greatly increased the available water supply in many regions and made possible a greater population in the towns. Trading missions were sent out by camel and ship, and land was cleared of forest to allow cultivation and the building of towns. The population and wealth of Israel both expanded substantially.

The Israelites of the time did not co-operate very well, and disliked the idea of a king ruling over all of them. Their social order was based on the tribal confederacy,

The Plain of Esdraelon as seen from near Nazareth (from a painting by William Holman Hunt). The plain was inhabited by people hostile to the Hebrews and presented an obstacle between the northern and southern halves of their land.

HEBREW INFANTRYMEN

The forces fielded by the Israelites (and many other nations of the time) were simply tribesmen who turned up with whatever weapons and equipment they possessed. A few men had swords or helmets, but most were armed with the most basic gear: a spear and shield. Nor were these well-drilled spearmen fighting in a phalanx-like formation. They were bound by kinship, loyalty to their tribe or to friends who fought alongside them, and by the charisma of their leaders.

with each tribe doing more or less as it pleased and consensus on any given matter consequently difficult to obtain.

A charismatic individual could lead a large undertaking in the short term but, eventually, the tribes would drift back to their own affairs. Under other circumstances, this would have left Israel wide open to reconquest by Egypt. However, the Egyptian empire was having difficulties of its own.

After a long struggle with the Sea Peoples, a loose label applied to the great variety of groups who raided around the coasts of the Mediterranean, the Egyptians at last managed to drive them off. However, the collapse of the Nineteenth Dynasty threw Egypt into turmoil and resulted in the loss of all its Asian holdings.

Although stability was eventually restored and an attempt made to regain the lost territories, Egypt never reconquered anything beyond the Plain of Esdraelon and soon came under renewed attack by the Sea

Peoples and tribes from Libya. This distracted attention from Asia and allowed the Israelites a chance to secure their hold on the region – if they could only deal with their own troubles.

In the event, Egypt, exhausted by war, was never again to be a power in Asia. However, with the Philistines growing in might, Sea Peoples controlling large sections of the coast and Arameans moving into Syria, Israel's position was also shaky.

The emergence of the Judges occurred some years after the death of Joshua and the conquest of Canaan. During this period, the Israelites were suffering at the hands of their enemies. As happened several times in their history, they had turned from the worship of Yaweh and begun to follow local gods, including Baal, who was favoured by the defeated Canaanites.

As usual, according to the Bible, this turning-aside from the true path resulted in suffering for the people of Israel. This time, it started with the depredations of bandits

LOCATION

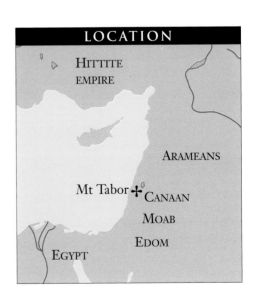

The geography of the region tends to funnel conflict into certain areas. Thus the coastal plain of what is today Israel has seen a vast number of battles, many of them in the same locations.

VICTORY OVER SISERA

The peak of Mount Tabor outlined against the sunset. The mountain has acquired a religious and cultural significance, perhaps because of the great events that have unfolded near it.

and robbers, followed by a string of defeats in battle against Philistine and Amorite attackers, and enemies among the people of Canaan who refused to accept Israelite rule. Where the righteous Hebrews under Joshua had enjoyed a spectacular victory over their pagan enemies, the generation that followed lost considerable territory to the invaders.

THE RISE OF THE JUDGES

After a period of misery at the hands of Israel's enemies, the Judges began to emerge. They were great leaders among the Israelites, whose function was partly religious, partly political and partly heroic, factors all intertwined in Jewish society. Personal charisma and great deeds were interpreted as a sign of God's favour and, in the end, all authority devolved from the same source. Even the Judges' function as chief magistrates was partly religious, as the laws of Israel were as much part of their religion as they were of daily life.

The laws of Israel began with Moses and had their origins in the Commandments he

brought down from Mount Sinai. Moses himself added much to the body of law, while others continued his work as the need arose. Lawgivers were greatly respected in Jewish tradition, as it was held that law came from Yaweh and was, at least in part, an expression of divine will. Those who made the law were therefore speaking for God and with his blessing.

Justice in most common matters was something for the elders of the tribe or village to deal with, guided by tradition and the body of law. The priests handled more difficult cases. This intermingling of religion and day-to-day law is a reflection of Jewish society at the time.

The great lawmakers and leaders of Israel, the Judges, ruled on the weightiest matters. Their role was somewhat different from that of modern-day judges, since they not only dealt with matters of law but also guided their people in other ways. The role was neither hereditary nor elected, but more a function of personal charisma and suitably great deeds.

THE OPPOSED FORCES

HEBREWS (estimated)
All infantry
Total: **10,000**

CANAANITES
Unknown, but probably
over 10,000

Once an individual became a Judge, he or she wielded a great deal of power. Judges, however, were not kings. They led rather than ruled, and there is at least one case of a Judge being referred to as 'king' once his actions ceased to be seen as in the best interests of his people. However, the office of Judge had much in common with kingship – Judges led their people in war and guided them through peacetime.

The Judges were 'elders' of their people (which does not always mean that they were particularly old; wisdom and the respect of the people made someone an elder, not age), and according to the Old Testament they were sent to lead their people back to righteousness. When the people listened to the Judges and embraced once more the correct religious practices, Israel did well. When they did not, Israel suffered accordingly.

DEBORAH THE GREAT JUDGE

Twelve Judges are identified in the Book of Judges, with five of them given the title of Great Judge. There is some question as to what divides these Great Judges from their lesser counterparts. It seems likely that the main distinction was whether or not the Judge in question had led a successful, large-scale military campaign. However, most of the Judges fought against one foe or another. Othniel, who was not a Great Judge, fought a foe referred to as Cushan of Double Wickedness, who was probably an Edomite. The first of the Great Judges, Ehud, defeated Moab.

Of the great individuals named in the book of Judges, only one, Deborah, is female. Little is known about her life. It seems that she was married and may have lived in Ephraim. She is known to have dispensed wisdom and justice from there, and to have written poetry.

In the time of Deborah, the Israelites had not managed to conquer the people of the Plain of Esdraelon. This region jutted across the lands of the Israelites and, since it was occupied by hostile peoples, more or less cut Israel in half. In the middle of the twelfth century BC, the plain was dominated by a confederacy of Canaanite tribes and city-states that had come to dominate some of the nearby Israelite tribes and oppress

them heavily. Chief among the peoples of this confederacy was King Jabin of Hazor, whose ancestor had been slain by Joshua and his city burned. There was cause for deep hatred between the combatants.

The dominance of Hazor over the nearby tribes was well established and was maintained by the ruthless use of terror. So frightened and despondent were the local Israelite tribes that the very idea of rebellion was unthinkable until Deborah appeared to lead her people to freedom.

THE ISRAELITES RALLY

With her potent oratory and obvious charisma, Deborah was able to rouse the tribes to defiance against their overlords.

Mt. Tabor, Israel – the windy road to the summit of mountain in the Galilee. Here the Biblical prophet Deborah was said to have led an army of 10,000 Israelites to defeat their idol-worshiping enemies.

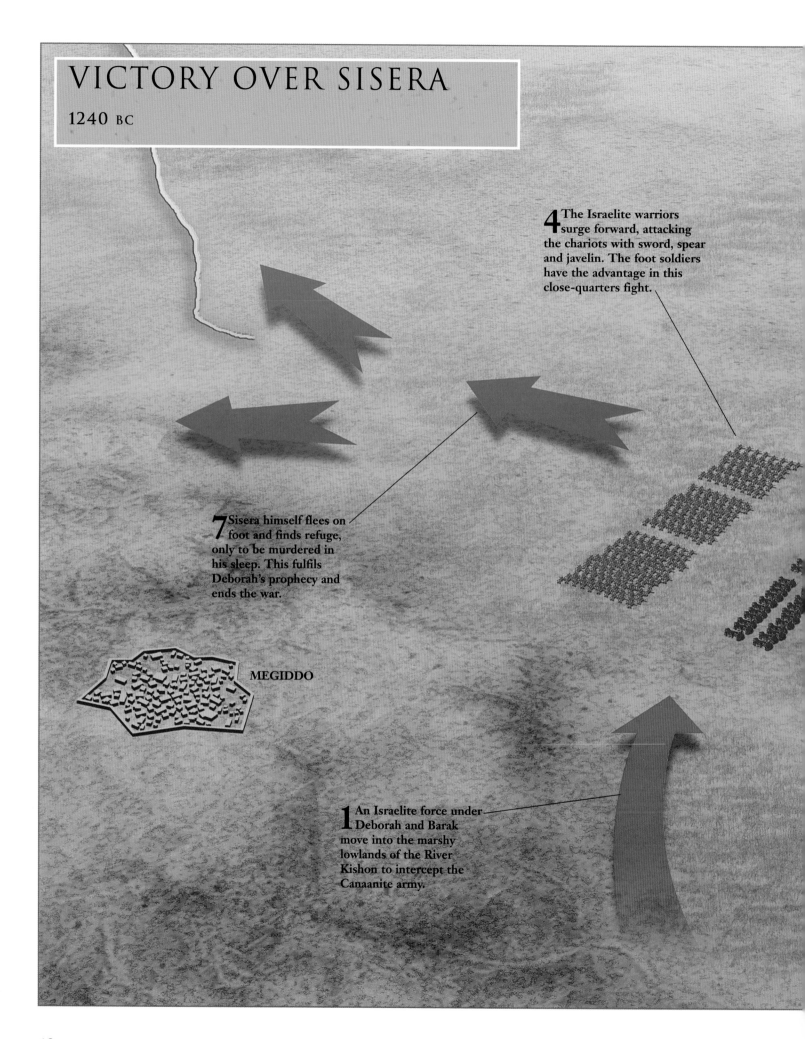

VICTORY OVER SISERA

1240 BC

4 The Israelite warriors surge forward, attacking the chariots with sword, spear and javelin. The foot soldiers have the advantage in this close-quarters fight.

7 Sisera himself flees on foot and finds refuge, only to be murdered in his sleep. This fulfils Deborah's prophecy and ends the war.

MEGIDDO

1 An Israelite force under Deborah and Barak move into the marshy lowlands of the River Kishon to intercept the Canaanite army.

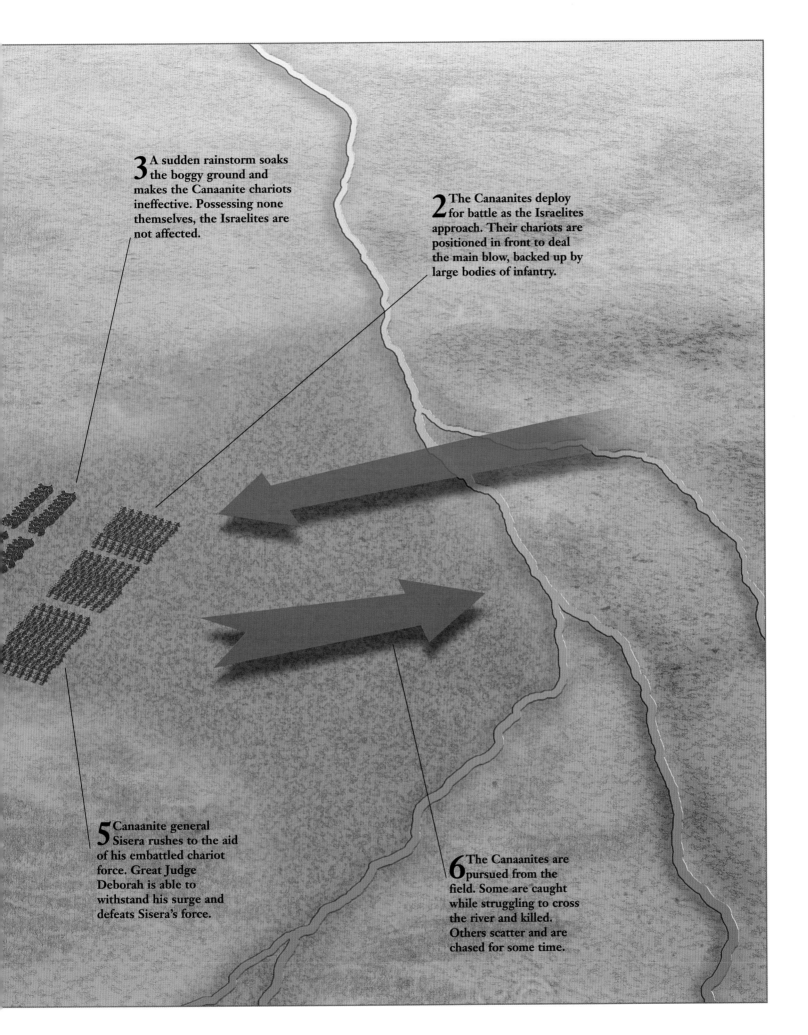

3 A sudden rainstorm soaks the boggy ground and makes the Canaanite chariots ineffective. Possessing none themselves, the Israelites are not affected.

2 The Canaanites deploy for battle as the Israelites approach. Their chariots are positioned in front to deal the main blow, backed up by large bodies of infantry.

5 Canaanite general Sisera rushes to the aid of his embattled chariot force. Great Judge Deborah is able to withstand his surge and defeats Sisera's force.

6 The Canaanites are pursued from the field. Some are caught while struggling to cross the river and killed. Others scatter and are chased for some time.

VICTORY OVER SISERA

The Great Judge Deborah. Being named a Judge was an honour few individuals ever earned. A combination of charisma, religious fervour and success was necessary.

She appointed Barak as general to lead the fight against the Canaanites, and called all the tribes of Israel to her assistance.

The response was mixed. Some local tribes were still too cowed to react, while many of those more distant decided that fighting Jabin and his followers was either not their concern or not in their interests. However, Deborah was able to inspire many of the people of Israel to rally to her – enough, in fact, to launch a campaign.

No Judge ever led the whole of Israel into battle because the tribal confederacy was simply too disorganized for that to happen. The positive side of this was that a great leader like Deborah could garner at least some support from any tribe, regardless of whether or not its elders believed that they should get involved.

And so the hosts of Israel assembled to fight the Canaanites, who were led by King Jabin's General Sisera. Handfuls of men came from some tribes, while those whose elders thought the cause both winnable and worthy sent large numbers of warriors. Under the command of Barak, the Israelites marched to meet their Canaanite foes at Mount Tabor.

BATTLE OF MOUNT TABOR

The Israelites were at a disadvantage against the Canaanites, as they had often been. Theirs was a tribal host, composed mainly of men without armour, equipped with spears, shields and, in some cases, swords. The Canaanites had infantry of the same sort but were also lavishly equipped with chariots. The chariots of the time were fairly light and were not intended for close-quarters combat.

Instead, they could dash about the battlefield, acting as a mobile platform from which the crew could shoot their bows or throw javelins.

This painting by Italian artist Francesco Solimena (1657–1747) shows Deborah meeting with general Barak, who commanded the army of the Hebrews in her name. Apparently the Hebrews could accept a female Judge, but needed a man to lead them in battle.

This mobility allowed the Canaanites to bring extra firepower to bear where it was needed and to speed off when threatened, enabling their troops to avoid hand-to-hand assaults. There was also the psychological effect of a great many chariots thundering about, raising dust to inspire fear among their foes.

Against this combination of firepower and mobility, the Israelites could only get stuck in and hope for the best. However, they did have one advantage: Yaweh, speaking through the Great Judge Deborah, had told them that they would win.

Deborah had prophesied that the Canaanites would be defeated, but not totally. She also claimed that a woman would kill General Sisera. Though this seemed a somewhat odd suggestion, the Israelites, nevertheless, went to battle inspired by her words.

Just before the battle opened, a sudden and massive rainstorm caused the nearby river to flood, soaking the ground all around. This severely impeded the Canaanites' chariots and allowed the Israelite warriors to come to hand-strokes.

Under aggressive close-quarters attack by the inspired Israelites, the Canaanite troops began to break. Sisera tried to rally his men. Normally, according to the Old Testament, the sound of his voice was enough to frighten off the bravest enemy, to shake town walls and even to kill wild animals. Deborah could withstand it, however, and Sisera was unable to prevent his force from melting away. Although the Israelites could not achieve a total victory, they were able to pursue their foes off the battlefield and inflict upon them a massive defeat.

AFTERMATH

Sisera was exhausted from the battle and sought refuge with Heber the Kenite. There, Heber's wife, Jael, gave him food and drink and a place to rest. While he was asleep, she killed him by hammering a tent peg through his temples, pinning his head to the ground and thereby fulfilling Deborah's prophecy.

Although the Israelites were unable to conquer the Plain of Esdraelon entirely, Deborah and General Barak's victory broke the Canaanites' power, and thereafter the

people of Israel were able to settle in and around the region without being troubled. The plain no longer presented an obstacle to travellers, making communication and commerce between the two halves of Israelite territory much simpler.

The Old Testament records that after Deborah smashed the Canaanites, the Israelites did not have to do battle with them again for a generation.

As prophesied by Deborah, the Canaanite leader Sisera dies at the hand of a woman. Here, he is depicted being killed in his sleep by Jael, wife of Heber the Kenite.

SPRING OF HAROD CAMPAIGN
1194 BC

GIDEON'S CAMPAIGN AGAINST THE MIDIANITES DEMONSTRATES THE USE OF DECEPTION AND PSYCHOLOGY TO DEFEAT A SUPERIOR FOE. WHETHER THE IDEA CAME FROM GIDEON HIMSELF OR WAS SENT BY GOD AS THE OLD TESTAMENT SAYS, THE OPERATION WAS ENTIRELY SUCCESSFUL.

WHY DID IT HAPPEN?

WHO An Israelite army under Gideon, opposed by the Midianite tribes.

WHAT Gideon raised a great host to defend Israel but only deployed part of it.

WHERE Near the Springs of Harod.

WHEN 1194 BC.

WHY The Midianites and their allies were subjecting the Israelites to constant heavy raids.

OUTCOME The Midianites were routed by a clever deception and subsequently smashed in battle.

Israel faced one crisis after another during its early history. Raids by other states and tribal groups were a constant nuisance, and at times became a severe threat to the survival of the tribal confederation. As a loose organization without central leadership, the confederation could never respond coherently. Instead, those tribes threatened must deal with the problem. Assistance from neighbouring tribes, who might owe a favour or feel threatened by the same enemy, was sometimes available, especially when a charismatic leader called for assistance.

Gideon was one such charismatic leader. He was propelled to prominence by the need to deal with intense raiding by

Midianite nomads. These raiders rode camels since they were a desert people, and were assisted by Amalekites and the people of Bene Qedem.

This was a new phenomenon. The camel had been domesticated for some time in Arabia, and its use was becoming widespread among the tribes living to the south and east of Israel. With much greater mobility than before, these tribes were now able to strike wherever they pleased.

This was bad enough, but the raiders quickly discovered that they could profit most by launching organized attacks around harvest time. This not only netted them considerable booty, but it also severely damaged the economy of the Israelite tribes

Such was the nature of Hebrew society that important events were seen as having a divine component. In this seventeenth-century antique German print, Abimelech is depicted returning Sarah to Abraham, complete with beams of light from heaven.

46

dwelling on the plain of Esdraelon and the surrounding region. In fact, had this situation been allowed to continue, Israel might have collapsed.

Predictably, according to the Old Testament, the Israelites had brought these difficult times upon themselves. Once again, they had forgotten that their prosperity and national security were both dependent upon remaining faithful to Yaweh. Having begun to worship false gods and idols once more, the Israelites needed to be taught a lesson. This time, the instrument of divine retribution was to be the Midianites and the Amalekites.

THE ENEMY

The Midianites were worshippers of Baal-peor and other gods disapproved of by the Israelites. There have, however, been suggestions that at least some of the Midianites worshipped Yaweh, which is certainly possible given the amount of contact between the two groups.

The Midianites came from a land east of Canaan, across the River Jordan, though in the past they had been more widespread. They had at times managed to get along peacefully with the Israelites, but there had also been bloody conflict in the past. Moses himself had ordered the Israelites to make war on Midian, and the resulting conflict was typically savage.

In the past, there had been five tribes of Midianites, but in Gideon's time only two are mentioned. Perhaps the others had been broken up by Moses or had moved away. Whatever the case, King Zalmuna and King Zebah ruled these tribes, while Generals Oreb and Zeeb led the forces of Midian. Some sources refer to these men as princes instead; the two terms were often interchangeable in this period.

Perhaps the Midianites were motivated by plunder or vengeance. It is also possible that they perceived themselves as conquerors with a manifest destiny. They had, after all, recently thrown off the yoke of Sihon and might have felt this was the beginning of a new age of greatness.

The Amalekites also had a history of conflict with the Israelites. They had attacked the Hebrews as they wandered in the Sinai Desert and warred with them

intermittently thereafter. It is likely that some of these conflicts were very bitter. To this day, the Amalekites are presented as the deadly enemies of Israel, and the word is sometimes used to mean an enemy of the Israelite people. The Amalekites are sometimes also known as Agagites, as all Amalekite kings were named Agag during their reign.

ENTER GIDEON

By the time Gideon appeared on the scene, the Midianites had established camps on the western side of the River Jordan, and from there were raiding deeply into Israelite territory. Some of the local tribes had been subjugated and were now being oppressed. The harvest-time raids had been ongoing for six years and a crisis was approaching.

According to the Old Testament, Gideon, an otherwise ordinary man, was chosen by Yaweh to save the Israelites. Though sceptical of his calling, Gideon asked for proof in the form of a miracle, which was granted. He asked for further

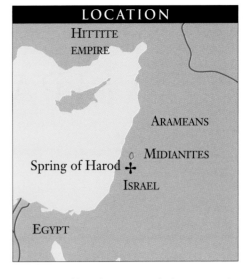

LOCATION

The Spring of Harod campaign took place on ground fought over by previous generations of Israelites. These were turbulent times with many tribes on the move.

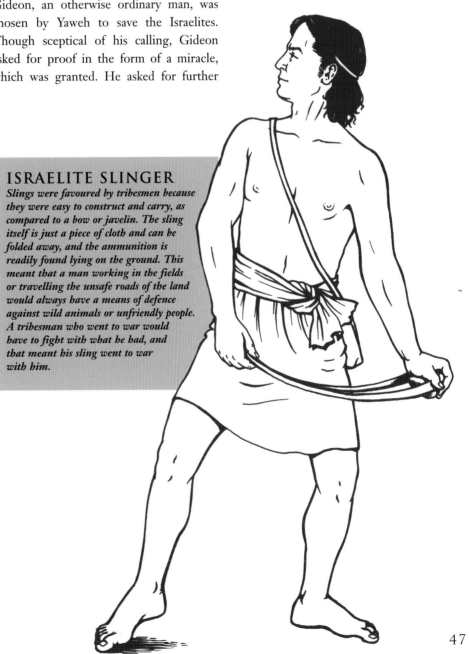

ISRAELITE SLINGER
Slings were favoured by tribesmen because they were easy to construct and carry, as compared to a bow or javelin. The sling itself is just a piece of cloth and can be folded away, and the ammunition is readily found lying on the ground. This meant that a man working in the fields or travelling the unsafe roads of the land would always have a means of defence against wild animals or unfriendly people. A tribesman who went to war would have to fight with what he had, and that meant his sling went to war with him.

In this nineteenth-century German wood engraving, Gideon asks for and is granted miracles to convince him that he was indeed favoured by God. In this depiction, an angel appears to confer the status of Judge.

THE OPPOSED FORCES

ISRAELITES (estimated)

Advance force:	300
Main force:	10,000
Total:	**10,300**

MIDIANITES
  Unknown, but a larger number
  of troops than the Israelites

proof and a second miracle occurred, which convinced him that he had been chosen to act in God's name.

Since the troubles faced by the Israelites resulted from their religious wavering, Gideon did not begin his military campaign before putting his own house in order. First, he went to the altars of Baal and Asherah in his hometown and destroyed them, chastising his people for turning away from the true God. No doubt, Gideon could cite many instances of troubles befalling Israel in which the cause was idolatry. In all these cases, the Israelites had ultimately been victorious, winning renewed peace and prosperity, but only after returning to the true path.

This sort of dramatic gesture, accompanied by suitably fiery preaching, was the hallmark of great leaders in Israel, and at some point thereafter Gideon began to be considered a Judge. Like other Judges before him, Gideon was able to rally support not just from his own people, but also among other tribes. He sent out messengers asking for help from the neighbouring tribes and soon a large number of men had gathered.

HOST OF ISRAEL ASSEMBLES

The warriors came from Gideon's own tribe, Manasseh, and also from Asher, Naphtali and Zebulun. There were more than 30,000 of them, which was far too many for Gideon's purposes. The Old Testament says that God wanted to make sure the credit for the coming victory went to him, presumably so that the Israelites would know that they could not thrive without their true religion.

A vast host such as this was big enough to win without divine assistance, or at least its members might think that the credit lay with them. This, the Bible says, did not suit God's purpose to show the Israelites that they needed divine help. Gideon was therefore instructed to send anyone who was afraid home.

It is possible that logistics might have played a part in the decision to field a smaller force. Feeding so many men would be a problem for a civilized nation with a regular army, let alone a tribal confederation like that of Israel.

Whatever the reason, by the time Gideon had finished, he commanded an army of about 10,000 men. These would be

An ox-drawn chariot of the Sea People, raiders who plagued the coasts of the region for many years. The exact origin of the Sea People remains a mystery, but they have been depicted on Egyptian reliefs from the period.

the best-armed, best-equipped and most fiercely motivated warriors that the four tribes could field. Such a force stood a good chance against its enemies; its fighting potential was probably not much less than that of the original gathering of less well-armed warriors.

This was still a problem, for if Gideon's army won in battle, its success could be ascribed to the experience, good equipment and skill of the men, and Gideon's wisdom in picking the best men he could find. It was therefore necessary to create a force that could not possibly win without the direct assistance of God.

So, when the army reached a river and stopped to drink, Gideon observed what the men did. Some threw themselves on their bellies and drank directly from the river. Others got down on their knees. While they were doing so, they were oblivious to their surroundings and vulnerable to attack.

A small percentage of Gideon's men did neither of these things. They scooped up water in their hands and lapped at it, all the time keeping watch for enemies. Gideon now ordered everyone else to remain behind. He would go on ahead with just these men. There were only 300 of them, but these were the most watchful and experienced of the 10,000 well-equipped men Gideon had rallied. They were the nearest equivalent to an elite special-forces unit that Israel could field.

It says much for the authority of the Judges that Gideon, who was no proven general or famous political leader, could call more than 30,000 men from four tribes, only to send two-thirds of them home again. Now, as the army neared the enemy, he wanted to dispense with most of his army and attack with a tiny force. Yet the army accepted his commands and waited.

GIDEON'S DECEPTION

Gideon had a plan. He moved his 300 men into position after dark. Each of them had a trumpet and a torch concealed in a clay jar. They approached the Midianite camp stealthily and, upon Gideon's signal, each man revealed his torch and blew his trumpet.

It may be that Gideon reached the conclusion – as Napoleon would do during his great Italian campaign so many years later – that psychology is far more important than physical fighting power. In any case, the effect was profound.

The Midianites woke from their slumbers to a great din of trumpets. The torches of an army were advancing towards their camp. They were sleepy, surprised and

An Ammonite nobleman. Although closely related to the Hebrews, the Ammonites were their enemies for many generations and fought bitter wars against them.

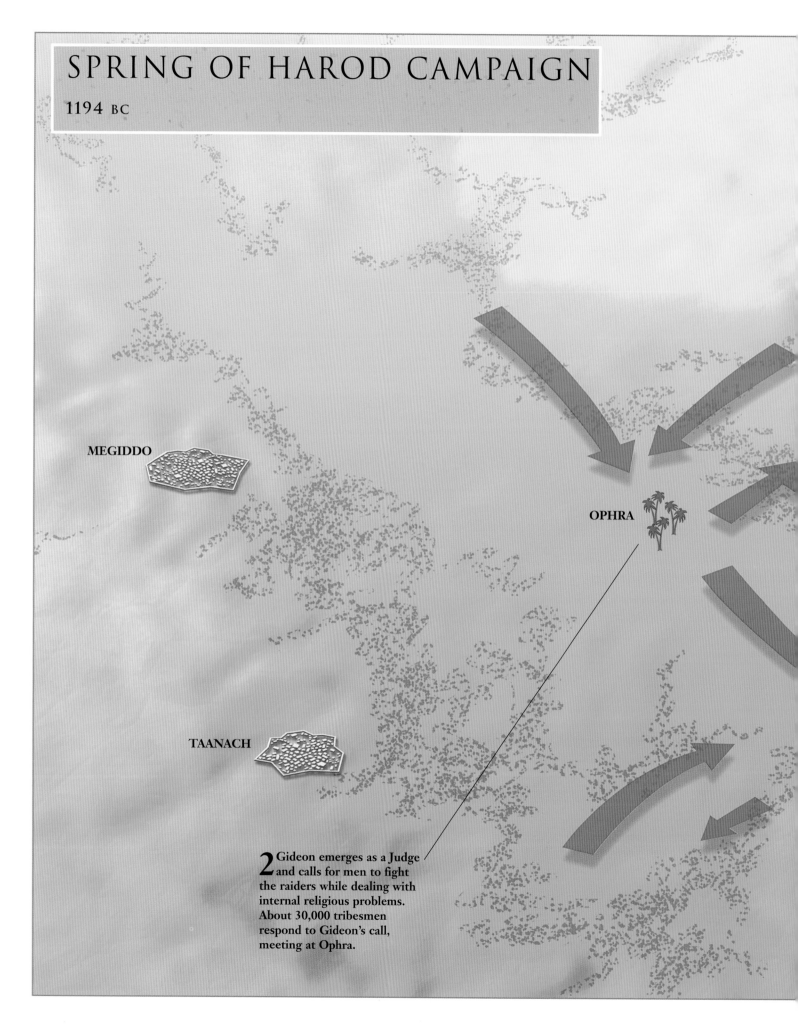

SPRING OF HAROD CAMPAIGN

1194 BC

MEGIDDO

OPHRA

TAANACH

2 Gideon emerges as a Judge and calls for men to fight the raiders while dealing with internal religious problems. About 30,000 tribesmen respond to Gideon's call, meeting at Ophra.

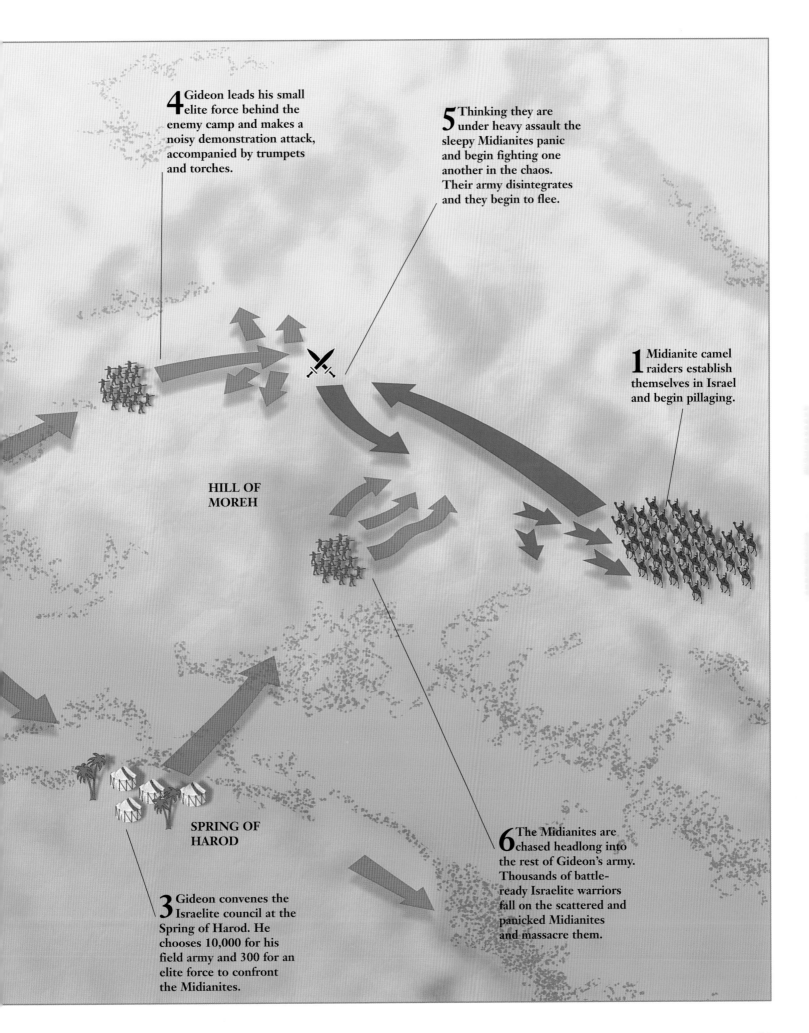

4 Gideon leads his small elite force behind the enemy camp and makes a noisy demonstration attack, accompanied by trumpets and torches.

5 Thinking they are under heavy assault the sleepy Midianites panic and begin fighting one another in the chaos. Their army disintegrates and they begin to flee.

1 Midianite camel raiders establish themselves in Israel and begin pillaging.

HILL OF MOREH

SPRING OF HAROD

3 Gideon convenes the Israelite council at the Spring of Harod. He chooses 10,000 for his field army and 300 for an elite force to confront the Midianites.

6 The Midianites are chased headlong into the rest of Gideon's army. Thousands of battle-ready Israelite warriors fall on the scattered and panicked Midianites and massacre them.

SPRING OF HAROD CAMPAIGN

confused, all of which quickly turned to fright. In the chaos, men mistook one another for enemies and fighting broke out in the camp. This added to the general panic and soon the Midianites were fighting among themselves, thinking that they were being overrun by a great army.

THE MIDIANITES ROUT

No attempt to rally or organize the Midianites succeeded, and men began to flee what they thought was a losing battle, pursued by trumpet blasts from their enemies. They fled through the darkness without order and in many cases without weapons or armour.

With trumpets sounding and the clash of weapons behind them, the Midianites rushed westwards seeking safety. What they found was the 10,000 men Gideon had brought with him. The Midianites, driven headlong onto the weapons of Gideon's army, stood no chance at all.

The fighting was extremely one-sided, and the Israelites were not inclined to be merciful. Their foes, who had made their lives miserable for years, were now delivered onto their spear points by God or Gideon's cleverness. It mattered little which, for the Israelites made the most of their opportunity.

The battle was not without tragedy for the Israelites. Gideon's brothers were killed in the fighting, as were many Israelite warriors. Things were much worse for the Midianites, who were already beaten when the fighting began and who were scattered, captured or massacred. The kings of the Midianites were captured, and Gideon put them to death to avenge his brothers.

AFTERMATH

The Midianites suffered terribly at Gideon's hand and ceased to be a factor in Israelite affairs. For their part, the Israelites thought so much of Gideon that they asked him to become their king. Gideon was not impressed and vigorously refused to accept the position, though years later his son Abimelech was appointed as king in his hometown. This was a local position rather than the overlordship of the tribes that Gideon was offered and, in any case, short-lived.

Though Gideon did not approve of the offer to install him as king of the Israelites, he did allow his followers to make him an idol from gold captured in the campaign.

Predictably, the biblical account relates that this piece of ill-advised paganism caused new troubles for Israel some years later, as it inspired others to make false idols. In the meantime, however, there was peace for many years. Gideon did not need to fight another campaign, and remained an influential figure for the rest of his life.

Above: Gideon observes his men drinking from the river. Only those that drank from their cupped hands, watching around them for enemies, were chosen for the attack.

Opposite: Gideon refused kingship of his people, but his son Abimelech had other ideas. Abimelech was a bad king who offended his people. He was mortally wounded by a millstone thrown from the wall above him, as depicted in this woodcut by Gustav Doré.

MICHMASH
1040 BC

FOR GENERATIONS, THE ISRAELITES, A CONFEDERATION OF TRIBAL PEOPLES, HAD STRUGGLED TO ESTABLISH THEMSELVES SECURELY IN THE 'PROMISED LAND'. EVEN PRIOR TO THE BIBLICAL EXODUS, WHEN MOSES LED THE CHILDREN OF ISRAEL OUT OF BONDAGE IN EGYPT IN THE THIRTEENTH CENTURY BC, THE HEBREWS HAD TREKKED INTO CANAAN, A PROVINCE OF THE EMPIRE THAT HAD ENSLAVED THEM.

WHY DID IT HAPPEN?

WHO The Israelites under King Saul against the army of the Philistines.

WHAT The individual heroism of Jonathan, son of King Saul, resulted in the rout of the Philistines, compelling them to retire from the interior of Canaan.

WHERE North of Jerusalem in the expanse of the Wadi es-Suweinit on the edge of the Judean Desert.

WHEN 1040 BC.

WHY The Israelites sought to remove the threat of Philistine expansion in Canaan.

OUTCOME Saul was established as a great warrior king and was further victorious against numerous enemies of Israel, although conflict with the Philistines would persist.

Following three significant victories – Joshua's over the Canaanites at the Waters of Merom; the defeat of General Sisera at the River Kishon by Great Judge Deborah, the warrior prophetess, in concert with Barak; and Gideon's annihilation of the Midianites – the Israelites had gained the upper hand in the disputed territory. However, a burgeoning threat loomed to the west, where the Philistines had slowly but steadily asserted themselves from the Mediterranean shores of southwest Canaan to the interior of the land.

The lineage of the Philistines is a topic of scholarly debate, but archaeological excavations and research indicate that they were a people related to the Myceneans of the Peloponnesus and the reaches of Greek influence. Their tactics of raiding and

expansion have been likened to those of the European Vikings. At the beginning of the twelfth century BC, the Philistines, who have been associated with a confederation called the 'Sea Peoples', were said to have undertaken a campaign to settle along the Canaanite coast. Defending their territory, the Egyptians, under Pharaoh Rameses III (1198–1167 BC), defeated the Philistines in a protracted naval battle, which occurred around 1190 BC.

According to ancient texts, Rameses III is reported to have subjugated the

---

This medieval illustration depicts King Saul greeting Samuel, the prophet of God. When the people of Israel clamoured for a king, the prophet chose Saul from the tribe of Benjamin.

conquered enemy, declaring that he had 'settled them in strongholds, bound in my name. Numerous were their classes, like hundred-thousands. I taxed them all, in clothing and grain from the storehouses and granaries each year.'

As Egyptian power began to wane, the Philistines undertook their venture into the interior of Canaan, which brought them into direct conflict with the Israelites. In fact, the very name by which these people have come to be known is said to translate from the Hebrew word *plishah*, which means 'Invader from the West'.

THE ASCENT OF SAUL

Little more than a century after their defeat at the hands of Rameses III, the Philistines had reached the foothills of the Judean Mountains. They now confronted the Israelites, who were experiencing difficulties maintaining cooperation between a coalition of tribes that had varied agendas and mutual distrust. The Philistines further appear to have extended their dominion into the regions of Judah and Benjamin. The threat to the Israelites was readily apparent, and compounding their predicament was the presence of the expansionist-minded Ammonites to the east of the River Jordan in the vicinity of Gilead.

During this unsettling time, the leadership of Samuel proved essential in preserving, protecting and defending the land of the Israelites. Samuel served foremost as the prophet and interpreter of the will of God. He had battled the Philistines and had occupied the seat of judgment, settling disputes among the people. Amid the growing threat from both east and west, the tribal leaders clamoured for the appointment of a king.

The Bible says that God spoke to Samuel, telling the prophet that he was being rejected by the Israelites in similar fashion to their rejection of the Almighty after their delivery from bondage in Egypt. Samuel was instructed to warn the tribes of what would happen during the reign of an earthly king.

He told the gathered chiefs:

When that day comes, you will cry out for relief from the king you have chosen, and the

PHILLISTINE ARCHER
A Philistine archer draws his bow. Prized as warriors, archers were the equivalent of artillery in the armies of the major kingdoms that fought for control of the Eastern Mediterranean a millennium before the birth of Christ. Once dominated by the Egyptians under Pharaoh Rameses III, who had defeated them in a great sea battle in 1190 BC, the Philistines began a foray into the interior of Canaan as Egyptian influence ebbed. After Michmash, the Bible records that Saul continued to win victories against the Philistines, until killed by a Philistine archer at the Battle of Mount Gilboa.

Lord will not answer you in that day (I Samuel 8: 18.)

The response was predictable:

But the people refused to listen to Samuel. "No!" they said. "We want a king over us. Then we will be like all the other nations, with a king to lead us and to go out before us and fight our battles." (I Samuel 8: 19-20.)

God then instructed Samuel to give the people a king. His choice was Saul, who is described as an impressive young man without equal among the Israelites, and who stood a head taller than any other man. The precise circumstances surrounding Saul's anointment as king are unclear, because they are recorded differently in various texts, but the decision was a logical one. Saul was a son of the tribe of Benjamin, the smallest of the Israelite tribes but also one

LOCATION

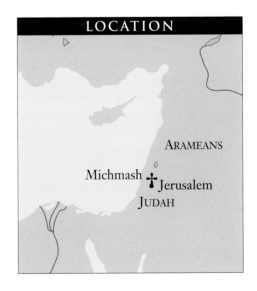

At Michmash, the difficult terrain hardly seemed suited for a major clash of arms. In the gorge of Wadi es-Suweinit, a single road led down to the narrow, rock-walled pass.

Dating from 1200-100 BC, this Egyptian bas-relief of an individual of the 'Sea Peoples' may depict a Philistine. The Philistines were said to have once been a seafaring people.

THE OPPOSED FORCES

ISRAELITES (estimated)
Infantry   600
augmented by returning
deserters and civilians
Total: **600**

PHILISTINES (estimated)
Charioteers: 6000
Infantry: 90,000
Total: **96,000**

with battle experience. Furthermore, with Saul as king, some of the internal quarrelling among the larger tribes might be quelled.

THE TEST AT JABESH-GILEAD

Only a month after becoming the first king of Israel, Saul received a call to action. The crisis was in the east, where Nahash and the Ammonites had laid siege to the town of Jabesh-Gilead. Capitulation would mean the establishment of a hostile lodgement in the Israelite heartland. When the people of Jabesh-Gilead offered to surrender on

favourable terms, the harsh reply from Nahash revealed the gravity of the situation.

No treaty would be negotiated with the inhabitants of Jabesh-Gilead unless every one of them submitted to having their right eye gouged out as a sign of submission and disgrace. The leaders of the town then requested seven days to send messengers throughout Israel with requests for assistance. Should they find themselves abandoned by their countrymen, they would surrender the city to the Ammonites.

For a brief period, Saul had returned to a life of farming at Gibeah. Upon his return from the fields one day, he was confronted with a messenger from Jabesh-Gilead bearing news of the horrific ultimatum. The people of Gibeah became distraught, weeping and wailing at the prospect of impending catastrophe. Saul took action, chopping a pair of oxen into pieces and dispersing them by messenger across Israel, decreeing: 'This is what will be done to the oxen of anyone who does not follow Saul and Samuel'. (I Samuel 11: 7.)

The call to arms was quite effective, and the Bible says that 300,000 men of Israel and 30,000 men of Judah were raised into an army. Word was sent back to Jabesh-Gilead: 'By the time the sun is hot tomorrow, you will be delivered.'

Saul marched his formidable force, aligned in three divisions, to meet the enemy. He attacked under cover of darkness, neutralizing any advantage of superior arms that the Ammonites might have. Saul's troops fell upon the Ammonite camp and wreaked havoc, killing until the sun was fully risen in the sky. The surviving Ammonites were scattered in such disarray that, according to the Bible, no two of them were left accompanying one another.

PHILISTINE MENACE

The raising of the siege of Jabesh-Gilead brought Saul tremendous prestige, and at Gilgal all of Israel affirmed his position as their sovereign. However, even as he rejoiced in the victory, the newly emboldened king made preparations to eject the Philistines from his country. For both offensive and defensive reasons, he established a small standing army, numbering only 3000, with 1000 soldiers under his son, Jonathan, at Gibeah, and the other 2000 with Saul at Michmash and in the neighbouring hills around Bethel in the territory of Benjamin. The remaining troops were instructed to return to their homes and farms.

This deliberate provocation of the Philistines may be viewed as simply the onset of the inevitable. Conflict had simmered for years and occasionally erupted into fighting. Now, flush with the victory over the Ammonites, the time seemed ripe for a decisive outcome. Jonathan, the eldest of Saul's sons, struck the Philistine outpost at Geba, which the interlopers had garrisoned to maintain control of the Israelites in the vicinity, and killed the Philistine governor.

This was followed by Saul's announcement of the action and a rallying cry to the Israelites to join him at Gilgal: 'Let the Hebrews hear!' So all Israel heard the news: 'Saul has attacked the Philistine outpost, and now Israel has become a stench to the Philistines'. (I Samuel 13: 3–4.)

During this time, Samuel took great care to remind the Israelites that God had delivered them from their enemies on several occasions but punished them when they had turned away from Him. Samuel

A triumphant King Saul leads the Israelite army during the rout of the Ammonites at Jabesh-Gilead. Saul's troops slaughtered the enemy in their camp and raised the siege of the city.

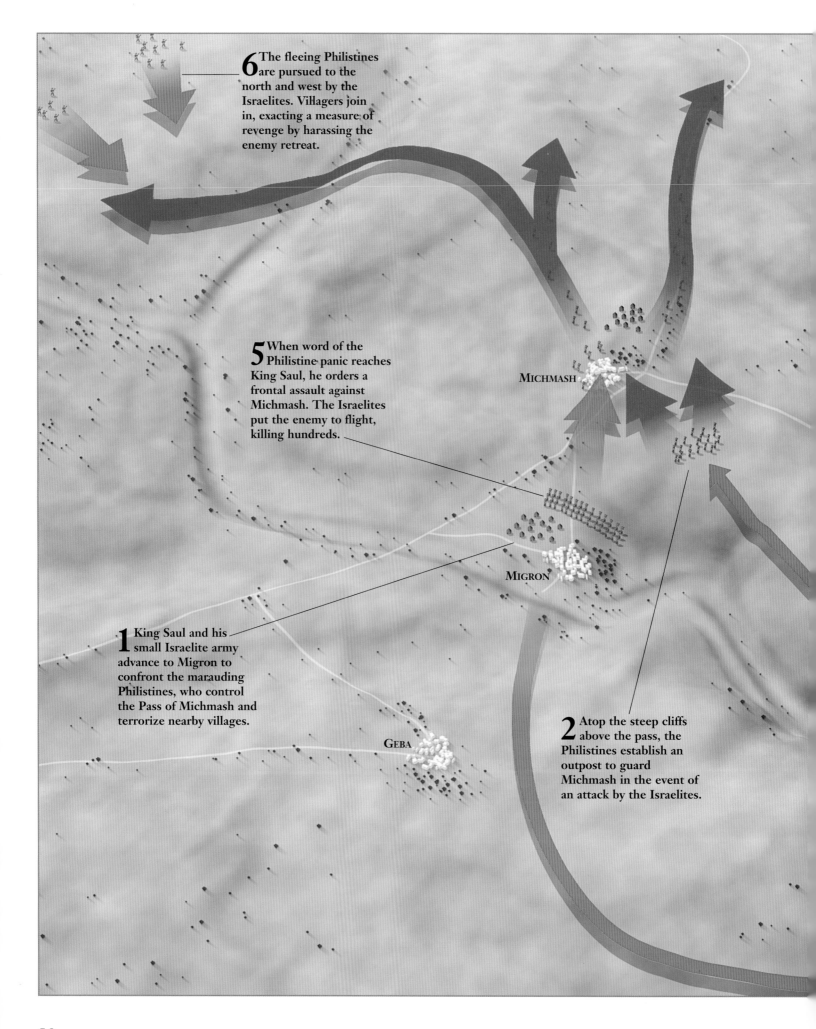

6 The fleeing Philistines are pursued to the north and west by the Israelites. Villagers join in, exacting a measure of revenge by harassing the enemy retreat.

5 When word of the Philistine panic reaches King Saul, he orders a frontal assault against Michmash. The Israelites put the enemy to flight, killing hundreds.

MICHMASH

MIGRON

1 King Saul and his small Israelite army advance to Migron to confront the marauding Philistines, who control the Pass of Michmash and terrorize nearby villages.

GEBA

2 Atop the steep cliffs above the pass, the Philistines establish an outpost to guard Michmash in the event of an attack by the Israelites.

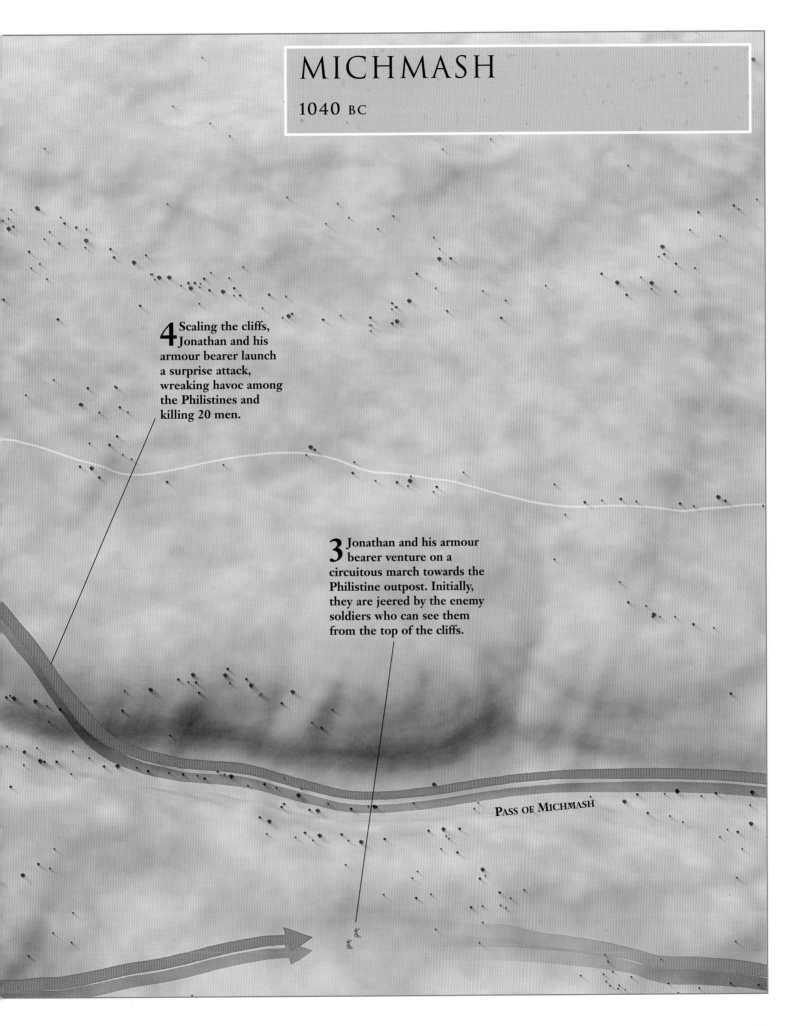

MICHMASH

1040 BC

4 Scaling the cliffs, Jonathan and his armour bearer launch a surprise attack, wreaking havoc among the Philistines and killing 20 men.

3 Jonathan and his armour bearer venture on a circuitous march towards the Philistine outpost. Initially, they are jeered by the enemy soldiers who can see them from the top of the cliffs.

PASS OF MICHMASH

MICHMASH

The prophet Samuel leads Israelites in the burning of a sacrifice to God upon an altar. When Saul failed to follow his instructions, Samuel pronounced that his kingdom would not endure.

warned the people that their continuing disobedience would have only one result: their destruction.

Certainly, the ability of both Samuel and Saul to arouse the religious fervour of the Israelites and spur them to military action played an important role in their subsequent efforts to rid the land of the Philistines. However, when confronted with the enemy host, the resolve of the Israelites began to weaken significantly, jeopardizing the future of their nation.

THE MICHMASH CAMPAIGN

The Philistine reaction was swift. The Bible says that they assembled a force of some 3000 chariots manned by 6000 charioteers and complemented by infantrymen who were as numberous as the grains of sand on the seashore. They advanced to Michmash, where, politically, their very presence was an overt challenge to Saul's sovereignty, and, militarily, they were able to contest any movement from the Desert of Judea towards the mountains. At Michmash, in the gorge of Wadi es-Suweinit, a winding road descends into a rugged valley near the present-day town of Mukhmas, approximately 11km (7 miles) north of Jerusalem. At the foot of the valley is the Pass of Michmash, with rocky walls on either side. Saul had relocated his force to Geba, which Jonathan had previously occupied. By that time, the Israelites had become aware of the Philistine advance. Many of them were seized with fear and fled, hiding in caves, thickets and even cisterns. Saul, his force now dwindled to a

A Philistine war chariot thunders forward. Swift, mobile and often decisive on the battlefield, the chariot was large enough to accommodate a driver and two additional foot soldiers or archers.

MICHMASH

mere 600 soldiers, had also raised the ire of Samuel, who had instructed him to wait seven days for the prophet's arrival at Gilgal. The Bible relates that Saul was disturbed by the desertions and chose not to wait for Samuel, taking it upon himself to offer a burnt sacrifice to God. Samuel chastised Saul for his lack of faith, pronouncing that Saul's kingdom would not endure.

Meanwhile, the Philistines, probably aware of the disagreement between Samuel and Saul and of the mass desertions that had occurred among the Israelites, sent three strong raiding parties against Ophrah, Beth-horon and the Valley of Zeboim along the rim of the Judean Desert.

With the Philistines now in control of the Pass of Michmash, and their destructive forays laying waste to the surrounding towns and villages, Saul marched his small army to Migron. Although he did not, apparently, plan to launch an offensive against the Philistines, he did attempt to prevent further incursions against the civilian population.

THE RECKONING DAY

According to the Bible, the Philistines subjugated the Israelites to the extent that they were not allowed to forge or fabricate farm implements or weapons of iron:

'Not a blacksmith could be found in the whole land of Israel, because the Philistines had said, "Otherwise the Hebrews will make swords or spears!" So all Israel went down to the Philistines to have their ploughshares, mattocks, axes and sickles sharpened.' (I Samuel 13: 19–20.)

On the day of the Battle of Michmash, it is said that only Saul and Jonathan were armed with either a spear or sword.

With Saul and the Israelite army in the most precarious of situations, it was Jonathan who seized the moment. Acting with both faith and courage, and without informing anyone else, he summoned his armour bearer and proposed that the two of them assault the Philistine position in the Pass of Michmash. When they revealed themselves to the Philistines, they were believed to be fugitives from Saul's army. The Philistines hurled insults at the pair and taunted them to scale the cliffs to their camp. According to the biblical account:

'Jonathan climbed up, using his hands and feet, with his armour bearer right behind him. The Philistines fell before Jonathan, and his armour bearer followed

A line of Philistine infantrymen, armed with spears and compact shields, steps forward. The Philistine army was well organized but fled before the onslaught of Jonathan and his armour bearer at Michmash.

and killed behind him. In that first attack, Jonathan and his armour bearer killed some 20 men in an area of about half an acre.' (I Samuel 14: 13–14.)

The sight of their fleeing comrades threw the main Philistine camp into disarray, and a confused retreat ensued. According to the Bible, it was God who sent panic among them. When Saul's lookouts observed what was happening, the king ordered his meagre forces to assemble and discovered that Jonathan and his armour bearer were missing. The Israelites executed a frontal assault against the disorganized Philistines, and in the mêlée many Hebrews who had been with the Philistines changed sides, joining Saul's force.

With their main avenue of escape cut off, the Philistines initially fled northwards before turning to the west, through and beyond Beth Aven and Aijalon. Word of the rout began to circulate throughout the

MICHMASH

countryside. Villagers who had fled the raiding parties and deserters from the ranks of Saul's army were now heartened enough to harass the Philistine withdrawal for miles.

THE SHADOW OF VICTORY

Saul had ordered his army to fast on the day of battle, possibly to prevent his soldiers from pausing in the pursuit of a beaten enemy and to maximize casualties. Jonathan, ironically, did not hear the command, and Saul ordered the hero of the battle, his own son, put to death.

Only the outcry of the soldiers and the possibility of a mutiny saved Jonathan's life that day. Saul had been vexed by both God's silence when he had asked for direction in continuing the battle against the fleeing enemy, and by Jonathan's impetuous act – even though the result was a victory. The

Opposite: Having severed the head of the giant Philistine warrior Goliath with a single stone from his slingshot, a victorious David brandishes his trophy in this late fifteenth-century rendering attributed to Andrea Mantegna.

Israelites did not pursue the Philistines further, and they were reported to have returned to their own land. Saul, the Bible says, was later victorious against the enemies of Israel on every side.

Campaigning against the Philistines continued. During one confrontation, the famed single combat of David and Goliath took place. During the ensuing years, Saul would fall into disfavour with God, and become a rival of David, the future king of Israel. Ultimately, he perished, along with Jonathan, at the Battle of Mount Gilboa.

The rugged Judean mountains were the scene of numerous battles during the reign of King Saul, and the inhospitable terrain at Michmash presented an opportunity for the heroics of Jonathan.

JERUSALEM
1000 BC

THE CAPTURE OF JERUSALEM WAS A PIVOTAL MOMENT IN WORLD HISTORY. KING DAVID MOVED HIS CAPITAL THERE AND RULED OVER A LARGE DOMAIN THAT INCLUDED THE FORMERLY SEPARATE KINGDOMS OF ISRAEL AND JUDAH.

WHY DID IT HAPPEN?

WHO A small Hebrew army under King David (c.1002–970 BC), opposed by the defenders of Jebus (Jerusalem).

WHAT Despite taunts from his enemy to the effect that they were secure in their fortress, David was able to storm and capture the city.

WHERE The city of Jebus (Jerusalem).

WHEN c.1000 BC.

WHY Having become King of both Israel and Judah, David set about pacifying the region and creating a unified kingdom.

OUTCOME King David made Jerusalem his capital; it has been referred to as the City of David ever since.

The modern-day city of Jerusalem has existed in one form or another since the fourth millennium BC, and possibly before even then. It gained vast importance when it became capital of David's united kingdom, and remains the spiritual, if not political, capital of the Jewish people to this day.

However, before the time of King David the city was known as Jebus and was the home of the Jebusites, a Canaanite tribe related to the Hittites and Amorites. The former had been a major power in the region, ruling a large empire for several centuries before it went into decline from around 1500 BC.

It is also possible that the Jebusites were Hurrians, a widespread people forming a segment of most regional populations but with little power of their own. As the Hurrians were absorbed into other cultures it is likely that they were an influence on the Jebusites. At this time, the Israelites were a tribal confederation that had managed to survive for about two centuries. However, conflict with the Philistines had been ongoing for many years and was gradually increasing in seriousness. The Philistines were formidable warriors and formed an aristocracy that ruled over a variety of conquered peoples, many of them Canaanites. The Philistines saw Israel as a threat to their security and moved against the loose tribal organization.

THE TWO SIDES

The Philistines had several advantages, not least the possession of good weapons and iron armour, which was uncommon in the region at that time. They were also well organized where the Israelites were not, and though the nearest tribes put up what

The remains of the Jebusite fortress on Mount Zion in Jerusalem. The Tomb of David is located here and this is where, according to tradition, the Last Supper took place.

ISRAELITE CHARIOT

An Israelite chariot. The horses of the period were not strong enough for really effective cavalry use, so the chariot filled that role. Several foot warriors could be outfitted for the cost of a single chariot. However, even though the chariot carried only a single fighting man in addition to the driver, it represented considerable fighting power, capable of striking anywhere on the field and escaping from a difficult situation. The psychological impact of a chariot assault was considerable; the terror it caused was sometimes enough to break an enemy force without any need to enter combat.

resistance they could, this was piecemeal at best and insufficient to deal with the Philistine advance.

Faced with a well-armed, disciplined and determined enemy who would not be dissuaded by setbacks, the Israelites were in mortal danger. Their tribal hosts were easily scattered by the Philistines and ridden down by their chariots. Even when the Israelites took the Ark of the Covenant into battle near Aphek in 1050 BC, it made little difference. The Ark was captured and the army scattered. Its home, the shrine at Shiloh, was destroyed, though the Ark itself was returned to the Israelites.

With much of their land under occupation and the practice of metalwork forbidden to them, the Israelites were in a difficult position. Some regions, especially those with difficult terrain such as mountains or desert, harboured resistance, but to all intents and purposes the old tribal confederation was destroyed. In this lay the seeds of David's kingdom.

GUERRILLA WARFARE

Throughout the Philistine occupation, the spirit of Israel was kept alive by bands of rebels and rabid prophets who travelled among the tribes inciting them to resist the invaders. The most famous of these prophets is Samuel, but although the men he inspired to fight made life difficult for the Philistines, they could not eject the invaders. That required something more than sporadic resistance by armed bands.

Reluctantly, and not without grave misgivings, the Israelites moved towards the idea of electing a king to unite and lead them all. The man chosen was Saul (1050?–1010? BC), who had already proven his leadership in battle against invaders from Ammon. Whether or not the prophet Samuel initially supported Saul (accounts vary), it was not long before he turned against the new king, weakening the fragile monarchy.

Despite these internal problems, Saul was able to rally sufficient support to challenge the Philistines, and at the pass of Michmash the Israelites won a great victory. This served to convince many doubters that Yaweh had chosen Saul as the instrument of Israel's salvation. His support grew massively and the Philistine occupation greatly weakened.

Saul spent his entire reign at war. Mostly he fought the Philistines, but he was also forced to deal with opportunistic incursions by neighbouring tribes. Although the idea of monarchy was alien to the Israelites, Saul was able to consolidate his power and enjoyed considerable popular support as the protector of his people. Saul's elevation to kingship did not radically change the lives of the Israelites. His seat of power was a fortress

LOCATION

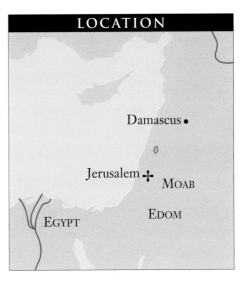

Damascus •

Jerusalem ✝ MOAB

EGYPT   EDOM

The location of Jerusalem in fertile land close to the Mediterranean has made it a desirable location for millennia, and thus the scene for many conflicts.

rather than a palace and he did not create a court nor set up a bureaucracy. He led the tribes as much as ruled them, and though he did begin to create a body of proven soldiers, there was no real move towards a formal standing army.

In the neighbouring land of Judah, also populated by Israelite tribes, Saul came to be accepted as a great leader, though he was not universally recognized as king. His leadership for a time forced back the Philistine threat, and the fortunes of the Israelite tribes rose accordingly. However, the strain began to tell on Saul and he became increasingly prone to irrational behaviour, which gradually alienated his supporters. His open dispute with the prophet Samuel did little to help matters. As the rift deepened, Samuel even accused Saul of usurping priestly functions and attempted to revoke his kingship.

Despite his best efforts, Saul was unable to drive the Philistines entirely from Israel. In part, this was due to their military prowess, but it had a lot to do with the nature of Israelite society too. The tribes were extremely independent and would cooperate for only a short time. Saul's efforts to create a reliable professional fighting force achieved little, and so he was constantly forced to fight against heavy odds with a scratch force of undisciplined tribesmen. Saul became prone to fits of depression, which were interpreted as the influence of an evil spirit. It was found that music improved his condition, and it was as a musician as well as a warrior that David rose to prominence.

ENTER DAVID THE HERO

David was a young man of Bethlehem who, it was said, was favoured by Yaweh. Like several others, he had become part of Saul's household. This little body of warriors was the only professional force the Israelites had, and its members functioned as a bodyguard to Saul as well as his trusted captains. However, initially David was not a warrior. He accompanied Saul to play music for him, helping to break the king's depression and keep him focused on the task at hand. It was in this capacity that David was present when Saul's army met that of the Philistine champion Goliath.

Goliath, a giant of a man and also an accomplished warrior, issued a personal challenge to the Israelites to send out their greatest warrior to confront him in single combat. When no one was prepared to accept the challenge, he cursed both the Israelites and their god.

David, who was 17 years old at the time, was shocked and offended, ashamed that

Egyptian depictions of various people of the region – from right to left: a Canaanite or Jew, a lower Egyptian man and woman, and two Jebusites.

THE OPPOSED FORCES

ISRAELITES
Unknown number of irregular infantry

JEBUSITES
Unknown number of townspeople

A statue (circa eighteenth century) of Saul, King of Israel. He is depicted as a strong yet wise character – a Patriarch of his people rather than their ruler.

none of his people would confront Goliath. Although he was not a warrior, he had considerable skill with the sling and claimed to have killed both a lion and a bear with it while protecting his family's flocks. He asked Saul for permission to fight the giant.

Saul, who was extremely fond of the young David, took off his armour and offered it to his new champion. It proved too big and too heavy for David, who did not know how to use effectively the weapons that he was offered. Instead, he went forth armed only with a staff and – perhaps showing rather more pragmatism than heroism – his sling. As Goliath taunted his foe, David let fly with his sling and killed him. The Philistines were dismayed and fled the field in disorder, granting Saul a great victory for no cost.

David became a great hero among the Israelites, and a close friend of Saul's son

5 The Israelites manage to gain the top of the walls. Recovering from their shock, the defenders counterattack vigorously.

JEBUSITE ACROPOLIS

6 After desperate close-quarters fighting, the defenders break and David's men enter the city. Unusually, the Jebusites are treated leniently. David makes Jebus the capital of a united Israel.

SILOAN POOL

2 According to some accounts, David's men enter the city through the water system. It is doubtful as to whether this would enable a major assault, but a diversionary operation might have been feasible.

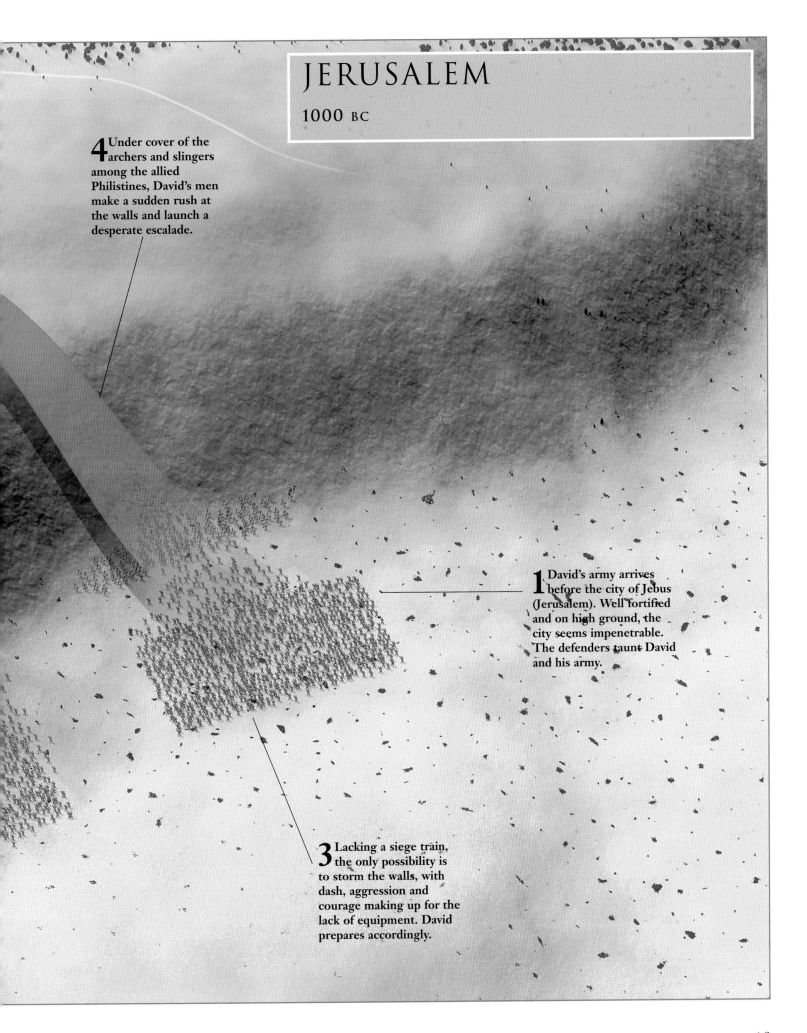

JERUSALEM

1000 BC

4 Under cover of the archers and slingers among the allied Philistines, David's men make a sudden rush at the walls and launch a desperate escalade.

1 David's army arrives before the city of Jebus (Jerusalem). Well fortified and on high ground, the city seems impenetrable. The defenders taunt David and his army.

3 Lacking a siege train, the only possibility is to storm the walls, with dash, aggression and courage making up for the lack of equipment. David prepares accordingly.

David's battle with Goliath as depicted in bronze by Lorenzo Ghiberti (1378-1455). Single combat between champions was an important part of warfare in the Old Testament period. Detail of the Doors of Paradise, *1425-1452, Florence Baptistery.*

Jonathon. He was offered the hand of Micah, daughter of Saul, in marriage. However, due to his increasingly unstable temperament, Saul could not cope with the adulation David now received. As David's popularity increased, so too did Saul's resentment until, eventually, he turned against his young friend and tried to have him killed.

DAVID AS OUTLAW

Saul's jealousy of David was increased by the fact that Samuel had anointed David as king to rule after Saul's death. David was forced to flee to the Philistines and was joined by others who had also been driven away by Saul's behaviour. He was given a vassal kingdom within Judah, in the hope that he would end up fighting Saul and weakening his kingdom.

David sent false despatches to the Philistines, claiming that he had been raiding into Judah when, in fact, he had been campaigning against enemy tribes of the Israelites. He thus strengthened his

position. He also had strong support among the priesthood. This was, in part, due to Saul's actions, for when he learned that the priests at Shiloh had helped David escape a murder plot, he had them slaughtered.

David's popularity and power continued to grow. He had opportunities to kill Saul and was urged to do so, but declined. Saul was eventually killed in battle at Gilboa, a massive defeat for the Israelites. The Philistines began to reoccupy their former conquests. The Israelites did what they could to oppose the new invasion, but could not muster effective resistance.

DAVID AS KING

David was proclaimed king in Judah. The Philistines approved of this development, since David was already a vassal of theirs. The other tribes of Israel gradually came to accept him as their leader, although some had a different allegiance. All but one of Saul's sons were killed at Gilboa. The survivor, Eshbaal, ruled a small segment of his father's territory. There was little open conflict between the two realms, though there were occasional skirmishes and a lot of political manoeuvring. Within a couple of years, it became obvious that Eshbaal was a weak leader and he was eventually murdered by some of his own officers.

David, meanwhile, was increasingly accepted as king throughout the Israelite tribes. He was a proven war leader who could protect his people and had the support of political figures as well as the priesthood. It soon became apparent to the Philistines that David was a threat – he was too popular and too powerful. He would have to be crushed. Thus the Philistine army marched against David's new kingdom.

David's reign was a time of great change for the Israelites. Not only did he create a standing force of professional troops, but he also led it to victory over the invaders at last. Backed by tribal levies, his force defeated the Philistines near Jebus (Jerusalem). Although outnumbered and faced by well-armed, strategic-thinking Philistines, David's small army defeated them twice. The second time was too much for the Philistines. They were harried out of the mountains and did not attempt to return.

David campaigned against the Philistines and broke their power, though he was unable to drive them from the region. It is probable that he came to an accommodation with his former foes, since there is no evidence that he took the cities of Ashdod, Ashkelon or Gaza. Indeed, it is known that Philistine troops served with David's forces in his later campaigns, so a peace deal seems likely. With the Philistine threat finally ended, the reason for the tribes to raise up a king over them was gone. David might have stood down and allowed his people to return to their old way of life, but too much had changed. He remained in power

and set about consolidating his control over the region.

At this time, David was king over several disparate groups, and his capital at Hebron in the far south was not acceptable to the northern tribes. David ruled from Hebron for several years but he knew that a better site was needed. He decided that the city of Jebus was ideal. The city had the additional advantage of being a stronghold of Canaanites within the lands of the Israelites. Taking the city would, therefore, remove the potential threat to David's realm.

THE TAKING OF JERUSALEM

Although, David's army was small and ill equipped, it was tough and experienced. All the same, the fortress city of Jebus was

The blinding of Samson as depicted by Rembrandt (1606-69). The Old Testament contains many individuals imbued with the superhuman powers atttributed to Samson, usually as a sign of divine favour or as enemies of Bible heroes.

JERUSALEM, 1000 BC

Some sources say that Saul was killed in battle at Gilboa. Others claim that he committed suicide, as depicted here, after being defeated. Either way, he and all but one of his sons perished (from The Suicide of Saul *by Pieter Bruegel, 1562).*

a formidable obstacle. Located at a height of 750m (2500ft) above sea level on a natural rock escarpment, the city had good walls, stout gates and strong towers. The defenders confidently taunted David's army that a handful of blind and lame individuals could defend the city.

David's army did not have the advantages of heavy armour or a large siege train. His force was composed mainly of light troops who, though highly effective in fluid combat in the mountains, were very vulnerable to missiles launched by the defenders. Many men wore no armour at all and were simply armed with a spear and a shield – not the ideal combination for a wall assault.

What David did have was a number of Philistine mercenaries under his command, as well as a fair number of archers and slingers. The latter provided covering fire while the rest of the infantry launched a do-or-die wall assault.

It has been suggested that David's men were able to enter the fortress through the water system, but archaeological research has discounted this possibility. More likely, the assault was sudden and covered by a hail of missiles, catching the defenders by surprise and keeping their heads down long enough for the Israelites to gain a foothold on the wall.

The desperate enterprise was successful and, after some hard fighting, the defence collapsed. The Jebusites were forced to surrender, and David treated them magnanimously. He did not put the populace to the sword and also allowed the former king of Jebus to live, which was remarkably merciful for the time. David even paid a fair price for private land seized in the capture of the city.

A UNITED ISRAEL

King David brought the Ark of the Covenant to Jebus, which became known as Jerusalem, and made his capital there. He ruled for many years over his large realm, benefiting from the city's excellent position between the north and south portions of his realm. This helped to avoid friction between the two groups since neither felt they were slighted by the capital's location.

David was able to pass a more or less united kingdom on to his son Solomon (d. 922 BC), who built the great temple at Jerusalem. The city's position was of great benefit to subsequent rulers, as it was not only central for political control, but also commanded the main trade routes between the two halves of the kingdom.

The election of Saul as king was an act of desperation and probably intended as a temporary measure until the Philistine threat receded. However, it led to the formation of a united kingdom under David and his descendents, and the rise of Israel as a major power in the region. Before the taking of Jerusalem, the Israelites were a collection of related tribes with a temporary king. Afterwards, Israel was a nation, and its people had a new identity.

King David brought the Ark of the Covenant to Jerusalem when he made it his capital. This combination of religious centre and administrative capital was entirely typical of Israel at the time.

SIEGE OF SAMARIA
890 BC

AS SO OFTEN HAPPENS IN HISTORY, THE DEATH OF A SOVEREIGN PRECIPITATES THE DECLINE OR DISMEMBERMENT OF A KINGDOM. SO IT WAS THAT WHEN KING SOLOMON DIED IN 922 BC, THE UNITED JEWISH KINGDOM WAS DIVIDED IN TWO. IN THE SOUTH WAS THE KINGDOM OF JUDAH, WITH ITS SEAT OF GOVERNMENT AT JERUSALEM. TO THE NORTH, THE KINGDOM OF ISRAEL EMERGED, WITH ITS ORIGINAL CAPITAL AT SHECHEM, SUBSEQUENTLY RELOCATED TO TIRZAH.

WHY DID IT HAPPEN?

WHO The Israelites under King Ahab against the coalition force of King Benhadad II of Syria.

WHAT The vastly outnumbered Israelites raised the siege of their capital city, putting the Syrian army and the drunken Benhadad II to flight.

WHERE The Israelite capital city of Samaria on the western edge of the Ephraimite uplands.

WHEN 890 BC.

WHY Syrian King Benhadad II initiated a pre-emptive strike against the growing strength of the Israelites, his traditional enemy.

OUTCOME The siege of Samaria was lifted, but the army of Benhadad II was not completely destroyed, setting the stage for renewed conflict.

The Israelite King Omri (c.883–872 BC) reigned at Tirzah for six years. Then, he sought a location to build a capital city all his own. About 14.5km (9 miles) east of Tirzah stands a hill called Shomron, which translated from the Hebrew means literally 'watchtower' or 'watch mountain'. From the high vantage point atop the hill, the surrounding countryside could be observed for miles, and a city could be defended against invaders, its steep sides providing a natural obstacle.

For two talents of silver, Omri purchased the hill from its owner, a farmer named Shemer, and set about constructing the third capital city of the kingdom of Israel. Over time, as the prestige of the new city grew, the region of the capital also came to be called Samaria, and its inhabitants Samaritans. Although the historical record is unclear, Omri apparently waged at least one unsuccessful war against the Syrians. The result was that the Syrians were allowed to establish trade areas in the region of Samaria. While such an arrangement may have been a condition of a peace treaty, it did not bode well for future relations between the Israelites and the nearby kingdom of Aram, or modern Syria.

Omri did apparently draw some strength through a close relationship with the Phoenicians, perhaps the most highly

This barren landscape of the mountains of Judea is typical of the area where the Israelite King Omri purchased a prominent hill and proceeded to build his new capital city.

skilled seafarers in the Mediterranean basin. The close relationship between the Israelites and the Phoenicians is evidenced by the marriage of Ahab (c.889–850 BC), the son of Omri and heir to the throne at Samaria, to Jezebel (d.842 BC), the daughter of Ethbaal, the Phoenician king of Tyre. The marriage of Ahab and Jezebel would prove to be the catalyst for the eventual ruin of the Israelite monarchy.

AHAB, IDOLS AND ARMS

Ahab ruled over the kingdom of Israel for 22 controversial and violent years. His marriage to Jezebel was marked by the introduction of the pagan gods Baal and Asherah into the kingdom, with the apparent approval and support of Ahab. On more than one occasion, Ahab proved himself to be irresolute when faced with the most difficult of decisions, bending to the will of others.

'Ahab son of Omri did more evil in the eyes of the Lord than any of those before him', the Bible says. 'He set up an altar for Baal in the temple of Baal that he built in Samaria. Ahab also made an Asherah pole and did more to provoke the Lord, the God of Israel, to anger than did all the kings of Israel before him.' (I Kings 16: 30, 32–33.)

The prophet Elijah then foretold of a great drought and famine that would ravage the Israelite kingdom until the day of repentance. Only at the utterance of Elijah, who fled into exile, would life-giving rain return. The Bible tells of a great contest atop Mount Carmel, in which the prophets of Baal and Elijah, who had returned to confront the ruler after the prolonged agony of the people, would determine whose god was the true god. Each of the 450 prophets of Baal and Elijah were to build an altar. The god who responded to the pleadings of his prophets by lighting the fire of the altar would prevail.

When the god of Elijah sent lightning to strike his altar, the contest was over. According to custom, the consequences of failure were dire. The Bible recounts: 'Then Elijah commanded them, "Seize the prophets of Baal. Don't let anyone get away!" They seized them, and Elijah had

SIEGE OF SAMARIA

them brought down to the Kishon Valley and slaughtered there.' (I Kings 18: 40.) When Ahab related the series of events, including the execution of the prophets of Baal, to Jezebel, her anger was so strong that she vowed revenge: 'So Jezebel sent a messenger to Elijah to say, "May the gods deal with me, be it ever so severely, if by this time tomorrow I do not make your life like that of one of them."' (I Kings 19: 2.) Elijah again fled for his life, and the clouds of war gathered over Israel.

BENHADAD II BIDS FOR PRE-EMINENCE

Despite the difficulties chronicled in the Biblical text, archaeological excavations reveal that Samaria prospered for a time. Despite facilitating the introduction of the worship of pagan gods into Israel at the behest of his wicked wife, Ahab had wealth enough to construct a magnificent palace with furnishings and fixtures richly embellished with ivory. Commerce and trade seemed to flourish.

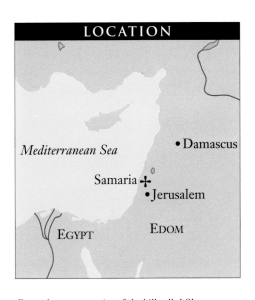

LOCATION

Mediterranean Sea

• Damascus

Samaria ✛

• Jerusalem

EGYPT

EDOM

From the vantage point of the hill called Shomron, lookouts were able to see an approaching enemy far in the distance, while the Israelite army would possess a strong defensive position.

SIEGE OF SAMARIA

This map shows the military and transport infrastructure of Solomon's (c.970–931 BC) realm. Solomon had constructed a series of fortified towns and ports, connected by an effective road network. With the introduction of the chariot, Solomon's forces were able to move quickly through the country to counter any invasion force.

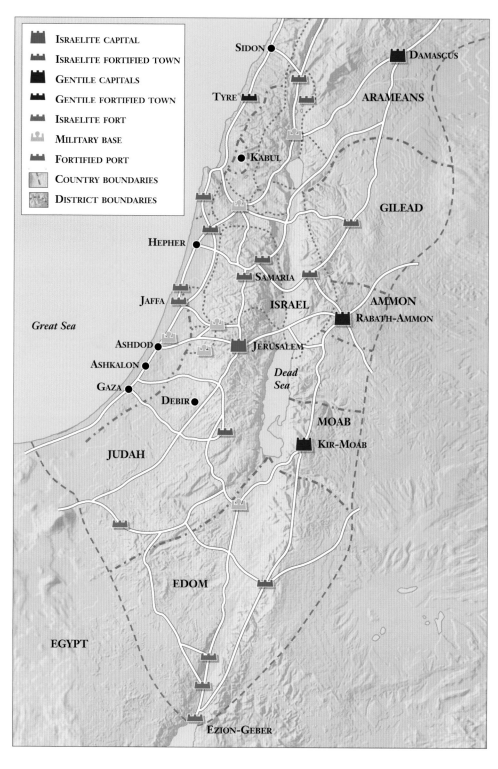

Israelite capital

Israelite fortified town

Gentile capitals

Gentile fortified town

Israelite fort

Military base

Fortified port

Country boundaries

District boundaries

THE OPPOSED FORCES

ISRAELITES (estimated)
Infantry and Charioteers: 8000
including the 232 soldiers
of the elite ne'arim
Total: **8000**

SYRIANS (estimated)
Infantry and Charioteers: a
coalition force comprised of the
army of Benhadad II and those of
32 vassal and allied kings.
Total: **Unknown**

Wary of his neighbour and the apparent return of prosperity to the Israelite kingdom, Benhadad II, the king of Aram (modern Syria), set out from Damascus to quell the perceived threat from his neighbour, which seemed to be growing stronger by the day.

Benhadad II was probably also motivated by the need to secure territory, such as the Golan Heights, which had belonged to the Israelites during the days of King Solomon and was subsequently wrested from them during the conflict with Omri. Benhadad II assembled a confederation of 32 kings and their armies, marching from the area around Damascus to the gates of Samaria. Presumably, these allies of the Syrian king were the heads of vassal states or related kingdoms that may also have felt threatened by the burgeoning strength and prosperity of the Israelites.

While Benhadad II and his host bore down upon Ahab's capital, the Israelite king was in conference with a group of leaders from the various districts of the kingdom and provincial commanders of militia.

As precious time ebbed away, Ahab was unable to organize an effective defence. Either Benhadad II had moved with unanticipated speed, or there may have been confusion among the Israelites. Given Ahab's penchant for indecisiveness, the latter may well have been the case. Whatever the reason, he found himself cut off from the main body of his army. According to the Bible, the effective number of troops actually available to Ahab in the besieged city numbered fewer than 8000 men.

SETTLING DOWN TO SIEGE

Benhadad II considered the eventual fall of Samaria to be a foregone conclusion as he drew his forces into a tight cordon around the city. The Syrian king determined to settle in for a protracted siege, observing that only a relatively small number of troops defended the prize, while those Israelite soldiers who might attempt to organize and

march to the relief of the besieged capital would be required to do so without their senior leadership.

Confident that his campaign would end, sooner or later, successfully, he now delivered an ultimatum to Ahab. His messengers were admitted within the city's walls and declared: 'This is what Benhadad says: "Your silver and gold are mine, and the best of your wives and children are mine."' (I Kings 20: 2–3.) Ahab, confronted with insurmountable odds and intent on self-preservation, was quick to accept the terms of surrender.

At this point, however, the Syrian king committed a grave error. Raising the stakes for Ahab and the Israelites, he heaped even greater humiliation on them with yet another demand. The messengers returned to them and said: 'This is what Benhadad says: "I sent to demand your silver and gold, your wives and your children. But about this time tomorrow I am going to send my officials to search your palace and the houses of your officials. They will seize

The ruins of Amri Ahab Palace in the hills of Samaria are preserved as part of the archaeological site of Sabastiya. The location is within the modern Israeli Occupied Territories.

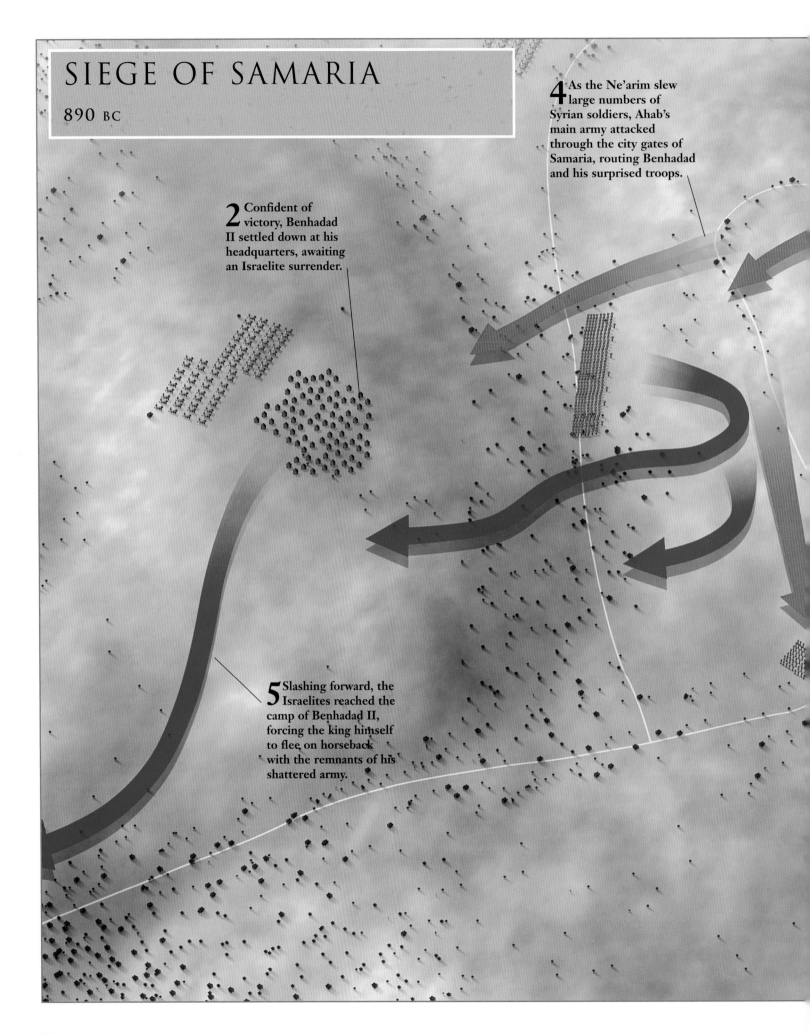

SIEGE OF SAMARIA

890 BC

2 Confident of victory, Benhadad II settled down at his headquarters, awaiting an Israelite surrender.

4 As the Ne'arim slew large numbers of Syrian soldiers, Ahab's main army attacked through the city gates of Samaria, routing Benhadad and his surprised troops.

5 Slashing forward, the Israelites reached the camp of Benhadad II, forcing the king himself to flee on horseback with the remnants of his shattered army.

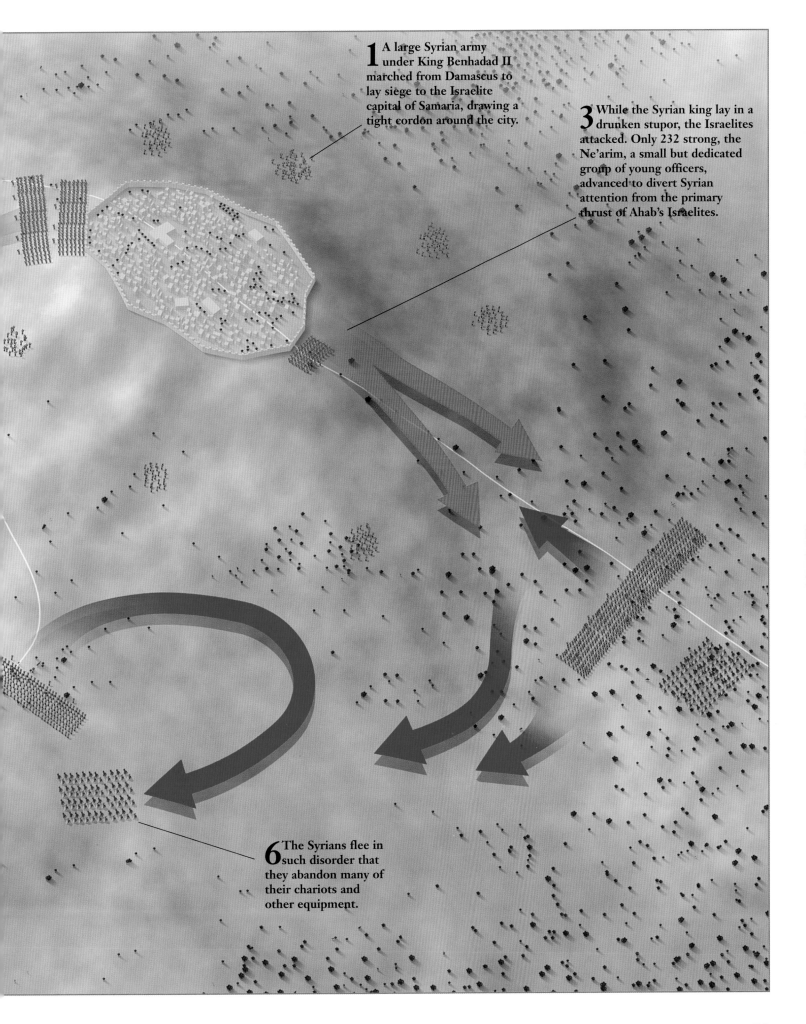

1 A large Syrian army under King Benhadad II marched from Damascus to lay siege to the Israelite capital of Samaria, drawing a tight cordon around the city.

3 While the Syrian king lay in a drunken stupor, the Israelites attacked. Only 232 strong, the Ne'arim, a small but dedicated group of young officers, advanced to divert Syrian attention from the primary thrust of Ahab's Israelites.

6 The Syrians flee in such disorder that they abandon many of their chariots and other equipment.

everything you value and carry it away.'" (I Kings 20: 5–6.)

In response, Ahab summoned his advisors once again. In unison, they implored the king to refuse the Syrian demands. While the historical record is vague, it clearly reveals Ahab's perspective

on the situation. He may have found himself in a genuine quandary when faced with the prospect of losing everything.

He may also have shrewdly played for time, judging that the greed of Benhadad II would get the better of the Syrian king and hoping that just such a turn of events would

galvanize support to make a stand against the invaders.

AHAB TURNS THE TABLES

When Benhadad received word of Ahab's refusal to submit, he issued a final missive to the Israelite king through his messengers:

Left: A romanticized medieval illustration of Samaria under siege portrays a growing sense of panic among the citizenry. However, the overconfidence of King Benhadad II resulted in defeat for the Syrians.

'May the gods deal with me, be it ever so severely, if enough dust remains in Samaria to give each of my men a handful.' (I Kings 20: 10.) The dramatic response from Ahab is still quoted in a proverbial context in modern times. Apparently bolstered by a newfound resolve to fight, his stinging

Above: An iconic stele of a pair of Assyrians driving a chariot illustrates the elaborate grooming and costuming of both drivers and horses. This carving was completed during the eighth century BC.

SIEGE OF SAMARIA

Opposite: The prophet Elijah duels with the 450 prophets of Baal on Mount Carmel, calling down fire from heaven to ignite his altar. Elijah decreed that the pagan prophets should be executed.

retort to the messengers of Benhadad no doubt rallied support within the besieged city. The king of Israel answered: 'Tell him: "One who puts on his armour should not boast like one who takes it off."' (I Kings 20: 11.) With that, Benhadad II ordered his troops to prepare to assault the city.

As Benhadad II made preparations, so, too, did Ahab. The Bible says that a prophet addressed the Israelite king, telling him that God would deliver the Syrian enemy into Israelite hands if Ahab himself would lead an attack to raise the siege. While Benhadad II and his lieutenants drank to excess in their tents outside the city, Ahab decided to divide his small force.

A cadre of only 232 young officers, known as the ne'arim, was gathered to march out of Samaria in full view of the Syrians. While the enemy was preoccupied with this small force that was apparently bent on self-sacrifice, Ahab and the remaining Israelite troops would deliver the decisive blow.

Meanwhile, Benhadad II and the commanders of the Syrian army lounged in their tents and fell into a drunken stupor. Lookouts reported the sighting of a small force marching from Samaria toward the siege lines, and the cavalier Syrian king was captivated with the opportunity to annihilate these brave but foolish Israelites to a man, or take them prisoner and parade them as human trophies through the streets of Damascus. 'If they have come out for peace, take them alive; if they have come out for war, take them alive', he ordered. (I Kings 20: 18.)

THE ROUT OF THE SYRIANS

The ne'arim, though few in number, proved to be a formidable foe, reportedly slaying all those who stood to oppose them and putting the great army of Benhadad II to flight. At the appropriate time, Ahab and the main Israelite force advanced through the city gates and fell upon the confused Syrians, whose commanders were

inebriated and apparently oblivious to the impending debacle.

So great was the rout of the Syrian army that Benhadad II was caught completely by surprise. As his soldiers began streaming past, the Syrian king realized that his only option was to flee the field. Evidently, there was little time to spare. The Bible says that Benhadad II fled on horseback, indicating a hasty retreat without the relative comfort of his personal chariot and bodyguard.

Ahab's soldiers fell upon the Syrians and inflicted heavy losses on them. It is also likely that the garrisons of Israelite outposts along the escape route, near the former capital cities of Shechem and Tirzah, joined in the harassment of the fleeing enemy.

From a tactical perspective, Ahab made good use of the terrain surrounding the hill of Samaria. His decision to take the offensive negated the mobility of the Syrian chariots, while the deception of the ne'arim lessened the invaders' advantage in numbers. Benhadad, however, was the greatest contributor to his own defeat, failing to maintain overall command and control, and falling drunk with his senior commanders on the eve of battle.

With siege towers, rams and scaling ladders to the fore, this colourful illustration shows the storming of the city of Samaria by the victorious Assyrians, as imagined by artist Don Lawrence (1928-2003).

AFTERMATH

Although Ahab had emerged from a desperate situation victorious, the Syrians were far from being thoroughly defeated. The Israelites do not seem to have vigorously followed up their triumph, and the reasons for this decision remain shrouded in mystery. It is known that, after the siege of Samaria had been raised, the prophet returned to Ahab with a warning that a renewed conflict with the Syrians was but a short season away. 'Strengthen your position and see what must be done,' he declared to the Israelite king, 'because next spring the king of Aram (Syria) will attack you again.' (I Kings 20: 22.)

Dark days lay ahead for Ahab and the Israelites. While there was victory on the battlefield, wickedness, idol worship and intrigue festered in the palace. Jezebel remained a blight on the kingdom, and continued unrest was a certainty.

GOLAN HEIGHTS
874 BC

FOLLOWING HIS DEFEAT AT SAMARIA, SYRIAN KING BENHADAD II RECEIVED THE COUNSEL OF HIS ELDER ADVISORS. THEY APPARENTLY IGNORED THE FACT THAT THEIR KING AND HIS SENIOR COMMANDERS HAD BEEN DRUNK AT THE TIME OF THE BATTLE. INSTEAD, THEY IDENTIFIED OTHER CAUSES FOR HUMILIATING DEFEAT AT THE HANDS OF KING AHAB'S SMALL BUT HIGHLY MOTIVATED ISRAELITE ARMY.

WHY DID IT HAPPEN?

WHO The Israelite army of King Ahab (889–850 BC) against the Syrian army of King Benhadad II.

WHAT Ahab undertook a campaign to defend against a second invasion by the reconstituted army of Benhadad II, defeating the Syrians.

WHERE The Golan Heights, northwest of the Israelite capital of Samaria.

WHEN 874 BC.

WHY Following his defeat at Samaria, Syrian King Benhadad II intended to invade the kingdom of Israel a second time. Ahab, the Israelite king, was determined to prevent another invasion.

OUTCOME The Syrian army was routed a second time and, after begging for his life, Benhadad was spared by Ahab.

King Benhadad II's advisors reasoned that three key points would ensure a victory against the Israelites when the contest was renewed:

Their gods are gods of the hills. That is why they were too strong for us. But if we fight them on the plains, surely we will be stronger than they. Do this: Remove all the kings from their commands and replace them with other officers. You must also raise an army like the one you lost – horse for horse and chariot for chariot – so we can fight Israel on the plains. Then surely we will be stronger than they. (I Kings 20: 23–25.)

Benhadad agreed and set the effort to reverse his military fortunes in motion. He

King Benhadad II of Syria laid siege to Samaria. Starving, the populace resorted to cannibalism, but the prophet Elijah caused the Syrians to flee with the noise of a great horn.

would choose more favourable ground on which to fight, allowing better deployment of his infantry and charioteers when the struggle was renewed. He would strengthen the central government of the coalition, replacing kings with military men and minimizing the difficulties of command and control that are inherent in any attempt to wage coalition warfare. He would also raise a force equal to that which had originally begun the trek from Damascus to Samaria, when his first campaign against the Israelites ended in ignominious defeat.

AHAB ALERTED

Although the biblical timeline relates that the period of time between the raising of the siege of Samaria and the Battle of the Golan Heights was a matter of months, a degree of uncertainty exists as to the exact interval. Whether a period of months or years passed, the joining of battle once again was inevitable. There were old scores to be settled, and Ahab had been warned by the prophet to expect another invasion by the Syrians. It is likely that Ahab was watching as Benhadad II carried out his prewar plans.

Just as Benhadad II had launched a pre-emptive campaign against the Israelites to prevent them from growing too strong, Ahab, in turn, measured the relative progress of the Syrians. When he believed the time to be right, Ahab launched an offensive of his own to prevent the Syrian host from invading his homeland and bringing war once again to the heart of the Israelite kingdom. Therefore, Ahab determined that a campaign to the north and west, into the region of the Golan Heights, might solidify Israelite control of this territory (which remains disputed to this day) and shield the kingdom from another incursion.

During the reign of King Solomon (c.970–931 BC), the Golan Heights had been Israelite territory, but the area had apparently been lost during at least one unsuccessful war with the Syrians during the reign of Ahab's father, King Omri (c.883–872 BC). The result of the

territorial, political and trade concessions that had previously been made to the Syrians in exchange for a tenuous peace was a lingering influence that extended to the establishment of trade zones within the Israelite kingdom and to the population itself, which undoubtedly included a substantial Syrian ethnicity. It is possible that Ahab saw in the present military venture an opportunity not only to remove the immediate threat of continuing trouble with Benhadad II, but also to cleanse Israelite territory of Syrian influence in general, and in particular the enclaves of trade and commerce.

IMPOSING GOLAN HEIGHTS

Ahab's army trekked into the Golan Heights, the remnant of an ancient field of tremendous volcanic activity and a

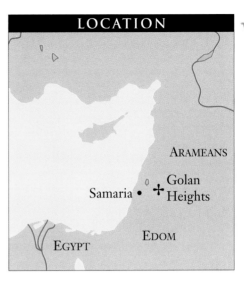

The Golan Heights became the focal point of Israelite King Ahab's campaign to assert control in the region and create a buffer against Syrian incursions.

ARAMEAN CAMEL RIDER

Bearded and bare-chested, an Aramean camel rider sits atop the 'ship of the desert'. An effective form of cavalry or transportation for lightly equipped infantry units, the camels provided a degree of mobility to the forces of King Benhadad II. This warrior is depicted holding the reins and a riding crop in his right hand, and the bow, his principle instrument of war, in his left. A primitive saddle is secured to the animal's back with a system of straps. The Bible relates that Benhadad fielded a complement of thousands of camel riders in his vast and imposing army.

GOLAN HEIGHTS

THE OPPOSED FORCES

ISRAELITES
Unknown

SYRIANS
Unknown, although they suffered an estimated 127,000 casualties during the battle.

Atop the Golan Heights in modern Syria, the Memorial Stone for the Fallen is pictured in 1991. The Golan Heights have been the scene of heavy fighting between the modern state of Israel and neighboring Arab states for more than 30 years.

substantial plateau that rises 122–518m (400–1700ft) above sea level. To the west, the Golan extends nearly to the Sea of Galilee and the River Jordan, its imposing escarpment rising sharply from the plain. The southern border is the River Yarmouk, southwest of the Israelite capital at Samaria. To the east lies the wide expanse of the plain of Haraum, and to the north is the modern border with the Arab nation of Lebanon.

While the Golan Heights is the descriptive term given to territory that has been under the military and political control of Israel since the Six Day War of 1967, the Syrian government continues to assert that it should be sovereign over the disputed area. The boundaries of the modern Golan Heights differ somewhat from those in the days of Ahab and Benhadad II. However, the passage of time has not diminished the importance of the Golan Heights in regard to national prestige and security.

The historical record of the Battle of the Golan Heights is extremely vague. It does seem logical that the terrain itself played a major role in the outcome of the fighting. Peaks, valleys, gorges and ravines scar the landscape, while rivers carve their beds through the otherwise arid and inhospitable expanse. Ahab's campaign is thought to have made reasonably good progress initially, and the Israelites were well into the Golan Heights before the Syrians managed to halt their progress.

The Bible relates that Benhadad assembled his mighty army and advanced to the vicinity of the town of Aphek, which lies slightly northeast of an area where two rivers run parallel and constrict passage to a narrow defile between the gorges on either side. It is believed that the Syrians established a base of operations at Aphek and blocked the path of further advance by Ahab at the narrows.

EYE TO EYE
The two armies, long-time enemies, now confronted one another on the Golan

Heights. The Bible intimates that the Israelites were, once again, seriously outnumbered:

The next spring Benhadad mustered the Arameans (Syrians) and went up to Aphek to fight against Israel. When the Israelites were also mustered and given provisions, they marched out to meet them. The Israelites camped opposite them like two small flocks of goats, while the Arameans covered the countryside. (I Kings 20: 26–27.)

At this point, the prophet of God is said to have approached Ahab and revealed to him that the Syrians were convinced of securing victory if the battle were joined in the valley. Ahab was also told that he would vanquish the enemy yet another time. According to scholarly research, the area

In this painting by artist Leighton Frederic (1836–96), the wayward King Ahab and his notorious wife, Jezebel, a worshiper of Baal, are confronted in a doorway by the prophet Elijah.

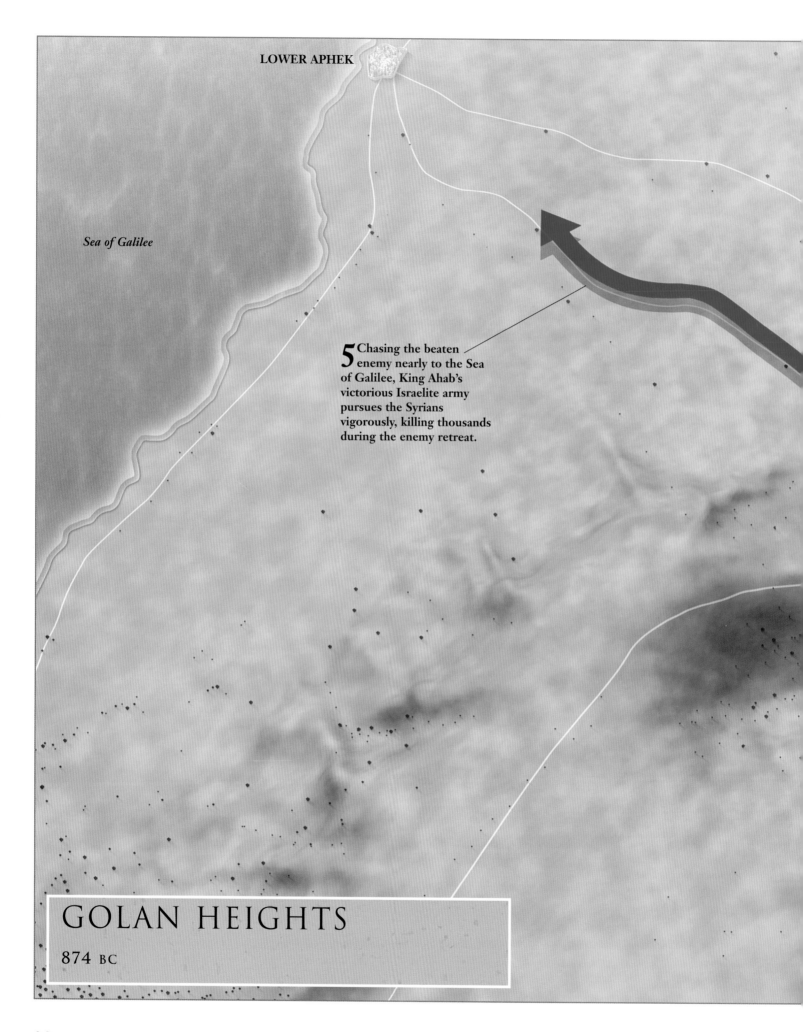

LOWER APHEK

Sea of Galilee

5 Chasing the beaten enemy nearly to the Sea of Galilee, King Ahab's victorious Israelite army pursues the Syrians vigorously, killing thousands during the enemy retreat.

GOLAN HEIGHTS

874 BC

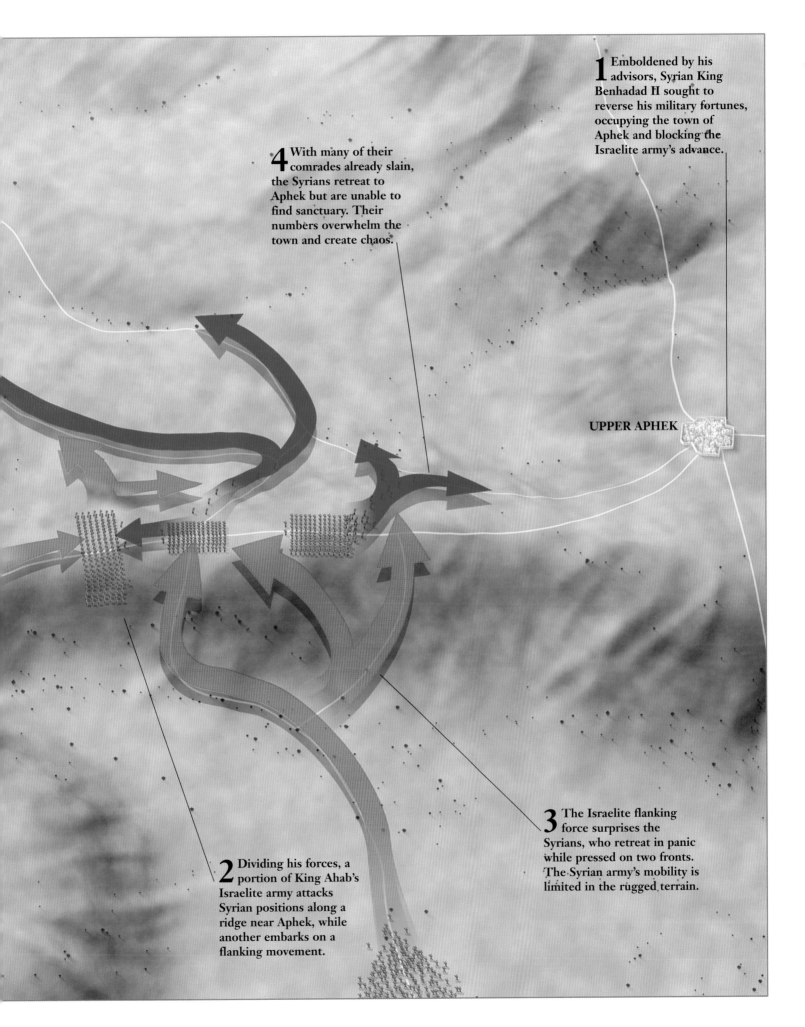

1 Emboldened by his advisors, Syrian King Benhadad II sought to reverse his military fortunes, occupying the town of Aphek and blocking the Israelite army's advance.

4 With many of their comrades already slain, the Syrians retreat to Aphek but are unable to find sanctuary. Their numbers overwhelm the town and create chaos.

UPPER APHEK

3 The Israelite flanking force surprises the Syrians, who retreat in panic while pressed on two fronts. The Syrian army's mobility is limited in the rugged terrain.

2 Dividing his forces, a portion of King Ahab's Israelite army attacks Syrian positions along a ridge near Aphek, while another embarks on a flanking movement.

A pair of Assyrian cavalrymen scan the horizon, brandishing a spear and bow and arrow. Capable of delivering a lightning blow, the swift movement of cavalry could encircle enemy troops and cut off their retreat.

Most Aramean infantry were levies and consequently lightly equipped. Typically, an Aramean infantryman would have been armed with a simple spear and shield, and sometimes a bow. His clothing was made of rough woolen cloth with a simple decorative border.

where the battle is thought to have taken place is only about 100m (330ft) wide for a distance of just under 411m (1350ft). Therefore, it seems logical to conclude that a frontal assault alone would have been doomed to failure.

An attacking commander might, however, consider two options to outflank the easily defended pass between the rivers. To the south, ancient footpaths lead to the rim of a neighbouring gorge, while to the north a steep trail crosses a ridgeline. Both might have provided avenues of approach to a force marching to outflank the eastern end of the defensive position.

In the absence of a definitive record of the battle, historians Chaim Herzog and Mordechai Gichon further theorize that the Aphek referenced in the biblical text could actually have been one of three different locations:

Lately, some scholars have located Aphek not at the Arab village of that name behind the defile, but at En Gev, near the shores of the Sea of Galilee. In that case, the Israelites must have turned the Arameans' flank along the Golan slopes. Others propose to identify Aphek with an assumed 'Lower Aphek'. Accordingly, the Arameans set out from 'Upper Aphek' and fled to the lower town, some four miles distant. We hold to the first proposal and cannot rule out the third alternative.

ISRAELITE ONSLAUGHT

The standoff, Israelite versus Syrian, was undoubtedly one of nervous tension. Perhaps there was a parlay between the two sides, or one army waited for the other to lose its nerve and withdraw. The Bible relates little of the actual fighting, only that there was great carnage:

For seven days they camped opposite each other, and on the seventh day the battle was joined. The Israelites inflicted a hundred thousand casualties on the Aramean (Syrian) foot soldiers in one day. The rest of them escaped to the city of Aphek, where the wall collapsed on twenty-seven thousand of them. And Benhadad fled to the city and hid in an inner room. (I Kings 20: 29–30.)

If Ahab had actually developed a plan of battle that involved a flanking movement followed by a frontal attack on the defile, Herzog and Gichon argue that the discovery by the Syrian soldiers of Israelite troops on their flank and rear might have caused the panicked retreat. Further, the torrent of fleeing soldiers seeking refuge at Aphek was simply too much for the city to withstand, the press of humanity literally causing a wall to collapse and contributing to the tremendous loss of life at the hands of the marauding Israelites.

Apparently, Benhadad II had failed to execute his own plan. Fighting the Israelites in the narrow confines of the defile limited the mobility of his larger army. It is likely that the sheer weight of Syrian numbers became a hindrance rather than an advantage during the battle.

BENHADAD BEGS

In the midst of the debacle on the Golan Heights, Benhadad II again held an audience with his advisors, presumably in the temporary refuge of the inner room:

His officials said to him: 'Look we have heard that the kings of the house of Israel are merciful. Let us go to the king of Israel with sackcloth around our waists and ropes around our heads. Perhaps he will spare your life.' Wearing sackcloth around their waists and ropes around their heads, they went to the king of Israel and said: 'Your servant Benhadad says: "Please let me live."' (I Kings 20: 31–32.)

In a magnanimous gesture, Ahab spared

Circa 850 BC, the prophet Elijah (left) pronounces judgement on Ahab (third from right), who has taken possession of Naboth's vineyard in Jezreel, and on his evil queen, Jezebel (second from left), daughter of the king of Tyre and Sidon.

Queen Jezebel, pushed from a window by an angry crowd, falls to her death. Her body was devoured by dogs. According to the Bible, Jezebel's evil influence contributed to Ahab's undoing.

done on previous occasions, a sullen Ahab returned to his palace and the company of Queen Jezebel (d.842 BC). Benhadad II returned safely to Damascus, and the two would soon fight as allies in another coalition, which shattered the invading Assyrians under King Shalmaneser III (858–824 BC) at Qarqar.

END OF AHAB AND JEZEBEL

Between the battles at the Golan Heights and Qarqar, Ahab and Jezebel descended to even greater depths of evil. The royal pair plotted to condemn to death an innocent neighbour, Naboth, along with his sons, in order to take his vineyard. At this point, the

the life of Benhadad II in exchange for the return of lands taken from the Israelites by the Syrians during the previous generation and for trade privileges in Damascus similar to those previously afforded Benhadad in Samaria. Ahab's action has been deemed as politically astute by some, potentially bringing to an end years of armed conflict between the two peoples. Herzog and Gichon assert that Ahab could never have hoped to gain dominion over the Syrian population and that he also recognized another threat, the aggressive posture of neighbouring Assyria.

Nevertheless, it stands to reason that Ahab's gesture was not universally well received among the Israelites. The Bible relates that a prophet then spoke of God's displeasure that Benhadad's life had been spared and that Ahab's life and his people would be tendered in retribution. As he had prophet Elijah revealed to Ahab that his own death would occur in the very vineyard he had coveted. His family was also condemned to extermination in the following generation.

Three years after the Battle of the Golan Heights, Ahab again fought Benhadad II, who had not lived up to his agreement with the Israelite king to return the occupied lands. During the Battle of Ramoth Gilead, Ahab was struck by a random arrow and did in fact die in the vineyard of Naboth. Later, Jezebel was thrown from a window and died. Dogs licked the blood of Ahab and devoured the body of Jezebel. Benhadad II was reportedly murdered in the night by

Hazael, who also succeeded him as king of Syria, c.842–805 BC. Some historians conclude that Hazael was Benhadad's own son.

In the days following the Battle of the Golan Heights, Samaria endured more siege warfare. The Syrians returned and were again unsuccessful in capturing the city. More than a century after the reign of Ahab, the Assyrians also returned, laid siege to the city for three years, and eventually established dominion over capital and all of the Israelite land, which became a province of their empire. The survivors were deported to the east, and the fall of Samaria marked the end of the northern kingdom of Israel.

Israelite King Ahab fights the Arameans at Ramoth Gilead in this renaissance-era painting. Mortally wounded by a stray arrow, Ahab died in Naboth's vineyard as foretold by Elijah. Dogs licked his blood.

WAR AGAINST MESHA
850 BC

THE REBELLION OF THE MOABITES WAS JUST ONE OF A SERIES OF PROBLEMS BESETTING THE KINGDOM OF ISRAEL. DEFEATED, THE ARMIES OF ISRAEL RETREATED TO THE CITY OF KIR-HARASHETH, WHERE THEY WERE BESEIGED. THOUGH THE SEIGE WAS BROKEN OFF AND MOAB WAS NOT CONQUERED, THE REBELLION WAS ENDED.

WHY DID IT HAPPEN?

WHO Moabite rebels under their King Mesha (ruled ninth century BC), opposed by the armies of Israel under King Jehoram (846–841 BC).

WHAT A series of Israelite victories led to a somewhat inconclusive end to the campaign.

WHERE Moab, to the east of the Dead Sea.

WHEN 850 BC.

WHY The Moabites rose in rebellion and took several towns before being defeated.

OUTCOME The rebellion was more or less quelled and Israel was able to confront other threats.

Moab and Israel shared a common ancestor, Terah, but this did little to ease tensions between the two. After the exodus from Egypt, the Israelites wandered in the wilderness for many years before encountering the lands of the Moabites. Their southern border was the Zered River, which the Israelites reached after 38 years of wandering.

The Moabites' realm had extended all along the eastern shore of the Dead Sea, but theirs was a turbulent history. By the time the Israelites arrived, they held only the southern half. The rest had been lost to the Amorites. Despite the Moabites' troubles, the Israelites did not attack them, because

God had 'spoken' to Moses and enjoined them not to.

Instead, Moses asked Sihon, King of the Amorites, for safe passage. This was denied, so the Amorites attacked the Israelites, whose response was to overthrow the Amorites and seize a segment of their land. This became the Israelites' new home.

The Israelites then settled down with Moab on their borders. However, the manner in which territory changed hands meant that Moab had a territorial claim to parts of Israel – a claim rejected by the new residents there. Conflict, which sometimes included open fighting, went on between Israel and Moab for many years. By far the

The prophet Moses was a great lawmaker, who set down most of the fundamental laws of the Hebrew people. Here he is depicted receiving the Ten Commandments from the hand of God.

most important arena in which this conflict was fought was that of religious belief.

Cultural and religious influences from Moab resulted in one of several occasions when the people of Israel strayed from the path their God had laid out for them. According to the Bible, worshipping false gods caused Israel to suffer great adversity until various prophets and kings got the nation back on the path of righteousness.

At one point, Moab conquered Israel and oppressed its people for some time until they were led in revolt by Ehud, who assassinated the Moabite king, Eglon, and freed his people. According to the prophets, Ehud's success was due to the people of Israel once more embracing their God and rejecting Moabite idolatry. Whatever the reasons, this conflict made future friction between Moab and Israel virtually certain.

During the time of Saul and Samuel, Israel was fighting for its life. The principal foe was Philisitia, but other tribes and kingdoms took the opportunity to settle scores or capture territory from Israel. Among them was Moab, though few gains were made.

DAVID AND SOLOMON

When King David (c.1002–970 BC), Saul's successor, had finished with the Philistines, he set about consolidating his power. Much of his activity was internal but, deciding that it was not possible for Israel to tolerate a hostile Moab on the eastern border, he set about conquering the Moabites. He was successful, and for a time Israel returned the favour and oppressed Moab.

Israel's fortunes over the next few decades were mixed. At times there were periods of prosperity and peace, in which the kings of Israel were able to build a powerful army with large numbers of chariots, as well as impressive fortifications to defend the key cities of the realm.

However, Solomon undid much of this good work by becoming an idolater and losing Yaweh's favour. Moab revolted and was for a time free. Omri, a descendent of David, re-conquered Moab some time later.

Moab had been a vassal state for two generations when King Ahab (c.889–850 BC) of Israel fell into the familiar trap of

turning to false gods. Upon his marriage to Jezebel (d.842 BC), who worshipped Tyrian gods, Ahab permitted her to bring the trappings of her native religion to his court. At this time, the capital of Israel was at Samaria, and the construction of a foreign temple there was truly no great matter, according to Ahab and his supporters.

Solomon had similarly indulged his foreign wives, and that had also led to problems. However, Jezebel was allowed to push her own religion and it gained popularity, especially among the large population of Canaanites who lived under Israelite rule but were not wholehearted in their worship of the God of Israel. Although King Ahab remained true to his god, even his own sons became apostate.

The result was that Israel was beset by internal troubles as Jezebel's followers persecuted those who clung to the worship of Yahweh. During this period of internal struggle, the prophet Elijah arose as a champion of Yaweh's worship and led a resistance that became holy war.

Not long afterwards, there was a successful revolt in Moab. Exactly when this

JUDEAN SOLDIER
This Judean soldier is typical of the sort of fighting-man who served in the campaigns of the period. He is lightly equipped with a spear and shield, with a short sword or long dagger for close combat. His weapons are his own possessions; professional soldiers armed by the state were uncommon at the time. His light gear is an advantage when operating in the field in hot conditions. With little to weigh him down, he can march further and faster than a better protected soldier, and since most other nations fielded mostly the same sort of troops he is not at a disadvantage.

LOCATION

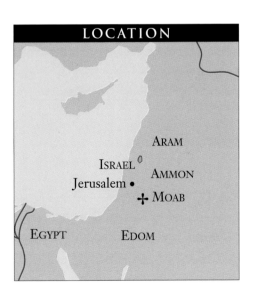

The kingdom of the Moabites lay to the south and east of the Hebrews. Conflict between the two was nothing new. The Hebrews had conquered their foes on at least one occasion in the past.

WAR AGAINST MESHA

Justice and wisdom in ancient Israel. King Solomon determines a child's true parentage by observing the reaction of both claimants to an order that it be cut in half and shared between them.

occurred is unclear, but this was a confused and difficult time for Israel. Ahab was killed fighting the Arameans and was succeeded by his son Ahaziah, who reigned for just a few months (c.841–842 BC). His brother Jehoram replaced him.

Jehoram tried to restore the kingdom's fortunes by having the worst of the idols removed from places of worship, but he was not able to undertake any real reforms while his mother Jezebel's influence remained

strong. Consequently, the kingdom of Israel was internally divided at the time of the Moabite revolt, and a large segment of its army was engaged far to the north at Damascus, repelling Syrian raiders.

THE MOABITE REVOLT

Mesha, King of Moab, had been a vassal of Israel for many years. Indeed, he had recently paid a large tribute. The Book of Kings lists this as a hundred thousand lambs

in awe of the prophet Elijah; their initial raids began just after his death.

The Moabites did not follow Yaweh but instead worshipped Chemosh. It is therefore possible that the uprising had a religious dimension, given that the Israelites were not known for their tolerance of other peoples' gods. It is likely that the rising took some time to organize, as it was Jehoram, not Ahaziah, who responded to the Moabite rebellion.

MOABITE SUCCESSES

Mesha was initially successful in his rebellion. He recaptured territory taken from the Moabites by several enemies, including the Amorites. However, his attention was directed mainly towards Israel, as it was obvious that the former overlords of Moab would try to put down Mesha's rebellion.

Mesha sought allies among the neighbouring tribes and did receive some help from the Ammonites and Edomites. He hoped that a successful campaign might trigger a general anti-Israelite alliance. He was not strong enough, however, to take on the Israelite forces in northern Moab and so sought easy victories, advancing with his allies into Judah, capturing several garrison towns. It is possible that the Moabites pushed as far as the Mediterranean coast, and certainly they were able to take several towns that were held lightly or not at all. This encouraged Mesha and his allies, but the hoped-for alliance was not to be.

JEHORAM FIGHTS BACK

Jehoram, knowing that the Israelites were overstretched, fought back as best he could while seeking allies. Israel and Judah were in serious danger. Some towns, sensing weakness, rebelled and joined neighbouring powers or became independent. However, the Moabites were unable to achieve a decisive victory.

As the conflict grew in intensity, the allies of Moab, most notably the Edomites, took the brunt of it. Seeing little gain for themselves, prospective allies of Moab found reasons not to get involved, while the Edomites decided that their best interests lay in an alliance with the Israelites and changed sides.

and a hundred thousand rams, and calls Mesha a 'sheepmaster', which he must have been to be able to deliver such an immense quantity of livestock.

However, soon after paying this tribute, Mesha heard that Ahab had been killed in battle. There was never going to be a better time for rebellion. With the conquerors divided internally and their king dead, the time was right to throw off the Israelite yoke. The Moabites also seem to have been

THE OPPOSED FORCES

ISRAELITES
No figures available

MOABITES
No figures available

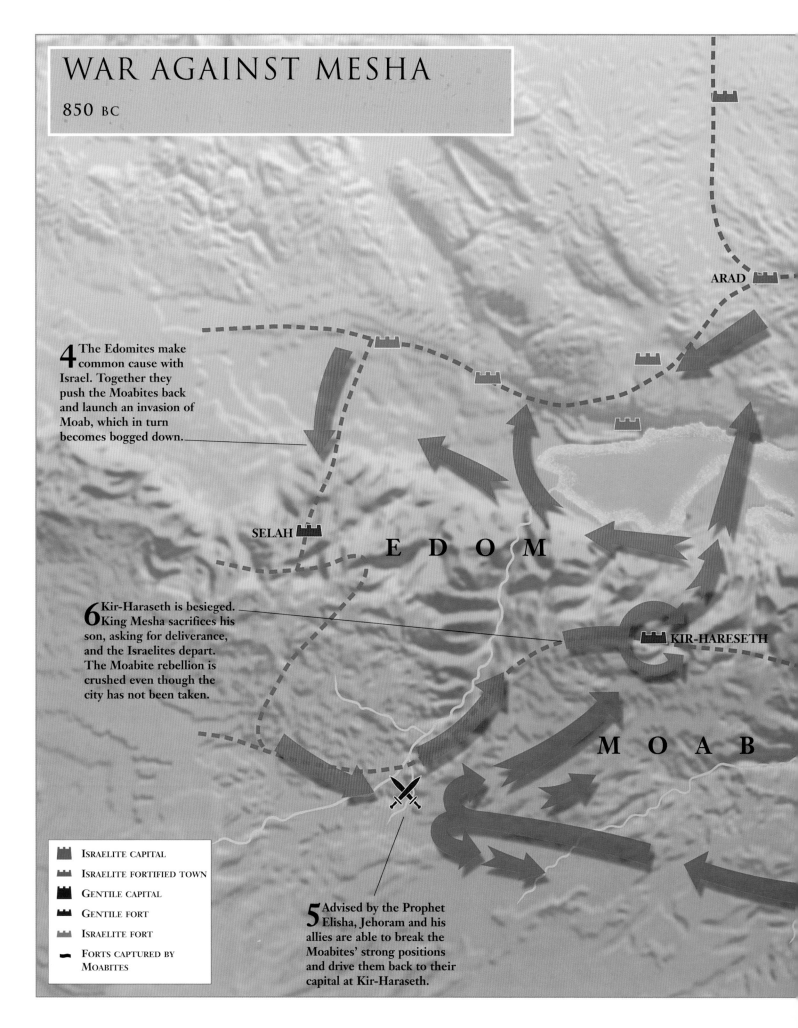

WAR AGAINST MESHA

850 BC

4 The Edomites make common cause with Israel. Together they push the Moabites back and launch an invasion of Moab, which in turn becomes bogged down.

6 Kir-Haraseth is besieged. King Mesha sacrifices his son, asking for deliverance, and the Israelites depart. The Moabite rebellion is crushed even though the city has not been taken.

ARAD

SELAH

E D O M

KIR-HARESETH

M O A B

🏰 ISRAELITE CAPITAL

🏰 ISRAELITE FORTIFIED TOWN

🏰 GENTILE CAPITAL

🏰 GENTILE FORT

🏰 ISRAELITE FORT

▬ FORTS CAPTURED BY MOABITES

5 Advised by the Prophet Elisha, Jehoram and his allies are able to break the Moabites' strong positions and drive them back to their capital at Kir-Haraseth.

J U D A H

3 Jehoram, King of Israel, struggles to prevent wholesale rebellion among his vassal towns but eventually manages to fight the Moabites to a standstill.

HEBRON

JERUSALEM

JERICHO

Dead Sea

2 Mesha, King of the Moabites, launches operations against several enemies, but his main thrust is against the Israelites, who are certain to try to put down his rebellion.

River Jordan

DIBON

RABATH-AMMON

1 Taking advantage of the Israelites' weakness, caused by the deaths of Elijah and Ahab, the Moabites rebel and capture several towns from their former overlords.

A M M O N

WAR AGAINST MESHA

Part of the fortifications of the city of Samaria, which was for a long time capital of the Israelites. It was here that Jezebel had the temple of Baal constructed.

Edom and Israel now took the offensive against Moab. Their intention was to advance into Moab from the south. This decision was, in part, due to politics and partly due to strategic reality. To enter from the north meant passing at first through Israelite-held territory in northern Moab, which would be easy. Then, however, the army would be forced to make an opposed crossing of the River Arnon. Against Mesha and his powerful army, this was obviously a recipe for disaster.

Coming in from the south also had political advantages. Edom had been a vassal of Israel for a long time and had freed itself in rebellion. Its army had recently changed sides but had started the campaign as an invader against Israel.

Jehoram can hardly have considered Edom to be a reliable ally, so moving his army through Edomite territory made sense. He would be able to watch his new ally for signs of treachery all the while, and would be well positioned to crush any attempt to switch allegiance again. The route through Edom also protected the line

of communications and allowed the Israelites to fall back in the event of a reverse. There was also the possibility of drawing the Moabites into the wilderness between Moab and Edom, and destroying them there.

THE INVASION GOES AWRY

Mesha was far too wily to be suckered into plunging his army into the wilderness, where his own supply problems might lead to the defeat of his forces without any need for battle. Instead, he positioned his army to meet the invasion. He waited at the Wadi El Ahsa for his opponents to come to him.

The allies advanced through the wilderness and found themselves confronted by the army of Moab waiting on the far side of the Wadi. The allies were short of water and, as they searched for a suitable source, light Moabite forces constantly harassed them.

Unable to advance across the formidable obstacle before them, short of supplies and harried constantly, Jehoram and his allies were in an uncomfortable position.

Taking counsel from the prophet Elisha, who had been at one time a follower of Elijah, the allies were scarcely encouraged. Elisha could proclaim only that God had brought the allied kings together to prepare for their destruction. After a time, however, Elisha made a prophetic announcement that the allies would receive divine help.

Elisha's advice was to send men down into the Wadi and dig pits, upon which the dry bed would fill with water despite a lack of rain. He also announced that the allies would win a tremendous victory. They would first be delivered from their present predicament and would then shatter the army of Mesha, capturing all the cities of Moab.

RENEWED SUCCESS

The allies did as they had been advised, and water was found in the Wadi. With the immediate problem of thirst solved, the allies were now able to renew their advance.

They made a forced crossing of the Wadi and inflicted a sharp defeat on the Moabites. Writings from the time state that the water disappeared quickly, so presumably the Wadi was again dry when the allies advanced across it.

Dismayed by the collapse of his defensive strategy, and perhaps uneasy about the omens, Mesha retreated towards the fortified city of Kir-Haraseth. The appearance of water in the Wadi had been seen by the Moabites, and to them it had appeared to turn blood red.

Mesha's priests advised him that this was an omen – the enemy kings had fallen on one another and victory now belonged to the Moabites. When this was disproved by a vigorous attack across the wadi, Mesha's resolve may well have been weakened.

RETREATS TO KIR-HARASETH

Mesha made a fighting retreat across Moab, evacuating towns along the way to add their troops to his host. The Jewish army and its allies followed all the way to Kir-Haraseth, laying waste the countryside in their path. This was commonplace in warfare in the period and was partly a deliberate policy to weaken the enemy, and partly the result of aggressive foraging.

Finally, the Moabites took refuge in Kir-Haraseth, a formidable fortress. The allies were unable to enter the fortress immediately, and instead laid siege to the city. They threw a ring of troops about it and posted slingers on high ground, where they could harass any defenders who showed themselves.

Kir-Haraseth is referred to by several names, including Kir-Moab (Fortress of Moab). One translation of its name is

A camp in the desert in Jordan. This forbidding landscape is the traditional home of the Moabite, Ammonite and Edomite people of biblical times.

WAR AGAINST MESHA

Above: A rampart of a Moabite fortification, ninth century BC. Fortress-building was a relatively new technique at the time of the Moabites' wars with Israel, but these ruins have survived from that time to the present day.

Left: The border town of Aroer contained this trading post which, although it dates from the ninth century BC, has survived to the present day in recognizable form.

Opposite: A Renaissance painting depicting the prophet Elisha, who succeeded Elijah after a long period as his disciple. After the defeat of Mesha, Elisha continued his work for many years, even performing a miracle after his death.

Fortress of Brickwork, suggesting that the city was a prominent work of fortification. In any case, its location high on a steep hill was formidable; an assault was therefore out of the question.

However, the allies did not need to make an assault. They had the city surrounded and the Moabite army bottled up within it. There was little chance of a relief force arriving and, without one, all the allies had to do was wait for the defenders to starve. Coupled with the availability of high ground outside the city, which allowed slingers to snipe at the defenders from above, this put the Moabite forces in an untenable position.

MESHA'S LAST ATTEMPT

King Mesha knew that if he simply sat inside his fortress, he would lose the war. He had to make a bold stroke to reverse his fortunes. Gathering to him some 700 swordsmen, Mesha came out fighting.

Mesha's assault was directed at the King of Edom. Various reasons have been postulated for this. Perhaps he sought revenge on his old ally or, possibly, he thought that the Edomites would put up less of a fight than the Israelites. It is even conceivable that Mesha thought the Edomites might change sides again if they got a bloody nose.

Whatever his reasoning, Mesha made a determined attack that inflicted many casualties but achieved nothing of any significance. His force was driven back into the city in total defeat.

Mesha was beaten, and he knew it. Perhaps in the hope of obtaining divine assistance or to turn aside the wrath of his god, Chemosh, Mesha then sacrificed his eldest son and heir. This was done in a particularly gruesome manner – as a burnt offering – and on the walls in full view of the besieging army.

In a perverse way, Mesha got what he wanted. For reasons that have never been explained, the allies disengaged and retired from Kir-Haraseth, withdrawing from the land of Moab. There was no pursuit: the Moabites let the invaders go unhindered and did not renew the campaign.

But neither was Moab reconquered. The southern part of the kingdom remained independent of Israel, and the Israelites turned to deal with other problems on their borders. Eight years after the death of Ahabin battle, the Israelite army was still engaged outside of Damascus. Now that the immediate crisis was dealt with, Moab was a problem that could wait for a more opportune time to achieve victory.

EDOM
785 BC

THE KINGDOM OF EDOM, WHICH OCCUPIED A HIGHLAND PLATEAU SOUTHEAST OF THE KINGDOM OF JUDAH, WAS SEVERAL TIMES THE TARGET OF EXPANSIONIST JUDEAN KINGS. THE DIFFICULTIES JUDAH ENCOUNTERED IN DEFEATING AND HOLDING THIS SMALL TERRITORY SHEDS IMPORTANT LIGHT ON MILITARY AND POLITICAL MATTERS IN THE AGE OF THE DIVIDED MONARCHY.

WHY DID IT HAPPEN?

WHO King Amaziah of Judah (c.801–783 BC) invaded Edom, to regain control of the province.

WHAT The Judean army defeated an Edomite force, then stormed the Edomite capital of Sela, allowing the reconquest of all northern Edom. However, an Israelite army led by King Joash routed Amaziah's force shortly afterwards.

WHERE The Valley of Salt, near the oasis of Zoar, in present-day southern Jordan. The battle with Israel took place at Beth-Shemesh in the Judean lowland region between the mountains and the plain of Philistia (the Shephelah).

WHEN c.785 BC.

WHY King Amaziah decided to regain the trade revenue and territory lost by his predecessor King Jehoram (846–841 BC) to Edom in the 840s BC.

OUTCOME The Judean army under King Amaziah won a victory over Edom and regained possession of the northern part of the country; however, King Joash of Israel then defeated the Judeans, taking Amaziah prisoner and sacking Jerusalem soon afterwards.

On its eastern border, Israel had a series of small states with large nomadic elements. Of them, Edom, southeast of the Dead Sea, was one of the most strategically important, since it controlled a significant trade route and access to Israel from the southeast. Thus, as Israel became a state, Edom was an early target. King David (c.1002–970 BC) had defeated the Edomites in the tenth century BC, subjecting the princes of Edom to Israelite overlordship. When Israel and Judah divided, Edom came under the authority of the southern kingdom of Judah as a dependency. Edom was sparsely populated and ill equipped to fight a 'modern' war with professional armies, armour, chariots and cavalry. It was, however, largely desert territory, making it difficult for Judean armies to control it with the typical military arsenal of the ninth and eighth centuries BC.

THE LOSS OF EDOM

In the ninth and eighth centuries BC, the Levant was deeply unstable politically. Edom seized its chance during the reign of King Jehoram of Judah to revolt and declared its independence under a dynasty of native kings. Jehoram, of course, could not accept such a blatant challenge to his authority. So he responded with an invasion of his breakaway province, taking infantry on the campaign as well as a sizeable chariot force. He must have believed that the chariots, the ultimate weapon of the most advanced armies of the time, would

Two tents pitch in the desert near Moab, modern-day Jordan. This arid region was the home of the Edomites and the Ammonites, traditional enemies of Israel in biblical times.

intimidate and easily overcome the more irregular forces of Edom, which probably did not include any chariots at all.

Chariots, while invaluable military tools in an open plain, were ill suited to a campaign against the territory of Edom. It proved to be very difficult to manoeuvre the chariots, light as they were, and their teams through the narrow, rocky and steep approaches to the rebellious vassal state. When the Judean army finally emerged from the defiles and deployed in a plain south of the Dead Sea, the charioteers found themselves on a terrain of cracks and crevices, over which it was very difficult to operate chariots.

The Judeans' run of bad luck – or insufficient army intelligence – continued. Jehoram put his army into camp at the oasis of Zoar, but did not post adequate sentries. The result was a highly effective Edomite surprise attack in the middle of the night, aimed above all against King Jehoram himself, and the Judean chariots and their horses; the Edomites apparently feared these instruments of war as much as Jehoram had hoped they would. Jehoram showed considerable presence of mind in the crisis, rallying his dismounted charioteers, and this hastily assembled force beat off the Edomite attack.

Although the threat was effectively ended, panic spread in the rest of the Judean camp, and so many of his soldiers fled for home that Jehoram had to call a halt to his campaign against Edom and beat an ignominious retreat. Edom remained independent for two generations thereafter.

JUDAH'S MILITARY RECOVERY

By the reign of King Amaziah, Judah was in a stronger military position. The Assyrians, the new power of the Middle East, were still too distant to pose a direct threat. In fact, Assyria's increasingly militant imperialism in this period was to the advantage of both Judah and Israel, since in two campaigns the Assyrian King Adad-nirari III (811–783 BC) weakened the strong Syrian state of Damascus, an ever-present danger to both. Furthermore, Amaziah was at peace with the rival Jewish state of Israel. The time seemed ripe for a campaign to regain the trade and territory that Jehoram had lost.

It is difficult to reckon Judah's military resources in this period. The biblical account of Amaziah's attack on Edom tells that the king was able to muster 300,000 Judeans, as well as an additional 100,000 Israelite mercenaries (2 Chronicles 25). Such numbers are impossible for a small and poor state like Judah. The best basis for

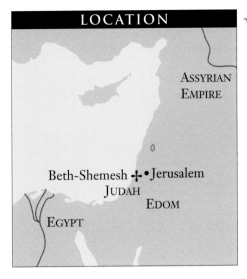

Situated on the far side of the Jordan River, south-east of Israel, Edom controlled much of the trade between Mesopotamia and Mediterranean states such as Judah.

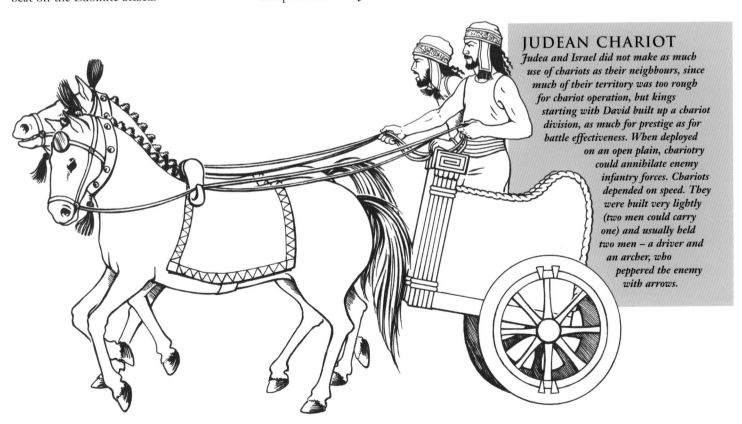

JUDEAN CHARIOT
Judea and Israel did not make as much use of chariots as their neighbours, since much of their territory was too rough for chariot operation, but kings starting with David built up a chariot division, as much for prestige as for battle effectiveness. When deployed on an open plain, chariotry could annihilate enemy infantry forces. Chariots depended on speed. They were built very lightly (two men could carry one) and usually held two men – a driver and an archer, who peppered the enemy with arrows.

E
D
O
M

A modern artist's impression of the Temple of Jerusalem, with the high priest presenting the child king Joash to the Judean army.

THE OPPOSED FORCES

JUDEANS (estimated)
Cavalry:	2000
Infantry:	10,000
Total:	**12,000**

EDOMITES (estimated)
Cavalry:	1000–2000
Infantry:	8000
Total:	**9000–10,000**

ISRAELITES (estimated)
Chariots (three-man crews):	4500
Infantry:	10,000
Total:	**14,500**

reckoning is an Assyrian record dating to 853 BC and stating that King Ahab had a force of 10,000 infantry and 2000 chariots at his disposal.

A century later, Judah may have been able to come close to the Israelite infantry force, but there is no evidence to suggest that it was wealthy enough to muster a comparable chariot force. Amaziah may also have employed mercenaries, since the use of mercenaries had been common in Judean and Israelite warfare since the time of King David. According to the account in 2 Chronicles, however, Amaziah never employed his Israelite recruits, since an unnamed prophet convinced the king to send them home before the battle.

Certainly, Judah still maintained a chariot force in the eighth century BC. However, there is no evidence that the king took any chariots with him on the Edom campaign, a decision that seems wise in light of Jehoram's earlier debâcle. There is evidence that Amaziah had a cavalry corps – which would have proved more useful for a campaign in Edom's difficult terrain. In fact, this is the first time that cavalry is attested in the military force of the kingdom of Judah.

Opposite: In biblical times as now, the inhospitable Negev Desert presented an almost impenetrable defence along Judah's southern border.

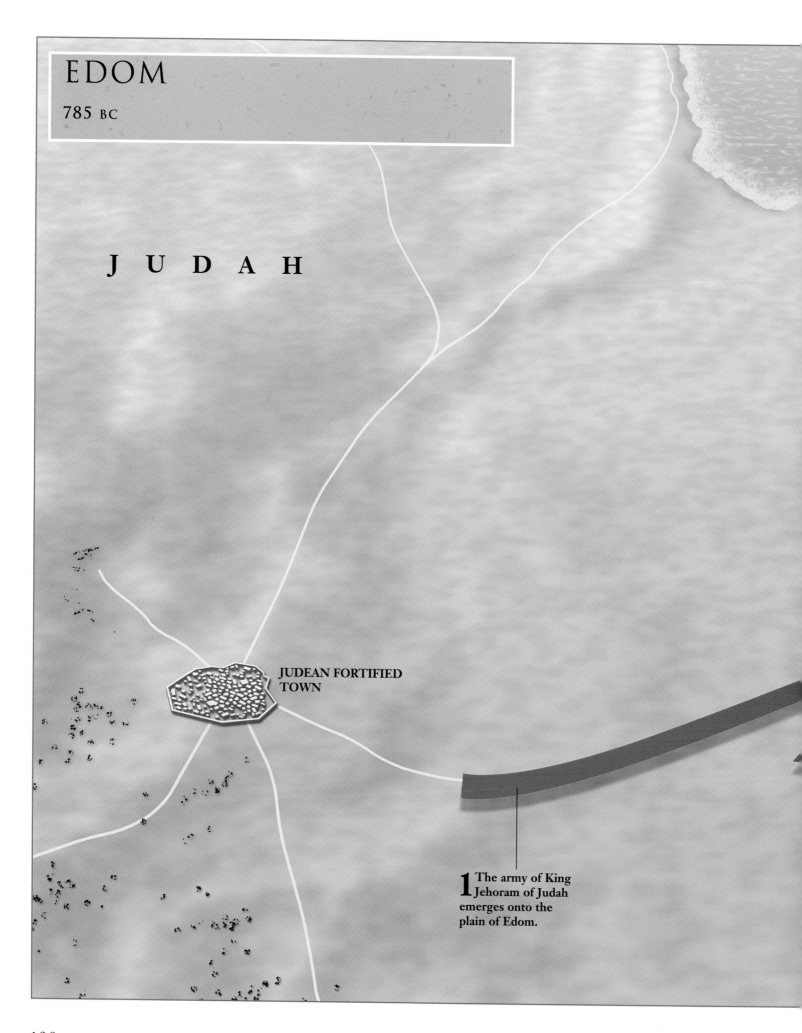

EDOM

785 BC

JUDAH

JUDEAN FORTIFIED
TOWN

1 The army of King
Jehoram of Judah
emerges onto the
plain of Edom.

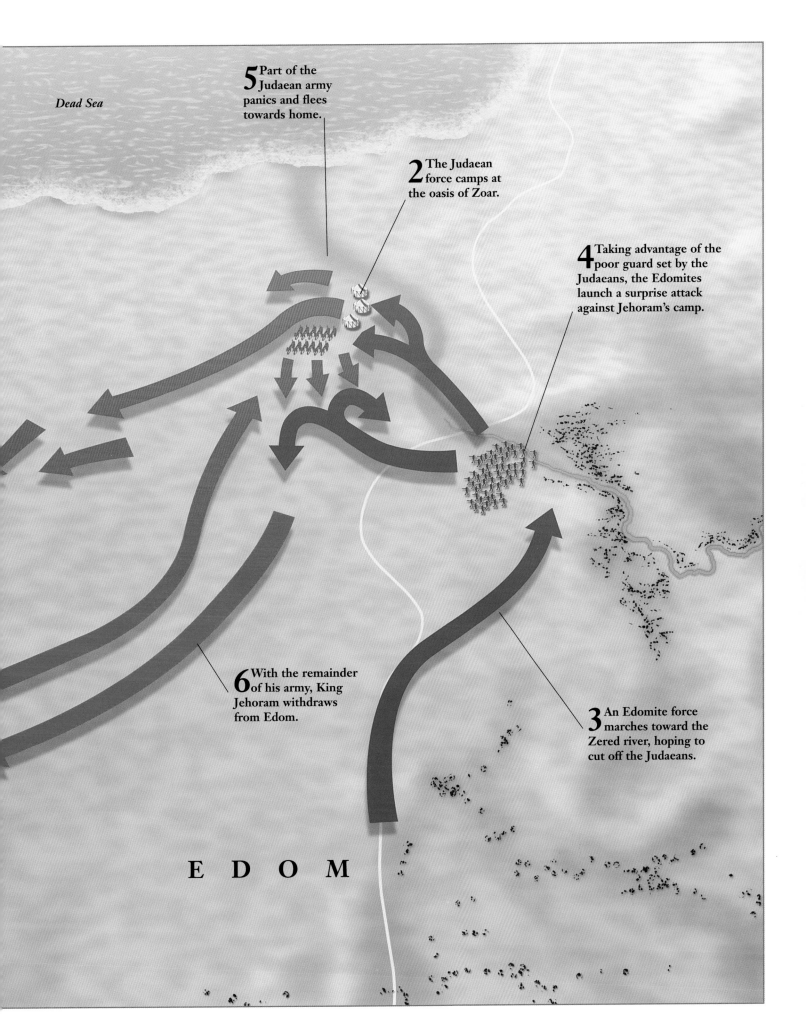

Dead Sea

5 Part of the Judaean army panics and flees towards home.

2 The Judaean force camps at the oasis of Zoar.

4 Taking advantage of the poor guard set by the Judaeans, the Edomites launch a surprise attack against Jehoram's camp.

6 With the remainder of his army, King Jehoram withdraws from Edom.

3 An Edomite force marches toward the Zered river, hoping to cut off the Judaeans.

E D O M

EDOM

THE EDOM CAMPAIGN

Amaziah's army marched southeastwards, probably skirting the Negev as they crossed the Judean mountains south of the Dead Sea. The Edomite army met the Judeans south of the Dead Sea, at a location the Bible calls the Valley of Salt. The battlefield was only a few miles from the oasis of Zoar, where Jehoram had been humiliated two generations earlier. In the battle that followed, the superiority of the Judean army was clearly apparent.

The majority of Amaziah's force consisted of local militias; before the campaign, the king held a census of the male population of Judah, during which he is known to have fixed the age at which young men were required to begin military service at 20 years. This occasional and still largely tribal force was supplemented with a strong professional element, including the king's bodyguard, garrison troops and any mercenaries hired for the occasion. Besides the advantages of a professional core, the Judean soldiers would, on the whole, have been better equipped than the Edomites. Judging from the evidence of better-attested battles, it is probable that Amaziah's army included a substantial number of

archers and slingers in addition to infantry equipped with spears, daggers and shields. The more elite troops would also have been clad in bronze lamellar body armour (bronze scales sewn onto leather), which would have been a rarity in the Edomite force. Best of all for tactical purposes, Amaziah apparently had a substantial cavalry force, probably comprised of mounted bowmen using powerful compound bows, who would have been able to manoeuvre much more easily on the broken ground than Jehoram's chariots had.

The Edomite warriors, by contrast, seem to have been much better equipped for raiding and guerrilla fighting, especially to judge from their night attack on King Jehoram. It is unlikely that many soldiers in the Edomite army possessed body armour. However, considering the Edomite's largely pastoral lifestyle in this period, it is likely that the Edomite king could muster at least some cavalry.

The result of the battle in the Valley of Salt was a major Judean victory. Extant accounts do not reveal how the victory was won, but Amaziah's triumph was clearly significant. The author of 2 Chronicles reports that the Judeans slaughtered 10,000 of the enemy in the course of the fight. It further relates that the Judean army also captured another 10,000 men, whom the Judeans slaughtered by throwing off a cliff. Amaziah was able to consolidate his victory by moving immediately against the fortress of Sela, the capital of Edom (perhaps the modern el-Sela southwest of Tapila, Jordan), which he took by storm. These successes allowed Amaziah to re-establish Judean overlordship over all of northern Edom.

THE QUARREL WITH ISRAEL

Scholars contest the chronology of events, but what appears to have happened next is that Judah became embroiled in an unnecessary war with Israel. Amaziah appears to have been puffed up by his victory over Edom, and sent defiant messages to his Israelite counterpart, King Joash, perhaps in the mistaken belief that the Israelite army was too preoccupied by war with Damascus to be able to respond. But Israel, the stronger of the two Jewish states, was enjoying its own military

This Assyrian horse archer from the period of the Edom campaign is probably very similar to his Judean counterpart. Note that the saddle and stirrup had not yet been invented.

resurgence at the time. King Joash had defeated Damascus in three campaigns between c.802 and 787 BC, recovering a number of Israelite towns in the process. The 2 Kings account reports that at first Joash simply exhorted Amaziah to pipe down and stop stirring up trouble, likening Amaziah's provocation to a thistle attacking one of the cedars of Lebanon (2 Kings 14: 9). When Amaziah continued his provocation, though, Joash accepted the challenge, rapidly assembling an Israelite army to confront Judah.

Joash led the Israelite army in an invasion that penetrated deeply into Judean territory. This force met Amaziah's probably smaller army at Beth-Shemesh in the Shephelah (the lowland region between the central mountain range and the plain of Philistia on the coast). In this pitched battle, it was the turn of the Judean army to be routed. Amaziah himself was taken prisoner, while the survivors of his army fled in all directions.

While no details of this battle survive, it is likely that Israel owed its victory above all to its substantial chariot force. If the king of Israel could still muster anything like 2000 chariots, as he had in 853 BC, it is unlikely Amaziah could hope to survive an encounter on open ground. Beth-Shemesh did indeed favour chariot warfare.

No Judean army remained in the field to offer the Israelites any effective opposition, so Joash was free to march where he wished. Clearly wanting to teach Judah a lesson, he proceeded to the eastern foothills, planning to vent his anger on Amaziah's capital city – Jerusalem.

Although Jerusalem is located in a naturally defensible position, its walls were apparently in a state of poor repair, and it must have been largely stripped of defenders at the time, thanks to the military catastrophe at Beth-Shemesh. It did not take long for the Israelite forces to breach the city's northern wall with a battering ram. The Israelites poured into the city, looted the palace and Temple treasuries, and then broke down a stretch of Jerusalem's wall 183m (600ft) long to make it even less defensible in the future. Before withdrawing, King Joash took hostages, perhaps in exchange for the hapless King

Amaziah, and returned to his northern home. Amaziah soon died, and his son Azariah (Uzziah) (c.786–758 BC) found himself in a state of near vassalage to Israel.

LESSONS OF THE EDOMITE CAMPAIGN

The Edom campaign of c.785 BC reveals how confused Near Eastern politics could be in the eighth century BC, as small states constantly squabbled over borders in an ever-shifting kaleidoscope of vassalage and military dominance. Not only did Edom escape from Judean overlordship, only to fall back under her control thanks to a successful campaign, but the apparently unnecessary war between Judah and Israel also suggests the complexity of the political and military game of the age.

The Edom campaign, especially paired with Jehoram's unsuccessful earlier invasion of Edom, also reveals the complicated landscape of ancient Palestine. The terrain was so varied that the usual rules of war of the age did not always hold true. Smart rulers adapted their armies to the conditions they expected to find, rather than relying too heavily on the technological norms of the age.

The site of Sela, ancient capital of Edom. 2 Chronicles reports that 10,000 captured Edomites were hurled from the cliff to their deaths after Amaziah's victory.

King Adad-nirari III (810–783 BC) was king of Assyria when Amaziah ruled Judah. He would have watched with great interest Amaziah's effort to expand Judah's power.

PALESTINE AND SYRIA
734–732 BC

ISRAEL HAD ITS FIRST REAL TASTE OF ASSYRIA'S OVERWHELMING MILITARY CAPABILITY IN THE YEARS 734–732 BC, WHEN TIGLATH-PILESER III INVADED PALESTINE AND SYRIA IN AN EFFORT TO ESTABLISH HIS CONTROL OVER THE REGION AND ITS TRADE. THE CAMPAIGN MARKS THE BEGINNING OF THE END OF THE NORTHERN STATE OF ISRAEL.

WHY DID IT HAPPEN?

WHO An Assyrian army led by King Tiglath-Pileser III (745–727 BC) carried out a three-year campaign against Israel, Damascus, Tyre, Ashkelon and Gaza.

WHAT The Assyrian army invaded Palestine and Syria, conquering fortified towns, annexing territory and carrying off much of the population on its return to Assyria.

WHERE In the first campaign, King Tiglath-Pileser's army marched down the coast of Phoenicia and Philistia, taking cities from Sidon to Gaza; the second and third campaigns were directed against Damascus; during the course of the third campaign, the Assyrians marched through northern Israel.

WHEN 734–732 BC.

WHY Tiglath-Pileser wanted to control access to Mediterranean trade, and also to reduce Egyptian influence in Palestine.

OUTCOME The Assyrians defeated Damascus and executed its king. Israel survived after its king was assassinated and his successor submitted to Tiglath-Pileser. Israel did, however, lose its dependencies.

King Tiglath-Pileser III of Assyria was a strong ruler who restored stability to his kingdom and launched reforms that made Assyria more formidable than ever. The lion's share of Assyria's resources was directed towards war. Most importantly, Tiglath-Pileser succeeded in creating a standing army of perhaps as many as 10,000 men, in addition to traditional provincial troop levies. The standing army, which included many foreign mercenaries, set a new standard of training and professionalism. It was a fully integrated force, complete with infantry, cavalry, a small chariot force (chariot forces had gradually got smaller since the ninth century BC and were eventually replaced by cavalry) and a corps of engineers.

Tiglath-Pileser is also credited with introducing bronze lamellar armour to the Assyrian troops – armour made of bronze scales sewn onto a leather tunic. Although no contemporary records report the size of Tiglath-Pileser's army, we can use an account of the army of King Shalmaneser III (858–824 BC) at the Battle of Karkar in 854 BC as a basis for comparison.

Shalmaneser was able to bring some 35,000 men to the battle – 20,000 infantry, 1200 chariots and 12,000 cavalry. A century later, the Assyrian cavalry force would have been larger and the chariot force smaller, but logistics would probably have limited Tiglath-Pileser's total campaign army to about the same size.

BIG PLANS

With such a formidable band of warriors at his command, Tiglath-Pileser was able to think big, which in his case meant conquest

The Assyrians experimented with chariots pulled by as many as four horses. Note the yokes, which severely limited the load each horse could pull; the horse collar was invented many centuries later.

of new territory. What Assyria needed above all else was access to Mediterranean trade. This need drew the king's attention to the west, to the small states of Syria as well as to Israel and Judah. But competition for Palestine, that invaluable land bridge between Asia and Africa, put Assyria into direct competition with the other great power of the age, Egypt. The small states occupying that vital region thus became pawns in an increasingly violent game for imperial power over the region. The kings in question found it difficult to accept such a limited role, and their efforts to retain full independence led to the downfall of several of these states, including Israel.

In his first western campaign of 743–738 BC, Tiglath-Pileser broke the power of Urartu, to the northeast of Israel. The king then marched on to the Mediterranean coast in an unmistakable demonstration of his power. King Menahem of Israel (747–738 BC) got the message, paying tribute and submitting to Tiglath-Pileser's overlordship rather than fighting a war likely to lead to Israel's extinction.

Not everyone in Israel was willing to give in so tamely to the Assyrian bully, apparently regarding their king's behaviour as craven or the Assyrian state as too far distant to intervene regularly in Israelite affairs. The anti-Assyrian faction came to power in 737 BC, when the army officer Pekah ben Remaliah succeeded in deposing and killing Menahem's son Pekahiah, taking the throne for himself.

The new king, Pekah (737–732 BC), would have known well that Israel by itself could not hope to face mighty Assyria. However, when King Rezin of Damascus began to organize resistance against Tiglath-Pileser, Pekah was happy to join a coalition that eventually included Rezin of Damascus, Pekah of Israel, Hiram of Tyre (969–936 BC), Mitinti of Ashkelon and Hanun of Gaza.

PROVOKING THE LION

The first fruit of the anti-Syrian alliance was an attack that the combined forces of Israel and Damascus launched against the smaller Jewish state of Judah to the south of Israel. The apparent motivation behind the attack

ASSYRIAN INFANTRYMAN

The Assyrian infantry consisted of two parts. The king employed a thoroughly professional full-time core of fighting men; such men spent most of their time in garrison duty, but could be mobilized rapidly for campaigns. There was also a militia that could be called up for major expeditions or in times of need. Most Assyrian infantrymen were equipped with helmet, shield, and short stabbing spear, as in this illustration. The king's professional troops would also have boasted body armour (including the first true military boots) and more specialized weapons, especially the expensive compound bows that were essential in siege warfare.

was to compel King Jotham of Judah (750–735 BC) to join in the anti-Syrian coalition that they had formed. Jotham, however, had paid tribute to Tiglath-Pileser, even though on his first western campaign the Assyrian army had never approached Judah. Jotham was clearly unwilling to foreswear his oaths to the Assyrian king – or to give in to the demands of his northern rival.

Damascus and Israel continued to increase their pressure, to the point of laying Jerusalem under siege, an event described in 2 Kings 16: 5–9. Jotham's successor Ahaz (735–727 BC) responded by sending messengers to Tiglath-Pileser begging for his assistance. Ahaz's messengers sweetened the message by presenting to the Assyrian king an enormous bribe of gold and silver garnered from both the palace treasury and that of the Temple in Jerusalem, but it is unlikely that Tiglath-Pileser needed much convincing. It was in his interest to have dutiful, subordinate vassals in strategically important Palestine.

The unprovoked attack against his vassal, King Ahaz, provided an excellent pretext for him to intervene. With luck, he

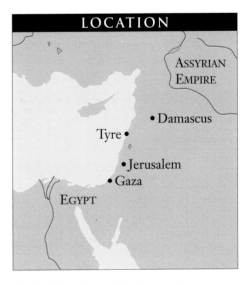

LOCATION

The landlocked Assyrian Empire wanted access to the Mediterranean's wealth. A first target was thus the Phoenician city of Tyre, after which Tiglath-Pileser's force moved southwards.

PALESTINE AND SYRIA

could defeat and depose his opponents in the region and thereby win the gratitude of King Ahaz.

'TO PHILISTIA'

A contemporary account, the Assyrian Eponym Chronicle, labels the first year of Tiglath-Pileser's second great western campaign 'to Philistia'. In spring of 734 BC, the king assembled his army and invaded from the north, marching along the Phoenician coast. His choice of invasion route was dictated by geography; since a mountain range and the deep cleft of the Jordan Valley limit the number of invasion routes into the coastal plain.

When he reached Phoenicia, Tiglath-Pileser set about subjecting the independent Phoenician city-states, important centres for Mediterranean trade. He took Byblos, apparently by escalade without an extended siege, and several smaller towns. It is likely that the king applied the Assyrians' usual terror tactics, meant to intimidate future enemies into surrendering without a fight. Judging from other eighth-century BC Assyrian accounts, it is probable that, once the city was reduced, leading citizens of Byblos were impaled and flayed, while other citizens were transplanted to regions far

Shalmaneser III (858–824 BC) of Assyria built a strong army, but did not attempt major expansion. This relief commemorates a treaty with his southern neighbour, Babylonia.

THE OPPOSED FORCES

ASSYRIANS (estimated)
Cavalry:	12,000
Infantry:	20,000
500 four–man chariots:	2,000
Total:	**34,000**

ENEMIES
None of the allied small states fielded an army against Assyria. Thus, the Assyrians met their enemies fortress by fortress, each containing garrison forces of 1000–5000 each.

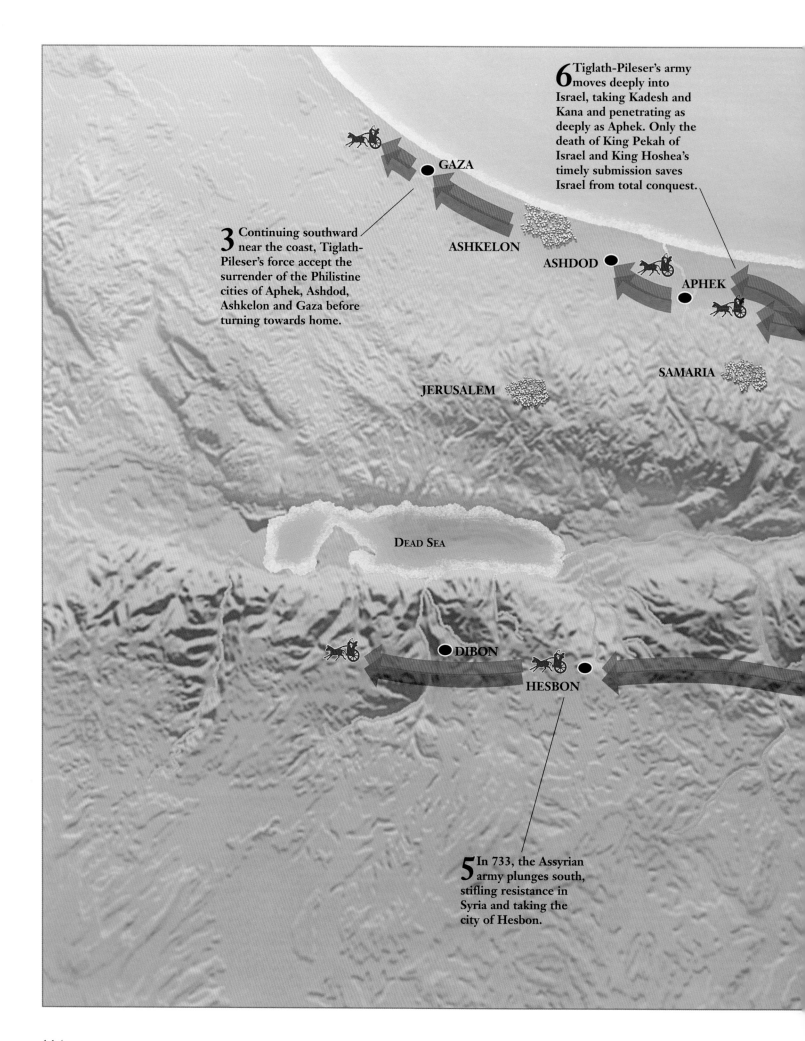

6 Tiglath-Pileser's army moves deeply into Israel, taking Kadesh and Kana and penetrating as deeply as Aphek. Only the death of King Pekah of Israel and King Hoshea's timely submission saves Israel from total conquest.

GAZA

3 Continuing southward near the coast, Tiglath-Pileser's force accept the surrender of the Philistine cities of Aphek, Ashdod, Ashkelon and Gaza before turning towards home.

ASHKELON

ASHDOD

APHEK

SAMARIA

JERUSALEM

DEAD SEA

DIBON

HESBON

5 In 733, the Assyrian army plunges south, stifling resistance in Syria and taking the city of Hesbon.

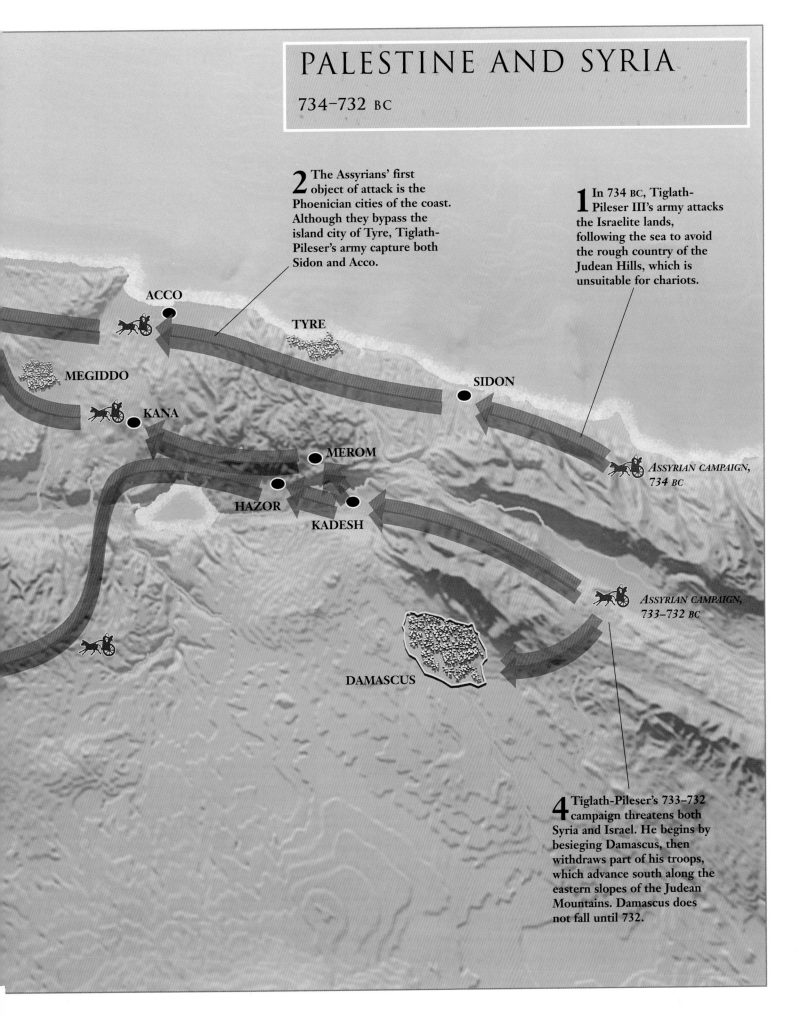

PALESTINE AND SYRIA

734–732 BC

2 The Assyrians' first object of attack is the Phoenician cities of the coast. Although they bypass the island city of Tyre, Tiglath-Pileser's army capture both Sidon and Acco.

1 In 734 BC, Tiglath-Pileser III's army attacks the Israelite lands, following the sea to avoid the rough country of the Judean Hills, which is unsuitable for chariots.

ACCO

TYRE

MEGIDDO

SIDON

KANA

MEROM

ASSYRIAN CAMPAIGN, 734 BC

HAZOR

KADESH

ASSYRIAN CAMPAIGN, 733–732 BC

DAMASCUS

4 Tiglath-Pileser's 733–732 campaign threatens both Syria and Israel. He begins by besieging Damascus, then withdraws part of his troops, which advance south along the eastern slopes of the Judean Mountains. Damascus does not fall until 732.

Besides great gods, the Assyrians enjoyed the protection of many other personal spirits, or 'demons', such as this ivory griffin-headed demon, which may have originally been part of a throne. Ivory carvings were widely used to decorate important pieces of furniture in antiquity, while griffin-headed demons were protective deities, and would therefore have been appropriate as giving divine protection to the throne's occupant. While similar creatures are depicted on Assyrian wall reliefs at Nimrud, this carving dates from the eighth century BC and comes from Toprakkale in Urartu, Anatolia.

The typical Assyrian infantry helmet would been very similar to this eighth-century BC helmet found at Urartu (Turkey), crafted of bronze with a simple design.

from their homeland, lessening the likelihood of future rebellion.

The Assyrian methods were rough but effective. When Tiglath-Pileser reached Tyre, King Hiram submitted and paid tribute before the Assyrians could formally initiate a siege. The next major town, Ashkelon, did the same, with King Mitinti swearing an oath of loyalty to the Assyrian conqueror. In similar fashion, Tiglath-Pileser worked his way southwards, reaching the Philistine plain. Arriving at Gaza, he discovered that King Hanun had fled to Egypt.

However, Hanun later returned to accept Assyrian overlordship. Tiglath-Pileser ended the year's advance at Wadi el-'Arish, the southern border of Palestine,

setting up a stele to commemorate his achievement.

'TO DAMASCUS'

The first year of Tiglath-Pileser's western campaign had been a noteworthy success. He was able to convert part of the conquered territory into an Assyrian province. Intimidation had also paid off, as the more easterly kingdoms of Edom, Moab, Ammon and Judah all sent ambassadors, bearing tribute and promising loyalty to Assyria.

In the second year of campaign, though, Tiglath-Pileser's grand strategy became apparent. His main objective was, in fact, King Rezin of Damascus, a much nearer neighbour to Assyria, who had, moreover, instigated resistance to Assyria in the first place. The 734 BC campaign had succeeded in subduing the other coalition forces, leaving Damascus isolated. Tiglath-Pileser could then deal with Damascus at his leisure.

The Syrian state of Damascus was a much more difficult military prospect than the small states of Phoenicia and Philistia. The campaign against the Syrian power lasted for two years; thus the Assyrian Eponym Chronicle labels the campaigns of both 733 and 732 BC as 'to Damascus'. Damascus was a flourishing trade centre, formidably defended.

The campaigns of 733 and 732 BC also began from the north, the easiest approach to the region. This time, however, the Assyrian forces stopped long enough to begin a siege of Damascus early in 733 BC. Finding no armies in the field to oppose him, Tiglath-Pileser then decided it was safe to divide his force. Leaving part of the army to maintain the siege, the king moved southwards with the rest of his force, this time following a line to the east of the Judean mountains. Tiglath-Pileser quickly took the fortified town of Janoah, after which he divided his army yet again. The eastern advance made a long loop to the east, culminating in the conquest of Hesbon.

The westward march was Tiglath-Pileser's opportunity to punish King Pekah of Israel for his rebellion. He pushed through northern Israel, taking Kadesh and Kanah, and eventually penetrating almost to the coast. In the process, the Assyrians took control of the Naphtali and Upper Galilee regions of Israel, as well as northern Transjordan. The only hint we have of the devastation he wrought in the region is a report that he deported 13,520 Israelite captives, sending them inland where they could not cause trouble and could help supply his voracious war machine.

Damascus itself did not fall until well into the year 732 BC, the third year of the western campaign. No details of the siege are available, but it was doubtless conducted with typical Assyrian thoroughness. The Assyrians would have begun with a demand that the city surrender. When that demand was

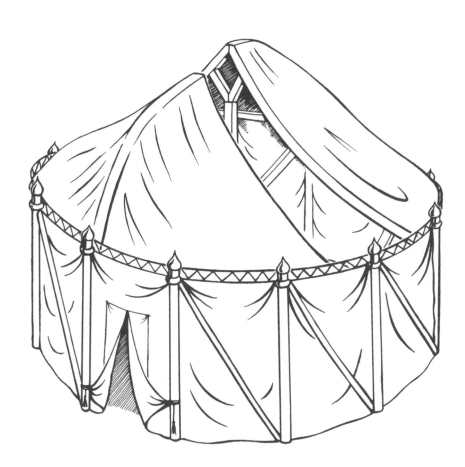

refused, all exits from the city would have been blocked, and the Assyrians would have constructed siege ramps that were gradually extended to touch the city's walls, the workers protected by comrades bearing enormous shields.

When the ramps were ready, Assyrian engineers would have had siege towers and battering rams hauled up the gentle slope. The rams, protected like tortoises in moving houses similar to modern tanks, would have begun their inexorable attack on the stretch of wall before them, their sharp points aimed at the mortar between stones. Suspended from a strong central beam and swung repeatedly on heavy ropes, the ram's action would gradually erode the mortar until at last a section of the wall gave way. Then the assault force would employ ladders to fight their way into the breach, while archers and slingers stationed at the top of the siege towers tried to clear the wall of enemy defenders. When they broke into the city, slaughter would begin, since a town that had forced the Assyrians into a lengthy and dangerous siege deserved no quarter.

When Damascus fell, King Rezim was captured. Tiglath-Pileser had him

A sign of Assyria's military professionalism was the issue of standardized tents to troops in the field, as in this illustration copied from a contemporary relief.

executed. Also, as a special sign of contempt, an Assyrian force purposely razed Hadara, Rezin's hometown. Damascus survived; it was too valuable as a trade centre to be destroyed. However, thousands of surviving Damascenes would have been taken into Assyrian exile.

AFTERMATH

Israel might have drawn upon itself the full weight of Tiglath-Pileser's wrath, but in 732 BC King Pekah was assassinated. His successor, King Hoshea (732–724 BC), immediately sent ambassadors promising his allegiance to Tiglath-Pileser. Only this saved Israel from annexation. Thus, although, it had lost a major segment of its territory – which became the three Assyrian provinces of Du'ria, Magidu, and Gal'aza – the kingdom continued to survive, at least for a short while.

Tiglath-Pileser's Palestine and Syria campaign proved conclusively that the little state of Israel could not hope to compete against the great empire of the eighth century BC. Its army was too small and amateurish to face the Assyrian military machine, and while its walls were strong, Assyrian kings had an impressive siege arsenal at their command. Israel, like Judah to the south, had only two choices: to accept Assyrian suzerainty, its kings dwindling until they were little more than puppets and provincial governors for rulers like Tiglath-Pileser; or to make common cause with the other small states of the region, hoping that they could form a coalition strong enough to drive Assyria from their borders. In the case of the alliance of Rezin of Damascus and Pekah of Israel, however, it is clear that this was based on wishful thinking rather than a coherent plan to work together to confront the superpower.

There is no evidence that the states of the coalition ever attempted to provide each other with military support, or fielded a coalition army that stood a chance of matching the army of Assyria. Instead, it was ultimately a simple matter for Tiglath-Pileser to pick off his enemies one by one, while each member of the coalition huddled behind his walls, wondering when the blow would fall.

A palace relief celebrating one of Tiglath-Pileser III's many victorious sieges. Such reliefs are a vital source of information about Assyrian equipment and fighting techniques.

Left: The ruins of Sidon, one of the Phoenician coastal cities successfully taken by Tiglath-Pileser III in his 734 BC campaign. The ruins date to a later period.

LACHISH
701 BC

KING SENNACHERIB OF ASSYRIA MARCHED AGAINST JUDAH TO SUPPRESS ITS REBELLIOUS KING, HEZEKIAH. THE FIRST MAJOR OBSTACLE IN HIS PATH WAS LACHISH, A POWERFUL JUDEAN FORTRESS THAT PROTECTED THE SOUTHWEST APPROACH TO JERUSALEM. SENNACHERIB RESPONDED WITH A CLASSIC ASSYRIAN SIEGE, EVENTUALLY TAKING AND SACKING THE TOWN.

WHY DID IT HAPPEN?

WHO King Sennacherib of Assyria (704–681 BC) led a large Assyrian army against the Judean fortified town of Lachish, subject to King Hezekiah of Judah (726–697 BC).

WHAT The Assyrians besieged the strategically located fortress, which guarded a major approach to Jerusalem.

WHERE Lachish in ancient Judah, the modern Tell ed-Duweir, southwest of Jerusalem, Israel.

WHEN 701 BC.

WHY King Hezekiah of Judah, along with his ally King Zidka of Ashkelon, had rebelled against Assyrian overlordship. In the expedition that culminated in the siege of Lachish, Sennacherib intended to defeat the rebels and consolidate his control on the region.

OUTCOME Lachish fell after a short Assyrian siege. Hundreds of its defenders died, and many others were deported from the region.

After the Assyrians destroyed the northern state of Israel in 724 BC, Judah found itself subordinated to the Assyrian juggernaut. The farsighted king of Judah, Hezekiah, spent years preparing his bid for independence. He refortified Jerusalem and guaranteed its water supply during a possible siege by means of an ambitious water tunnel. He also improved the defences of towns throughout Judah. On the diplomatic front, he threw in his lot with Egypt, Assyria's rival for control of Palestine. By 701 BC, Hezekiah and his ally King Zidka of Ashkelon were prepared for rebellion, counting on Egyptian assistance against Assyria's overwhelming power.

INVASION

King Sennacherib of Assyria's response was swift. By the end of the eighth century BC, Assyria had developed one of the most militaristic states ever seen on earth: it is

The wall reliefs that Sennacherib commissioned for Nineveh, many of which are now in the British Museum, are a priceless source of information for Assyrian military practices.

estimated that Sennacherib could draw on the services of as many as 150,000 soldiers, although many of them would have been needed for ongoing garrison duties in Assyria's conquered provinces. At a modest estimate, Sennacherib could easily have brought 25,000–35,000 soldiers to punish little Judah – which had probably never been able to muster a field army of more than 10,000 at any time in its history. In the biblical account of this campaign (2 Kings 18–19), the Assyrians sneer that the Judeans had to depend on Egypt even for their basic cavalry needs.

The Assyrian forces would also have been more professional – the core consisted of year-round paid troops, many of them foreign mercenaries, supplemented with provincial levies. Moreover, Sennacherib's army was a fully integrated force, with cavalry and a corps of engineers to support an infantry of archers, slingers and spearmen. The elite troops, at least, were equipped with excellent weapons and bronze lamellar body armour (bronze plates sewn onto leather).

King Hezekiah did not even attempt to meet the invincible Assyrian army in the field. Instead, he hoped that Judah's many strong fortresses would wear down the Assyrians until they gave up and left. That forced Sennacherib to fight a campaign of sieges – a task that the Assyrians did superlatively well.

Sennacherib followed the by-now familiar Assyrian invasion route, entering Palestine from the north and marching swiftly southwards along the eastern Mediterranean coast. Phoenicia and Israel were already Assyrian provinces, thanks to earlier Assyrian onslaughts, so Sennacherib met no resistance until he reached the Plain of Philistia. Although we can assume that King Zidka of Ashkelon did his utmost to win support from the other Philistine city-states, only two held out when Sennacherib arrived – Ashkelon itself surrendered without resistance, its king making his peace with heavy tribute.

His hapless allies were swiftly taken by assault, many of their inhabitants killed in battle or its aftermath, or taken into captivity far inland in Mesopotamia if they had skills useful to the conqueror.

At first, it appeared that Judah might be spared. Sennacherib destroyed several towns, including Joppa, but was stalled while besieging Ekron. An Egyptian relief force arrived and caught much of his army in an ambush at Eltekeh (Tell esh-Shallaf, north of Jabneh). It is unclear what happened then; the Assyrians may have defeated the Egyptians, or perhaps just evaded them. Whichever the case, Sennacherib was able to return to Ekron and capture the city. Then, Sennacherib and his army turned inland, towards Judah.

LACHISH

To control Judah, it was necessary to control the little state's many fortresses, constructed in the course of nearly two centuries of

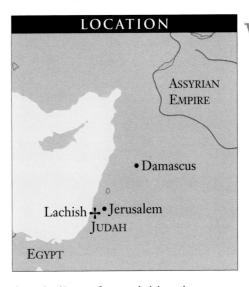

Sennacherib's army first marched down the Phoenician-Philistine coast, then turned inland to confront Lachish, a major fortress that defended the road to the Judean hills.

ASSYRIAN GUARDSMAN

The core of Sennacherib's army consisted of professional, year-round soldiers, who guarded the king, performed garrison duties, and provided the discipline and training that made Assyrian armies so formidable. Members of the guard were provided with standard equipment, including lamellar body armour (small plates laced together in parallel rows), helmet, shield, and the first standardized army boot in world history. These elite troops were diversified, with large numbers of archers and engineers as well as spearmen. For several centuries, these soldiers were the terror of Middle Eastern states.

LACHISH

While some armies considered archers to be light skirmishing troops, Assyrian archers were front-line fighters. If threatened, they could take to their swords and fight it out, but would more often rely on the protection of a shield-bearer and supporting infantry. Assyrian tactics were sufficiently well developed that infantry could be moved forward to protect the archers, then pulled back out of the way once its protection was no longer needed.

THE OPPOSED FORCES

ASSYRIANS (estimated)
Cavalry:	5000
Infantry:	30,000
Total:	**35,000**

LACHISH (estimated)
Population of town:	about 2000
Total:	**2000**

unremitting warfare. The first major obstacle Sennacherib faced was Lachish, which blocked a major western approach into the Judean Mountains, the Lachish–Hebron road. Without taking possession of Lachish, it would be impossible to move an army against Jerusalem, capital of Judah.

Lachish was a formidable obstacle. The town was situated on a steeply sloped tell, an artificial mound consisting of debris from earlier settlements on the site. A double line of walls with crenellated battlements and square towers at regular intervals surrounded the town. The whole wall complex had been rebuilt in solid stone, replacing earlier casemate walls – thin retaining walls filled with rubble. At Lachish, the defenders had also added to the height of the wall by erecting wooden frames along the top of the wall. They had shields mounted on them, behind which archers and rock-throwers could take shelter while harassing the enemy. To make

a near approach to the walls even more difficult, the slopes of the tell had been lined with a glacis, forming a steep slope of carefully laid rocks that would have been difficult to climb, much less assault. Beyond the walls and the glacis lay a deep ditch. Lachish's main gate was sited near the southwest corner of the wall. A narrow road led to it, making mass assault impossible.

The gate itself was actually double: the outer gate, defended by two strong towers, led to a courtyard with a low wall. If an attacker succeeded in penetrating that far, he still would have to turn right to approach the inner gate, which was also supported by two towers and led to a large gatehouse. Any force that broke into the city would also have to deal with a fortified palace complex before the city would be completely in their hands.

THE SIEGE

Before beginning the siege, Sennacherib sent a herald to the gates, offering moderate terms in return for immediate surrender. After all, sieges could hold up an army for weeks or even months, and Sennacherib must have feared pinning down his army for too long where it would be exposed to possible Egyptian attack, not to mention bad weather and disease. The royal governor in command of Lachish refused his offer, so the siege began.

Sennacherib established his camp about 960m (1050ft) yards from the southwest corner of the town, near the gate, where access to the city would be easiest for his troops. We know about the course of the siege in surprising detail, thanks to two excellent sources. Sennacherib himself regarded his successful siege of Lachish as a major accomplishment, and commemorated it with a relief panel on a wall of his palace of Nineveh (now in the British Museum).

The Assyrian depiction of the siege was clarified, and further details added to our knowledge, by large-scale excavations of the site in the 1930s. While 2 Kings and 2 Chronicles both deal with Sennacherib's campaign of 701 BC, they do not include any specific mention of the siege of Lachish.

Sennacherib's engineers began the construction of a siege ramp near the Assyrian camp, building it up at an easy slope towards the southwest corner of Lachish's main wall; they probably also constructed a ramp, a solid structure of stone and wood, up to the main gate at the same time. The ramps were constructed with a gradient of about 30°, with a gentler slope near the top. The main ramp was about 55m (60 yards) long, and wide enough for the Assyrians to operate five battering rams against the city wall.

The defenders, of course, did everything they could to slow or stop construction of the ramp. Catapults had not yet been invented, but the defenders would have had a good supply of arrows, spears and rocks to throw on the workers.

There must have been a high casualty rate among the labourers, many of whom would have been Judeans of the surrounding region, forced into service by

the invaders. The Assyrians also took steps to limit the damage inflicted from the wall.

Their own archers sniped at the defenders, using powerful compound bows with an effective range of over 274m (899ft) – although shooting upward against gravity would have lessened that distance. These archers were an important and privileged part of the Assyrian force, as can be seen by their ankle-length armour in the Nineveh reliefs – which would have severely hampered mobility but also greatly reduced the number of casualties.

Each archer was also protected by a shield-bearer, whose massive shield (or mantlet), curving partway over himself and his archer, could deflect most missiles. As the ramp approached the wall, the Assyrians drew up one or more siege towers. A siege tower, constructed to match the height of

This painting shows an Assyrian assault. The Assyrians have built a siege ramp, and now assault the wall with rams, supported by archers. Note the impalement of captured prisoners in the foreground.

4 After several days of bloody combat, the Assyrians enter the city. Many inhabitants are brutally killed.

3 At the same time, Sennacherib's men assault the city with rams and scaling ladders, the archers giving covering fire.

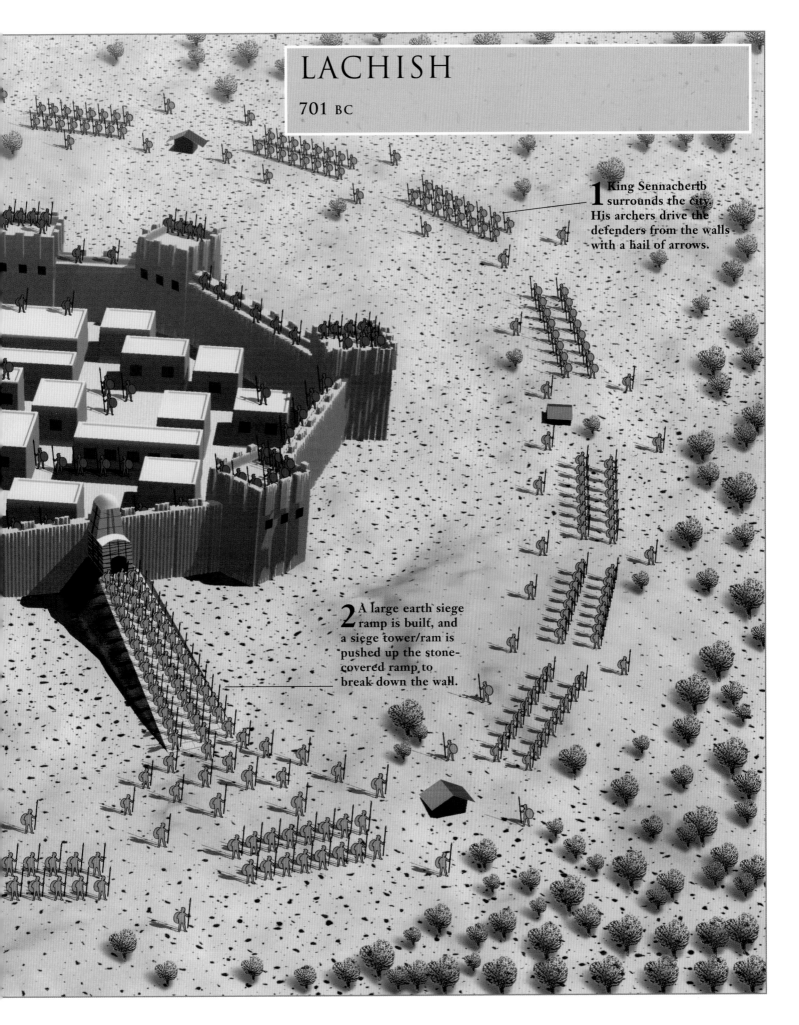

LACHISH

701 BC

1 King Sennacherib surrounds the city. His archers drive the defenders from the walls with a hail of arrows.

2 A large earth siege ramp is built, and a siege tower/ram is pushed up the stone-covered ramp to break down the wall.

LACHISH

The remains of the citadel of Lachish still give a good impression of the strength of the fortress that Sennacherib's troops had to assault.

Below: A nineteenth-century artist's impression of the Assyrian king Sennacherib (r. 704–681 BC), based on contemporary relief carvings.

the town wall, would allow archers to compete on equal terms with the defenders.

THE RAMS

When the Assyrian ramp reached the wall of Lachish, battering rams were hauled forwards. These were not just simple logs carried by teams of men, but complex pieces of siege equipment. The ram itself was a massive length of wood, with an iron head at the end that narrowed to a sharp point. It was suspended from beams by means of a cradle of ropes, making it possible for a few men to sway the ram back and crash it into the wall every few seconds.

The whole device was transported within a strongly built hut on wheels, pushed towards the wall from behind, or moved forward by teams pulling ropes that had been wrapped around stakes near the wall.

Although the ram house was constructed of wood, it was covered with fresh animal hides and perhaps even with metal plates – a necessary precaution, since the best way for the defenders to stop its gnawing attack on their wall would be to set fire to it. If enemy torches or fire

pots did succeed in kindling a blaze, a relief shows that ram teams even included a soldier whose task it was to reach out and pour large ladles of water onto the danger point.

The Lachish relief from Nineveh, as well as other illustrations of Assyrian siege warfare, shows that it was customary to aim the ram sharply upwards, striking as high on the wall as possible. With its sharp point, the ram's head would have been aimed as carefully as possible towards the joints between large building blocks, gradually eroding the mortar and, eventually, causing the rocks to fall. By aiming high on the wall, fallen debris could add to the ramp, making the eventual assault easier.

The defenders of Lachish did everything possible to postpone that day, doubtless hoping for relief from either Jerusalem or Egypt. They threw fire down onto the rams, and also tried to stop the ram's action by catching it with hooks they hung from the wall on long chains. The

Opposite: Two Assyrian courtiers from a palace relief at Nineveh. The militarization of Assyrian society can be seen from the fact that, although jewelled and well-groomed, the men still carry swords.

LACHISH

On this relief, Sennacherib, seated on a tall throne and fanned by court eunuchs, receives the surrender of Lachish. The king's head was defaced in antiquity.

fighting was fierce: archaeologists discovered a mass grave of 1500 Assyrian soldiers near the site.

Eventually, however, the battering rams did their work. Some Assyrian warriors poured into the town through the breach, while others swarmed up ladders and into the town. Hundreds of men, women and children were killed, as the victors looted the city. Sennacherib's relief also shows the special fate awarded to Lachish's leaders – they were impaled, to die slowly by the

walls of their city. Other citizens appear in the relief, beginning their march into Assyrian exile.

AFTERMATH

Lachish had delayed the Assyrian army, but at first it appeared that their sacrifice would not be enough to save Jerusalem. While Sennacherib was still at Lachish, King Hezekiah sent his submission, along with the contents of the Temple and palace treasuries. Nonetheless, after Lachish,

Sennacherib marched to the capital, and began to prepare for another siege, this time against Jerusalem's formidable defences. But those defences were never put to the test.

The biblical account of what followed is chilling: 'And that night the angel of the Lord went forth, and slew a hundred and eighty-five thousand in the camp of the Assyrians; and when men arose early in the morning, behold, these were all dead bodies.' (2 Kings 19: 35.) Not surprisingly, Sennacherib then went home.

It is difficult to determine what exactly happened. Historians have suggested that the Assyrian army was hit by a sudden large-scale epidemic, perhaps of plague. The Egyptian army may also have been in the vicinity, making it impractical to conduct the long siege that Jerusalem would require. And there is some evidence that Sennacherib received sudden word

of a rebellion in Babylon, forcing him to withdraw. Although his conquest was incomplete, Sennacherib had every reason to boast when he returned from his Judean campaign. He had captured 46 forts, including the major fortresses of Lachish and Ekron; he also boasted that he had deported 200,150 people, many of them destined to labour for the rest of their lives to support the Assyrian military establishment or to fight in future Assyrian armies.

Sennacherib's primary enemies, Ashkelon and Judah, had submitted to him, renewing oaths of loyalty and paying massive tribute. It appeared that the region was now sufficiently intimidated that future kings would not attempt to side with Egypt against mighty Assyria, so Sennacherib could return home without a qualm.

This seventeenth-century painting by the Dutch artist Lambert de Hondt depicts Sennacherib before Jerusalem, turned away from the city by divine wrath striking from heaven.

FALL OF JUDAH
588–586 BC

NEBUCHADNEZZAR II, SECOND RULER OF THE NEO-BABYLONIAN EMPIRE, WAS OUT OF PATIENCE WITH THE REBELLIOUS KING ZEDEKIAH OF JUDAH. IN A CAMPAIGN THAT LASTED FROM 588 TO 586 BC, HE CAPTURED A SERIES OF JUDEAN TOWNS, A CAMPAIGN THAT CULMINATED IN AN 18-MONTH SIEGE OF THE CAPITAL, JERUSALEM. AFTER HIS VICTORY, NEBUCHADNEZZAR DESTROYED THE TEMPLE OF SOLOMON AND LED THOUSANDS OF JUDEANS INTO CAPTIVITY IN BABYLONIA.

WHY DID IT HAPPEN?

WHO King Nebuchadnezzar II (or Nebuchadrezzar) of Babylon (605–562 BC) led a major army to punish his rebellious vassal, King Zedekiah of Judah.

WHAT Judah's efforts to align with Egypt against the Babylonian Empire threatened its control of the Levant. So Nebuchadnezzar decided to destroy the kingdom.

WHERE The southern Jewish kingdom of Judah (modern-day southern Israel), culminating in an 18-month siege of Jerusalem.

WHEN 588–586 BC.

WHY Although the northern kingdom of Israel had ceased to exist, Judah still hoped to preserve its autonomy. To that end, the Judean king Zedekiah accepted Egyptian support against his overlord, the ruler of the Neo-Babylonian Empire.

OUTCOME The kingdom of Judah ceased to exist. Its last king was blinded and carried off to exile in Babylon, while his territory became a Babylonian province. The capital, Jerusalem, including the Temple of Solomon, was destroyed, and thousands of Jews were enslaved.

When the mighty Assyrian Empire collapsed in 612 BC, rulers of the small states that dotted the Near East must have heaved a great sigh of relief, hoping that the demise of the superpower would allow their own states to regain independence. The dream proved to be illusory, however. Almost immediately, Babylon claimed a role as the new superpower of the post-Assyrian world. Thus, small states like Judah found themselves once again the objects of competition between a major Mesopotamian power and Egypt, since Judah lay on the land bridge between the rival Egyptian and Babylonian Empires.

A REBELLIOUS PROVINCE

The Babylonian King Nebuchadnezzar II was the second ruler of the newly ascendant Neo-Babylonian (or Chaldean) state. He spent much of his reign feuding with Egypt in an unrelenting struggle for control of the Middle East. As his ability to fight Egypt fluctuated, states that had passed directly from Assyrian control to that of Babylon

This illustration from a Spanish Bible shows King Zedekiah of Judah taken to Babylon as a prisoner by Nebuchadnezzar. Arms and armor are typical of the early fifteenth century AD.

hoped yet again to regain their independence. Hope was particularly aroused by Nebuchadnezzar's attempted invasion of the land of the Nile in 601 BC; when the invasion failed, it encouraged Babylon's unwilling vassal states, including Judah, to rebel.

Although Nebuchadnezzar could not defeat Egypt, he certainly had sufficient armed force at his command to destroy a puny vassal state like Judah – and it was necessary to teach Judah a lesson or he was likely to lose control of Palestine, that vital land bridge to Egypt. So in 597 BC Nebuchadnezzar personally led a large Babylonian army against the rebellious King Jehoiachin of Judah, who must have hoped that Egypt would defeat Babylon so decisively that the king would not be able to rally. Nebuchadnezzar could probably field an integrated army of 40,000–50,000 men, a strong professional force supported by militia.

It is very unlikely that Judah's army ever numbered much more than 10,000 men. Since Judah could not hope to field an army that could campaign against Babylon with its overwhelming resources, Jehoiachin's only possible response was to take refuge behind the strong walls of Jerusalem. Nebuchadnezzar therefore marched against Jerusalem, placing the city under siege. His wrath was satisfied, though, when Jehoiachin submitted and paid over an enormous tribute (including gold and silver from the Temple treasury). Jehoiachin was sent into exile far from his homeland, along with 10,000 leading citizens and useful craftsmen. However, Judah did at least continue to exist as a state.

Nebuchadnezzar replaced Jehoiachin on the Judean throne with Zedekiah, a supposedly more subservient vassal who, nonetheless, continued to dream of escape from Babylonian overlordship. The Egyptian Pharaoh Psammetichus II (594–588 BC) seems to have encouraged Zedekiah in his thoughts of rebellion, doubtless hoping to weaken the Babylonian state without wasting his own troops. Zedekiah appears to have begun to plot a second revolt as early as 593 BC. He negotiated with the Syrian states that lay under Babylonian hegemony (Edom, Moab and Ammon), as well as the major Phoenician city-states of Tyre and Sidon. In 591 BC, Zedekiah's plans were ready, and he declared his independence from Babylon.

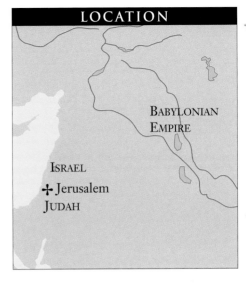

In the sixth century BC, the New Babylonian Empire became the dominant power of the Middle East. Judah lay between it and the other great power of the age, Egypt.

BABYLONIAN CHARIOT
(6TH CENTURY BC)

The sixth century BC was the last time chariots played a significant role in Near Eastern warfare. By the time Judah fell, Babylonian chariots had become much heavier, able to carry up to four men at a time. Such a heavy load needed four horses to pull it effectively, since the horse yokes in use at the time tended to constrict the horses' breathing. Babylonian chariots had a driver and an archer like earlier chariots, but they also had room for a shield bearer and a fourth man with a short stabbing spear, suggesting that chariots were driven into enemy formations instead of circling around them as they had in earlier centuries.

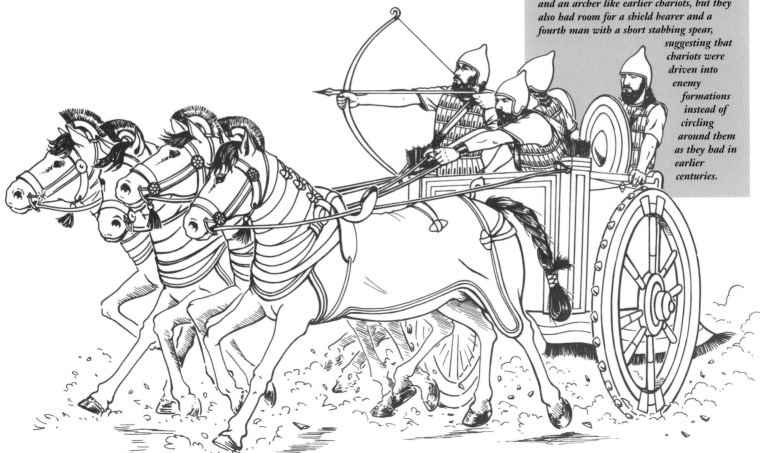

FALL OF JUDAH

An artistic impression of the Babylonian escalade that succeeded in capturing Jerusalem in 586 BC. In reality, the city was taken only after Babylonian rams had breached the wall.

THE OPPOSED FORCES

BABYLONIANS (estimated)
The full Babylonian field army, including siege train and cavalry detachments:
Total: 40,000–50,000

JUDEANS (estimated)
The population of Jerusalem, swelled by refugees from regions conquered by Nebuchadnezzar:
                                    40,000
The population of other towns:
                                    1000–5000
Total: about 45,000

Nebuchadnezzar did not turn his attention to his rebellious vassal immediately. When he did so in 591 BC, it is clear from his actions that he believed that the time for gentle treatment was over. Once more, he marched into Judah with a massive army, again a highly professional force that could have numbered as many as 50,000 men.

Certainly, Zedekiah did not even attempt to meet the angry Babylonian ruler in the field. Instead, he relied on the strong walls of his cities, and the promise of military aid from Pharaoh Apries (the biblical Hophra) of Egypt (589–570 BC).

Nebuchadnezzar invaded Palestine from the north in the spring of 588 BC, a roundabout route that was nonetheless easier than attempting to make his way through the cleft of the Jordan Valley and over the Judean Mountains. His troops marched down the coastal plain, snapping up the cities of Phoenicia before moving on to the provinces that had formerly constituted the state of Israel. Many cities did not even attempt resistance against such overwhelming force.

Kedesh, Megiddo and Aphek did try to hold out against the Babylonians, but they paid for their resistance with speedy destruction, although they put up a spirited resistance. Nebuchadnezzar's army enjoyed such overwhelming force that he could attack many points of a fortification at once, taking towns by escalade rather than having to endure a protracted siege. Evidence of the horror roused by Nebuchadnezzar's approach has been found in the excavations of the Judean city of Lachish, in the form of a letter from an outpost commander, reporting that he could no longer see beacon lights from the north. By the end of 588 BC, Nebuchadnezzar was able to move on to his chief target, Jerusalem.

JERUSALEM

Jerusalem was the capital of Judah and the greatest cosmopolitan centre of the region, with a population in the neighbourhood of 20,000. This number would have been swollen in 588 BC by refugees who had fled from the path of Nebuchadnezzar's advancing army, perhaps as much as doubling Jerusalem's population during the siege and placing an enormous strain on the city's food supply. Although Nebuchadnezzar had already intimidated the city into surrender once before, King Zedekiah determined on resistance this time, probably aware that he could expect little mercy since Judah had rebelled for a second time. He must have hoped that Jerusalem would be able to hold out against a Babylonian siege until the arrival of help from Egypt.

Such a hope was not unreasonable. Jerusalem, nestled in the Judean highlands, was sited in a nearly impregnable landscape. A century before, King Hezekiah (726–697 BC) had restored the city's walls, adding towers to aid in defence. He also built a second wall outside the first, a massive defence 6m (20ft) wide and constructed of large boulders that would be unlikely to yield easily to Babylonian battering rams. Hezekiah, at that time expecting attack from Assyria, had also served Jerusalem by securing the city's water supply with a massive engineering project that is still extant. He had a tunnel dug from within the city to the Gihon Spring outside the city walls, a distance of 533m (1749ft), and then completely sealed the spring off from access by any other means.

Thus, in a siege, the Jerusalemites were assured of an ongoing supply of untainted

water. Hezekiah's fortifications had proven their worth in 701 BC when the Assyrian Sennacherib had besieged the city and failed to take it. In that year, Sennacherib had broken the siege off quickly, probably because he received reports of rebellion in Babylon (although the biblical account suggests a large-scale epidemic among his troops). In the rapidly changing political

The warlike Nebuchadnezzar II is also famed as the creator of one of the seven wonders of the ancient world, the hanging gardens of Babylon, established for Nebuchadnezzar's mountain-born wife.

3 The Egyptian army marches north, intending to reinforce King Zedekiah, but is defeated and turns back.

2 The Assyrian army divides to take several Judean cities, moving on to besiege Jerusalem.

5 While besieging Jerusalem, the Assyrian army captures more southern Judean outposts, including Hebron, Azekah and Beersheva.

4 Nebachednezzar's army returns to the interrupted siege of Jerusalem. The city is captured.

6 King Zedekiah flees Jerusalem with a small entourage, but is taken captive in the Judean Mountains near Jericho.

RAPHIA

GAZA

ASHDOD

JAFFA

BEERSHEVA

LACHISH

AZEKAH

APHEK

BETH-SHEMESH

ARAD

HEBRON

BETH-HAKEREM

JERUSALEM

ENGEDI

DEAD SEA

JERICHO

FALL OF JUDAH

588–586 BC

GREAT SEA

1 Nebuchadnezzar's army crosses the Judaean Mountains into Judah, and soon captures the fortress city of Megiddo.

DOR

ACCO

SAMARIA

MEGIDDO

TYRE

RIVER JORDAN

FALL OF JUDAH

The Destruction of Jerusalem by the Italian painter Ercole de' Roberti (c. 1450–1496). This sort of large historic theme was popular with Renaissance artists.

A Babylonian siege ram, covered with protective metal plates. The ram was pushed from behind up to the wall, then swung repeatedly against a mortar seam.

environment of the ancient Near East, King Zedekiah must have had reasonable hopes that Nebuchadnezzar would be unable to mount a lengthy siege.

THE SIEGE

The siege began in the middle of the rainy season, on 10 January 587 BC. Nebuchadnezzar began by attempting a circumvallation, doubtless hoping to starve the recalcitrant inhabitants into submission. Such a decision also suggests that both he and his Babylonian siege engineers recognized that it would be difficult to penetrate Jerusalem's defences.

At first, Zedekiah's bold stance seemed to pay off. Nebuchadnezzar was forced to break off the siege when Pharaoh Apries did indeed cross the Egyptian border with a large expeditionary force to relieve his beleaguered ally. Nebuchadnezzar drew his army together and marched southwards to

meet Apries, rather than letting himself be pinned against the walls of Jerusalem. The two armies clashed north of Gaza. Unfortunately for King Zedekiah, the Babylonian army was triumphant. Nebuchadnezzar soon returned to Jerusalem to resume the siege. This time, Judah could no longer hope for salvation from beyond their borders.

Our best source for the siege is the prophet Jeremiah, who spent the siege in Jerusalem, imprisoned for having prophesied the imminent fall of the city. The picture he paints of the siege, in the biblical books of Jeremiah and Lamentations, is grim. Jeremiah tells that the Babylonian army built siege ramps – long, gently inclined slopes constructed of rock and wood, up which the besiegers could roll their siege engines. Although no

Opposite: This famous twelfth-century statue of the prophet Jeremiah forms the central pillar of a doorway of the abbey church of Moissac, France.

FALL OF JUDAH

One of the most impressive engineering feats of ancient Israel, Hezekiah's shaft and tunnel leading to the Gihon Spring of Jerusalem is still intact today.

account specifically mentions them, the Babylonian arsenal would have included siege towers, designed to match the height of the city walls and thus allow the attackers to shoot arrows and sling stones against the defenders – if, that is, they managed to clear enough defenders from the wall to allow battering ram crews to labour unscathed.

The key siege weapon, however, was the battering ram itself. This was a massive tree trunk bound with bronze or iron and with a sharp iron head, which was suspended from a frame so that it could be swung repeatedly at a weak point in the wall.

Nebuchednezzar would have had many such engines at his command. The task of those being besieged was, of course, to impede the work of the ram in any way possible, whether by killing its operators, burning the ram itself or cutting the ropes from which the ram was suspended by using knives affixed to long poles.

THE END

That the siege lasted 18 months is a tribute both to Jerusalem's impressive series of defences and to its defenders' skill. Eventually, though, the defenders weakened as famine and disease spread through the city. The books of Jeremiah and Lamentations both tell of starvation, Lamentations 4:10 in particular reporting that starving mothers boiled and ate their own children. Disease would have spread the more rapidly since the city was packed full of refugees, many of whom probably lived in hovels on the streets and in the Temple forecourt.

Finally, on 9 July 586 BC, the Babylonians succeeded in breaching the northern wall. Even after they were within the walls and fighting from street to street, some of Jerusalem's defenders successfully retreated to the Temple of Solomon, a strongly fortified complex.

They held out there for another three weeks, until August 4. Three days later, on 7 August (the ninth day of the Jewish month of Av), Nebuchadnezzar ordered the complete destruction of the Temple, along with the rest of Jerusalem.

AFTERMATH

When Nebuchadnezzar's troops breached the wall, King Zedekiah and his retinue attempted to flee. They headed eastwards into the Judean Mountains, apparently in an effort to elude pursuit. A Babylonian patrol caught them before they reached the Jordan River, however, and brought them back to Nebuchadnezzar at the northern town of Riblah, where he had established his headquarters.

Nebuchadnezzar exacted a gruesome revenge on the man he regarded as a disloyal, oath-breaking vassal. First, he had Zedekiah's sons slaughtered before their father's eyes. Then, Zedekiah himself had his eyes bored out, after which he was loaded with chains and sent into captivity in Babylon.

Nebuchadnezzar also took steps to dissolve the Judean state, thereby assuring that there would be no further rebellions. Following the standard Babylonian and Assyrian practice, he ordered a deportation of Jews to Babylonia. There is no agreement about how many Jews were taken off into this 'Babylonian captivity', but the fact that about 40,000 of their descendants returned 70 years later suggests a large initial number.

Nebuchadnezzar was not, however, ruthless. He appears to have left the farming populace, which would of course have constituted a large majority of the population, in undisturbed possession of their land. Those deported were important men (and their families) who could have stirred up fresh resistance to Babylonian rule, as well as skilled craftsmen and warriors of immediate use to the Babylonian king. A Babylonian governor was given authority over the region, and for the time being the independent Jewish state ceased to exist.

An artist's impression of grieving Judeans during the 'Babylonian Captivity of the Jews', mourning the loss of their homeland.

141

SIEGE OF TYRE
332 BC

THE PHOENICIAN CITY OF TYRE WAS ONE OF THE BEST-FORTIFIED CITIES OF ALL TIME, YET SUBDUING IT WAS VITAL TO ALEXANDER THE GREAT'S PLANS FOR CONQUEST OF THE PERSIAN EMPIRE. THE MOST CHALLENGING OF MORE THAN 20 SIEGES CONDUCTED BY ALEXANDER, THE SEVEN-MONTH SIEGE AND FINAL CONQUEST OF TYRE DISPLAY MACEDONIAN MILITARY SKILLS AT THEIR VERY BEST.

WHY DID IT HAPPEN?

WHO Alexander the Great's (356–323 BC) Macedonian and Greek army of about 30,000 men, aided by an allied fleet provided by several Phoenician cities and Cyprus, versus Tyre, a major Phoenician city subject to Persia, with a population of about 50,000.

WHAT Macedonian siege of Tyre, which resisted Alexander in his effort to control the eastern seaboard of the Mediterranean.

WHERE Tyre (modern Sur, southern Lebanon), at that time an island about 4.4km (2.75 miles) in circumference, approximately 0.8km (0.5 miles) off the Phoenician coast.

WHEN January to August 332 BC.

WHY Alexander's conquest of Persia was impossible without control of the sea. He did not have a sufficient naval force to meet the Persian fleet, so he set out to eliminate the threat by taking the Persian-held seaports of the eastern Mediterranean coast, including Tyre.

OUTCOME After seven months of increasingly desperate resistance, Alexander took Tyre, killing most of the male population and enslaving the women and children.

In 334 BC, the Macedonian king, Alexander the Great, launched his invasion of the mighty Persian Empire, which in this period controlled Phoenicia and Palestine. In his first encounter with the Persians, he defeated a Persian field army at Granicus. Instead of proceeding immediately inland to attack the Persian imperial heartland, though, Alexander next began a bold strategy to assure his supply lines before undertaking the march into the Asian hinterland.

Alexander did not have sufficient sea power to challenge the Persian-controlled Phoenician fleet; and although some of his Greek allies, such as Athens, were naval powers, Alexander did not trust their loyalty. His only option, therefore, to win the eastern Mediterranean from the hostile Persians was a plan to capture the Phoenician naval bases

Alexander and his Companion Cavalry cross the Granicus River. Although more famous for his field battles, some historians regard Alexander's sieges as the true mark of his military brilliance.

along the Mediterranean coast, making it impossible for their ships to work against Macedonian interests.

Thus, after Granicus, Alexander soon set out southwards along the Mediterranean coast of Anatolia and then Phoenicia. Most of the Phoenician cities, never very happy as Persian subjects, opened their gates to the Macedonian conqueror. Tyre, however, was at bitter enmity with its fellow Phoenician city Sidon, so when Sidon went over to Alexander, the Tyrians decided to resist.

THE PERFECT FORTIFICATION

The Tyrians had every right to be confident in their ability to withstand Alexander. Expectation was high that the Persian King Darius III would arrive soon with a much larger force than had been mustered at Granicus, an army that would wipe out the presumptuous barbarians. (In fact, Darius never appeared; his failure to respond in a timely fashion to Alexander's threat remains a mystery.)

Even without Darius, the townsmen felt they would have little to fear. Tyre was situated on an island 0.8km (0.5 miles) off the coast of the mainland. While strongly fortified all around, Tyre's walls on the landward side were a staggering 46m (150ft) in height, rising from the edge of the sea so that no attacker could gain a foothold from which to stage an assault. Catapults were mounted all around the walls. Even slow starvation of the defenders seemed unlikely, since two good harbours, on the north and south sides of the island, made supplying the city by sea an easy matter. A strong Tyrian fleet of about 80 ships, mostly triremes, was sufficient to keep the waterways open.

The Tyrians would also have known that their city had withstood sieges by the greatest military powers of earlier ages. The Assyrians had tried and failed to take Tyre in the seventh century BC. The Babylonians, successors to Assyrian power in the Levant, had also besieged the island fortress – for a staggering 13 years – but eventually gave up the attempt. It seemed very likely that Tyre would prove to be the rock upon which Alexander would break his army. Indeed, Darius might have counted on Tyre's ability

to hold the Macedonians as he slowly assembled his army.

OPENING MOVES

Alexander's siege began in January 332 BC. The most compelling military need was to find a way to approach the island city's walls. Therefore, Alexander almost immediately began construction of a mole, a causeway from the mainland that gradually inched towards the island city. The chief planners were probably Alexander's two greatest siege engineers, Charias and Diades, who had benefited from major advances in Greek siege warfare during the reign of Alexander's father, King Philip II (382–336 BC). Construction of the mole posed several challenges.

Although not technically demanding, the magnitude of the task called for major manpower resources. The manual labour was unpopular with Alexander's soldiers, but

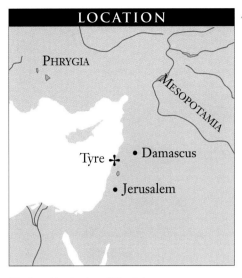

LOCATION

Tyre's position in the middle of the eastern Mediterranean coastline allowed it to dominate sea travel in the region, making its conquest essential to Alexander's success in Persia.

SIEGE DEFENCES
In ancient sieges, the advantage lay on the defenders' side. Artillery that could break walls had not yet been invented, and gravity-propelled missiles helped the defenders drive away enemies who tried to bring a ram up to the wall. The defenders were, however, vulnerable to enemy missiles shot from bows or early catapults, whether from the ground or from siege towers. Against these large shields or screens were mounted defensively on the wall.

THE OPPOSED FORCES

MACEDONIANS (estimated)
Macedonian and Greek infantry:
30,000
Phoenician and Cypriot triremes:
200
Marines and rowers: 40,000
Total: **70,000**

TYRIANS (estimated)
Men of military age: 15,000
Other civilians: 15,000
Tyrian triremes crews: 20,000
Total city population: **70,000**

Alexander dealt with the matter personally by impressing large numbers of locals into labour gangs to work alongside the soldiers. He also directed the men himself, and gave large gifts to encourage his soldiers. Stone was readily available, from the ruins of Old Tyre on the coast, and the nearby forests of Lebanon provided trees. At first, work proceeded rapidly, since the water was shallow near the mainland, although closer to Tyre it deepened to 5m (18ft).

As the mole inched towards Tyre, Tyrian soldiers attacked the workers, employing torsion catapults mounted on the city walls while also drawing close to the mole with their ships to pelt the workers with arrows and missiles from small shipboard catapults. Alexander responded to the threat of ship harassment by erecting a palisade to shelter

his work gangs. He also constructed two siege towers at the end of the mole. They stood 46m (150ft) high, perhaps the tallest siege towers ever built, a necessary measure if the arrow-shooting catapults placed in them were to be able to strike the catapults and their operators on Tyre's high walls.

The siege towers, draped with fresh hides, were impervious to ordinary measures to burn them down. So the ingenious Tyrians hatched a more comprehensive plan to destroy them. They modified a cavalry transport ship, filling it with combustibles, including sulphur and pitch; cauldrons containing more flammable materials were slung on the ship's yardarms. The crew weighted the ship's stern so that the bow would be able to run further up onto land. Tyrian triremes

Alexander's mole, an artificial causeway, was gradually built out to Tyre, allowing the Macedonians to bring two great siege towers against the island city's walls.

be resupplied by sea. Fortunately for the Macedonian king at this point, the surrender of the other Phoenician naval bases to the Macedonians paid off. A fleet of 80 Phoenician triremes arrived at Sidon, discovered that the city now supported Alexander and followed its lead in accepting Alexander's overlordship.

The Cypriot fleet soon also appeared to add itself to Alexander's command. Between them, the two fleets provided the Macedonian king with more than 200 triremes, more than enough to put a stop to Tyrian fleet activities. Alexander's new fleet promptly defeated the Tyrians in a naval battle, then proceeded to blockade both Tyrian harbours.

The Tyrian ships confined to the northern harbour (the Harbour of Sidon) made a spirited attempt to break the naval blockade. They screened their plans by hanging sails over the mouth of the harbour, and tried to break out with three quinqueremes, three quadriremes and seven triremes. Their surprise attack caught the Cyprian seamen off guard, sinking several ships and driving others onto the shore. Damage was limited, though, because Alexander quickly led the Phoenician

Alexander's father, King Philip II of Macedon (359–336 BC), was the creator of the Macedonian army that Alexander used to such magnificent effect. This gold coin from Tarsus is a symbol of Philip's wide reach.

then towed the fire ship towards the end of the mole, casting off at the last possible moment; the transport's crew started fires, then swam for their lives.

The ship succeeded in igniting both Macedonian towers. As the towers burned, Tyrian soldiers in small boats tore down the palisade that Alexander had erected to help protect the workers and set much of Alexander's smaller siege machinery alight. Soon afterwards, high seas submerged most of the mole. Clearly, the Tyrians had won the first round.

SIEGE FROM THE SEA

The assault on the mole exposed the key weakness of Alexander's position – he needed ships, without which the Tyrian fleet could harass his men at will, and Tyre could

1 The island city of Tyre was surrounded on all sides by high walls said to have been more than 50m (160ft) tall in places. These, together with the number of Tyrian ships that defended the seas around the city, and the very inaccessibility of the island itself, made the prospect of besieging Tyre a daunting one.

TYRE

5 As the mole reached the island, Macedonian catapults began bombarding the walls and defenders. These were joined by catapults from Alexander's ships. The Tyrians defended their city fiercely, but once their walls were breached south of the mole they could not stop the entrance of Macedonian soldiers, and Tyre fell.

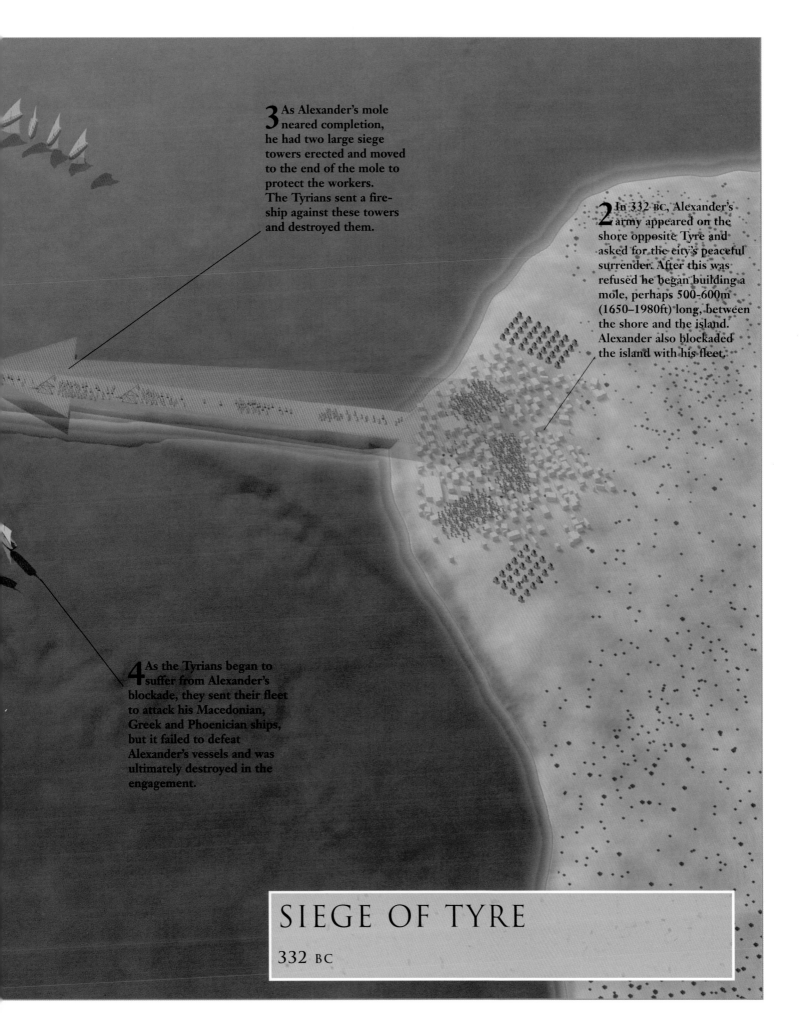

3 As Alexander's mole neared completion, he had two large siege towers erected and moved to the end of the mole to protect the workers. The Tyrians sent a fire-ship against these towers and destroyed them.

2 In 332 BC, Alexander's army appeared on the shore opposite Tyre and asked for the city's peaceful surrender. After this was refused he began building a mole, perhaps 500–600m (1650–1980ft) long, between the shore and the island. Alexander also blockaded the island with his fleet.

4 As the Tyrians began to suffer from Alexander's blockade, they sent their fleet to attack his Macedonian, Greek and Phoenician ships, but it failed to defeat Alexander's vessels and was ultimately destroyed in the engagement.

SIEGE OF TYRE

332 BC

squadron around from the south harbour and defeated the Tyrians.

Meanwhile, Alexander and his engineers began construction of a new mole, following a line rather further to the north and widening the causeway to about 61m (200ft) for greater stability against storms. The remains of this second mole can still be seen, forming the basis of the isthmus that now links Sur, Lebanon, permanently to the mainland. New siege towers protected the work, and this time the patrolling ships of Macedon's new allies made another naval attack impossible. Alexander also began to probe Tyre's sea walls with floating battering rams: he had ships tied together so that they could provide stable platforms for rams, the ship platforms moored close against a segment of wall with anchors all around.

Tyrian divers succeeded in cutting the ships' anchor cables, causing several to run aground. Then, however, Alexander

switched to mooring chains, and the onslaught continued. Alexander's new fleet also proved its usefulness by clearing away the large boulders the Tyrians had placed in the sea before their walls to keep ships away.

THE ASSAULT

As the summer progressed, the siege rapidly grew in intensity, the Tyrians fighting for their city with ever-increasing desperation. The Tyrians captured some of Alexander's men and paraded them on the walls before executing them and throwing their bodies into the sea. They also killed some Macedonian heralds, which might explain the violence of Alexander's revenge against the city.

The Tyrians also put up a highly innovative defence as the Macedonians approached their walls. The historian Diodorus Siculus tells that Alexander, contrary to normal ancient practice, used stone-throwing torsion catapults so large

Although Alexander's fleet mostly consisted of triremes, he also used lighter and more manoeuvrable biremes, propelled by two banks of oars, as in this illustration.

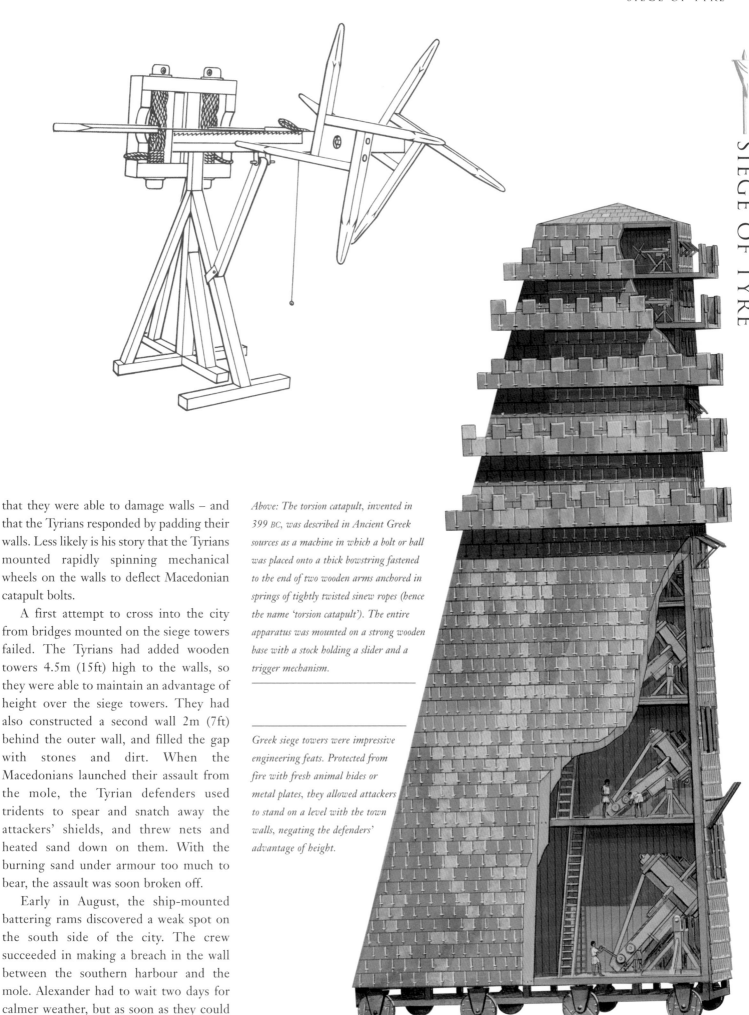

that they were able to damage walls – and that the Tyrians responded by padding their walls. Less likely is his story that the Tyrians mounted rapidly spinning mechanical wheels on the walls to deflect Macedonian catapult bolts.

A first attempt to cross into the city from bridges mounted on the siege towers failed. The Tyrians had added wooden towers 4.5m (15ft) high to the walls, so they were able to maintain an advantage of height over the siege towers. They had also constructed a second wall 2m (7ft) behind the outer wall, and filled the gap with stones and dirt. When the Macedonians launched their assault from the mole, the Tyrian defenders used tridents to spear and snatch away the attackers' shields, and threw nets and heated sand down on them. With the burning sand under armour too much to bear, the assault was soon broken off.

Early in August, the ship-mounted battering rams discovered a weak spot on the south side of the city. The crew succeeded in making a breach in the wall between the southern harbour and the mole. Alexander had to wait two days for calmer weather, but as soon as they could

Above: The torsion catapult, invented in 399 BC, was described in Ancient Greek sources as a machine in which a bolt or ball was placed onto a thick bowstring fastened to the end of two wooden arms anchored in springs of tightly twisted sinew ropes (hence the name 'torsion catapult'). The entire apparatus was mounted on a strong wooden base with a stock holding a slider and a trigger mechanism.

Greek siege towers were impressive engineering feats. Protected from fire with fresh animal hides or metal plates, they allowed attackers to stand on a level with the town walls, negating the defenders' advantage of height.

Above: This Roman floor mosaic, dating from the second century BC, gives a good impression of a trireme's grace in the water.

Left: The ruins of Tyre. After Alexander's conquest of the city, it was soon rebuilt and maintained its importance as a seaport in Roman times.

operate at sea, he sent ships with siege machinery to widen the breach.

When everything was prepared, Alexander launched a massive assault on all fronts. He himself led the attack on the breach, using, for the purpose, two transport ships loaded with his best infantry. The attack was co-ordinated with ship attacks all around Tyre, major fleet assaults on both harbours and a fresh attempt at escalade from the mole. The Tyrians did not have enough defenders to fight off so many challenges at once. Alexander's force beat its way through the breach, the fleets broke into both harbours and started fighting street to street, and the main Macedonian force was then able to enter the city along the mole.

AFTERMATH

Although Alexander was noted for his mercy to defeated enemies, he made an example of Tyre. In part, this was typical ancient fighting practice: if a city refused to surrender and had to be taken by force, the triumphant army had a widely recognized right to slaughter, rape and pillage indiscriminately.

It was not uncommon for all male defenders to be killed, especially if the defenders were members of another race. Alexander might have been more generous, but the Tyrians themselves had not 'played fair'. In particular, they had killed not just Macedonian prisoners but also heralds.

So Tyre was burned, and the assault is known to have cost the lives of about 8000 Tyrians. There were about 2000 adult male survivors, and Alexander now ordered their crucifixion. Still, he showed himself surprisingly kind by the standards of the age by saving everyone who had taken refuge in the temple of Melkart, whom Alexander identified with the Greek god Heracles.

Those who survived included the king of Tyre, who was treated honourably. However, the Tyrians had decided partway through the siege to send their women and children to their colony of Carthage in North Africa – a decision made too late. Alexander took control of the sea before it could be carried out, and those non-

combatants who had survived the assault were now sold into slavery.

The Macedonians had lost a valuable seven months besieging Tyre, but the Persian king's lethargy prevented this delay from being catastrophic for Alexander. Morevoer, he lost only about 400 troops, a sign of how careful he was to protect his men whenever possible.

In return, the young Macedonian king won control of the eastern Mediterranean, thereby gaining a foothold in Phoenicia and Palestine (which would remain in Greek hands for nearly two centuries). He was perhaps the greatest siege commander of all time.

Alexander on horseback, from the 'Alexander Sarcophagus' (c. 310 BC). Note the ram's horns, a sign of Alexander's divinity as son of the Egyptian god Ammon.

EMMAUS
165 BC

WHY DID IT HAPPEN?

WHO The Jewish rebel army of Judas Maccabeus against the Seleucid army of Ptolemy, Gorgias and Nicanor.

WHAT The punitive expedition of the Seleucid government was defeated and put to flight as Judas Maccabeus adapted his original battle plan to exploit his enemy's vulnerability.

WHERE Emmaus near the foothills of Judea, a short distance from the Mediterranean Sea in the west and Jerusalem in the east.

WHEN 165 BC.

WHY The Seleucid government sought to put down the troublesome revolt of the Jews led by Judas Maccabeus.

OUTCOME The Jewish rebels continued a string of victories against the numerically and technologically superior Seleucids, defeating them again at Beth-Zur a year later, entering Jerusalem and rededicating their Temple.

WHEN THE SELEUCID PUNITIVE EXPEDITION DISPATCHED BY THE CHANCELLOR LYSIAS MARCHED INTO JUDEA IN THE SPRING OF 165 BC, THE JEWISH REVOLT AGAINST THE HELLENISTIC REGIME OF ANTIOCHUS IV EPIPHANES WAS IN ITS THIRD YEAR. FOR MORE THAN A CENTURY, THE INHABITANTS OF JUDEA HAD LIVED WITH A GREAT DEGREE OF RELIGIOUS FREEDOM, FIRST AS PART OF THE PTOLEMAIC EMPIRE BASED IN EGYPT, AND THEN AS SUBJECTS OF THE SELEUCID GOVERNMENT AFTER THE PROVINCE HAD BEEN TAKEN BY FORCE IN 198 BC.

Under Antiochus IV Epiphanes (175–164 BC), the pragmatic view that the growing influence of Rome would present a threat to Seleucid security required that Judea serve as a buffer against Roman invasion through Egypt. Actually, Antiochus had invaded Egypt and been forced to withdraw under the threat of war with Rome. As his army marched back to Antioch, the embittered king attacked Jerusalem.

The historian Flavius Josephus recorded what happened next:

Now Antiochus was not satisfied either with his unexpected taking of the city, or with its pillage, or with the great slaughter he had made there; but being overcome with his violent passions, and remembering what he had suffered during the siege, he compelled the Jews to dissolve the laws of their country, and to keep their infants uncircumcised, and to sacrifice swine's flesh upon the altar.

Thus, Antiochus initiated a campaign to 'Hellenize' Judea, forbidding Jewish religious and cultural practices and attempting to replace them with the gods

Having undertaken the mission to 'Hellenize' Judea, an expedition of Seleucid soldiers prepares to ford a stream as its leader points the way toward the stronghold of the Jewish rebels.

and mores of their own Greek tradition. Seleucid soldiers massacred Jews and again sacked the city of Jerusalem. They established a garrison in the city and persecuted the population. The spark that ignited the Jewish revolt was the pillaging and desecration of the Temple.

When Mattathias, a Jewish priest, was brought before the people by the Seleucids and ordered to slaughter a pig as a sacrifice and then eat its flesh, the righteous indignation of the priest boiled over. He killed a Seleucid officer and led his people into the hills. Although outnumbered by a well-trained and well-equipped army, the Jewish rebels remained elusive, adding to their number and training with the few weapons they had. Within a year, Mattathias had died; however, he had appointed his third son, Judah, as leader of the continuing rebellion. Judah was destined to become one of the great warriors in Jewish history, but the prospects for success appeared remote at best.

THE HAMMER

Judas Maccabeus was compelled to resist the Seleucid onslaught because of his faith in God, and the Jewish insurrection may be viewed as one of the first wars for religious freedom in recorded history. The surname Maccabeus translates from the Aramaic word *maqqaba*, meaning 'the hammer'. The name was well earned, as Judah commanded a once ragtag band of patriots against overwhelming numbers of professional soldiers.

On more than one occasion, Judas Maccabeus proved himself an innovative tactician, refusing to take on the Seleucid enemy unless conditions were favourable. He recognized that his force could not win a direct confrontation. The historians Chaim Herzog and Mordechai Gichon describe the reality of what he faced:

Armed with farm implements of a primitive nature and home-made weapons such as the mace and the sling, Judah's small group prepared to give battle to an up-to-date Greek army. The Seleucids were well trained, well organized, and tried in battle. Their ranks were composed of heavy and light infantry, heavy and light cavalry, chariots, elephant units and 'artillery' units operating ballistas (engines for

hurling huge stones), not to mention the various service units. Their weapons included swords, javelins, spears, bows, slings, ballistas, and battering-rams.'

Judah determined that the employment of guerrilla tactics would best serve his purpose. His general philosophy was to attack the Seleucids in the confines of valleys, where they would be unable to deploy the large and ponderous phalanx, which consisted of soldiers bearing lances with shields locked to provide maximum protection, advancing steadily and overrunning the enemy before it. The element of surprise, the ambush, and the hit-and-run were key tactics, which not only obliged the enemy to be wary of operating

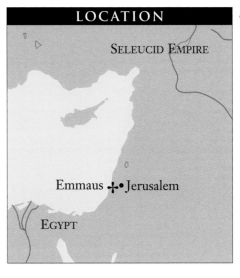

LOCATION

SELEUCID EMPIRE

Emmaus ✝•Jerusalem

EGYPT

Judeans had lived for some time under Greek, or Seleucid, dominion, but the growing threat of Roman invasion from Egypt compelled Antiochus to create a buffer against the potential enemy.

SELEUCID HOPLITE
Armed with a traditional round shield and short sword in the Greek style, this Seleucid hoplite is typical of those who sought to bring the Jewish rebels under Judas Maccabeus to heel. His crested helmet fits tightly and provides protection for the neck, while his chainmail armour is fastened over a cloth tunic. Although the soldiers in the Seleucid ranks were well trained, they had not previously faced an enemy such as this, willing to fight a guerrilla war under only the most favorable circumstances. The rebels repeatedly employed tactics that neutralized the greater numbers and heavier armament of the Seleucids.

This painting, entitled the Generosity of Mathias, *fancifully depicts the slaying of a Seleucid soldier by the elderly priest, an act that sparked the Jewish revolt and the rising of his son, Judas Maccabeus, to prominence.*

THE OPPOSED FORCES

JEWISH REBELS (estimated)
Infantry: 6000
Total: **6000**

SELEUCIDS (estimated)
Infantry: 20,000
(40,000 in I Maccabees; half
that number in II Maccabees)
Cavalry: 7000

Total: **27,000**

too far from supply bases but also eroded the morale and combat efficiency of the Seleucids. Judah was also a visionary, capable of stirring religious fervour and nationalistic spirit among his people.

The inhabitants of Judea became the eyes and ears of the Jewish rebels, gathering intelligence that allowed Judah to set traps for Seleucid patrols, threaten supply lines, and gather better arms for the growing number of fighters. They also provided sustenance for the rebels who hid in the virtually trackless hills of Judea.

NAHAL EL-HARAMIAH

Soon, it became apparent that the unrest in Judea could not be tolerated. Antiochus IV directed his military governor in Samaria, Apollonius, to deal with the upstart Jews. Apollonius gathered together a force of about 2000 soldiers, outnumbering the

rebels by more than three to one. With only about 600 effectives at his command, Judah was determined to dictate the course of the campaign. He tracked the Seleucid advance and chose the most favourable ground to attack the enemy.

A few miles east of the town of Gophna, the route of advance chosen by Apollonius reached the valley of Nahal el-Haramiah. Here, Judah reasoned, the Seleucid advantages of numbers and superior weaponry could be neutralized. He divided his force into four groups, intent on trapping the Seleucids in the narrow valley by closing avenues of escape and also attacking from the hills on both flanks.

Continuing southwards, the Seleucid troops entered the valley of Nahal el-Haramiah in the late afternoon, marching four across in two lengthy columns of 1000 soldiers, with Apollonius at the head of the second column. At Judah's signal, the leading elements of the first Seleucid column came under frontal attack from the south. Not immediately aware of the situation ahead of them, the following troops continued to march into the valley, which soon became choked with Seleucid soldiers. First from the east and then from the west, the Jewish rebels fell upon the mass of the enemy.

Apollonius was killed early in the fighting, and Judah himself led the fourth group of rebels in the north, sealing the Seleucids in the slaughter pen of Nahal el-Haramiah. The invading force was wiped out, and Judah claimed the sword of Apollonius, which he would wear in future engagements to inspire his fighters.

The immediate impact of the battle was to further legitimize Judas Maccabeusas as the military and political leader of this fight for religious freedom. His strategy for doing battle with the Seleucids was also validated and became a model for those waging guerrilla war against a superior enemy for millennia to come.

BETH-HORON

When news of the total defeat of Apollonius reached Antiochus IV, the king ordered another general to quell the uprising in Judea. Seron, a politically motivated commander who led a force twice the size of the Seleucid army destroyed at Nahal el-Haramiah, commented: 'I will make a name for myself and win honour in the kingdom. I will make war on Judah and his companions, who scorn the king's command.' (I Maccabees 3: 14.)

Seron did apparently learn one important lesson from the fate that had befallen Apollonius. His troops marched

The Seleucid phalanx was a formidable military formation and could crush most enemies face on; however, it was vulnerable to flank attack. Judas Maccabeus recognized this fact and used it to great advantage, neutralizing his enemy's superior strength.

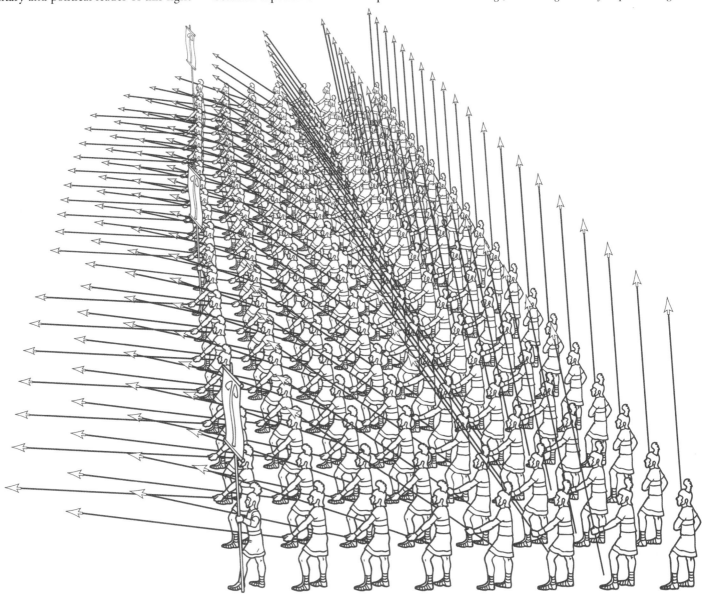

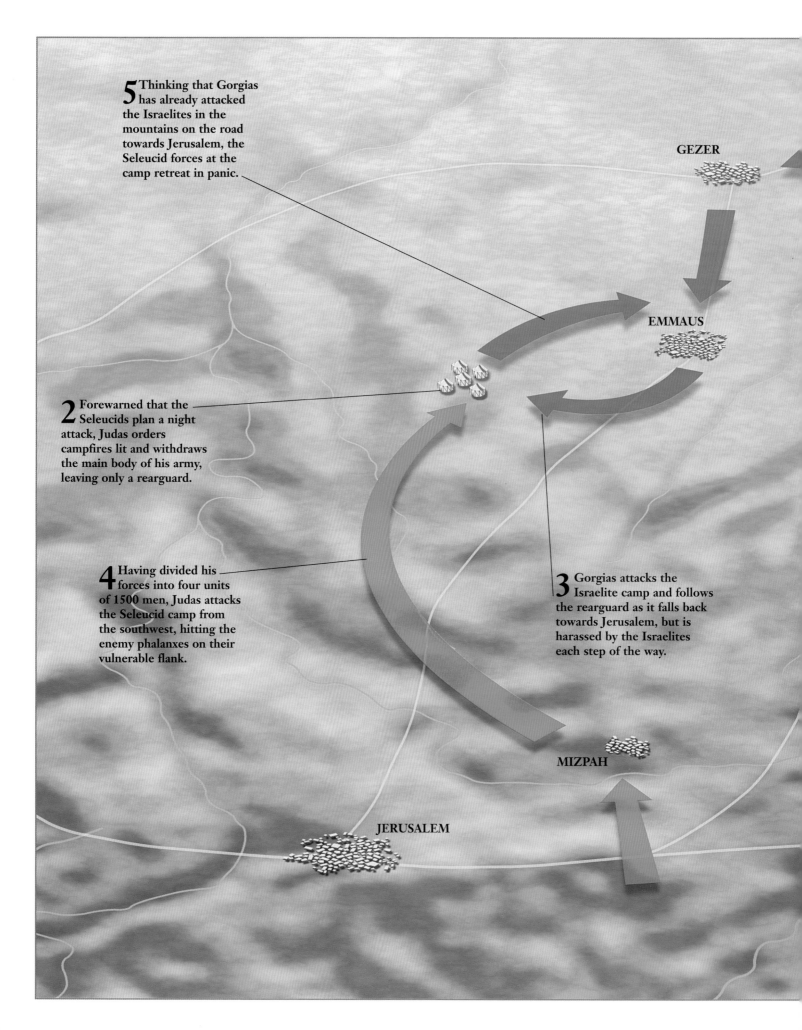

5 Thinking that Gorgias has already attacked the Israelites in the mountains on the road towards Jerusalem, the Seleucid forces at the camp retreat in panic.

GEZER

EMMAUS

2 Forewarned that the Seleucids plan a night attack, Judas orders campfires lit and withdraws the main body of his army, leaving only a rearguard.

4 Having divided his forces into four units of 1500 men, Judas attacks the Seleucid camp from the southwest, hitting the enemy phalanxes on their vulnerable flank.

3 Gorgias attacks the Israelite camp and follows the rearguard as it falls back towards Jerusalem, but is harassed by the Israelites each step of the way.

MIZPAH

JERUSALEM

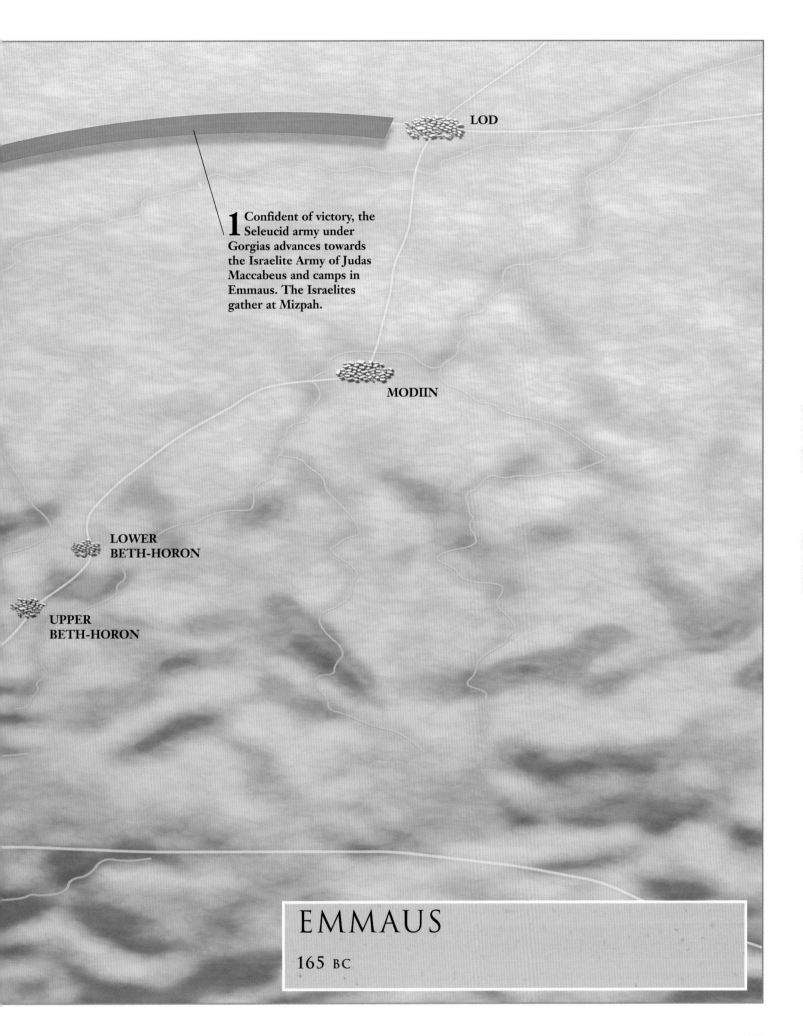

LOD

1 Confident of victory, the Seleucid army under Gorgias advances towards the Israelite Army of Judas Maccabeus and camps in Emmaus. The Israelites gather at Mizpah.

MODIIN

LOWER
BETH-HORON

UPPER
BETH-HORON

EMMAUS

165 BC

along the coast of the Mediterranean Sea for a great distance to avoid being trapped in a confined space. He intended to unite with the Seleucid garrison at Jerusalem and then overwhelm the rebels. Wary of a possible ambush, Seron also kept a larger interval between his columns while traversing the countryside.

With the formidable enemy formations less than a day's march from Jerusalem, Judah brought his men out of the mountains near Gophna, divided his forces again, and prepared an ambush. A superb orator, Judah addressed his soldiers on the eve of battle to steel their resolve:

But when they saw the army coming to meet them, they said to Judah, 'How can we, few as we are, fight against so great and so strong a multitude? And we are faint, for we have eaten nothing today.' Judah replied, 'It is easy for many to be hemmed in by few, for in the sight of Heaven there is no difference between saving by many or by few. It is not on the size of the army that victory in battle depends, but strength comes from Heaven. They come against us in great insolence and lawlessness to destroy us and our wives and our children, and to despoil us; but we fight for our lives and our laws. He himself will crush them before us; as for you, do not be afraid of them. (I Maccabees 3: 17–22.)

Because of Seron's route of advance, Judah was forced to clear a narrow gorge at Beth-horon as his site of battle. The plan was almost identical to that which had led to the annihilation of the Seleucids at Nahal el-Haramiah – cut off the enemy's escape route from the pass and strike hard at both flanks. This time, Seron was killed at the head of his troops, 800 Seleucid soldiers died and the rebels pursued the panicked survivors from the height of the pass at Beth-horon to the open plain.

YET ANOTHER PUNITIVE EXPEDITION

Antiochus IV flew into a rage when he heard of Seron's failure. His plans for an offensive towards Persia to collect revenues for his depleted treasury were put on hold until he could decide how to deal with the situation in Judea, which was obviously getting out of hand. The king appointed Lysias as regent in his absence and placed a sizable army under his command prior to

departing for the east. Lysias, in turn, received a blunt order from Antiochus. Flavius Josephus recorded that Lysias was 'to conquer Judea, enslave its inhabitants, utterly destroy Jerusalem and abolish the whole nation'.

With a clear understanding of his responsibility, Lysias appointed three

commanders – Ptolemy, Nicanor and Gorgias – and ordered them to proceed to Judea to put down the Jewish rebellion. In comparison to the forces employed in previous Seleucid expeditions, this army was immense. According to the Book of I Maccabees, it numbered 40,000 infantry and 7000 cavalry. Although this number is reduced to 20,000 in II Maccabees, it remained a formidable foe – against which Judah could muster only approximately 6000. In addition, these Seleucid generals stayed clear of the highlands and advanced along the coast, eventually establishing a base of operations at Emmaus, near the Valley of Ajalon.

In this vivid painting, from around the seventeenth century, Judas Maccabeus and the Jewish rebels fight with Seleucid forces under the command of Gorgias, a lieutenant of Lysius, at the Battle of Emmaus.

This seventeenth-century illustration of Judas Maccabeus depicts the war leader in clothing and armour more typical of the period in which it was drawn.

camp at Emmaus. He organized his army into units ranging downwards in size from 1000 to squads of as few as 10, and appointed captains and junior officers to command them. He placed his 6000 men in divisions, 1500 strong, and commanded by Judah and his three brothers, Jonathan, Simon and Johanan.

Intelligence reports confirmed that the Seleucid host had encamped at Emmaus, so the Jewish army advanced southeast from Mizpah. Judah was also warned that Gorgias planned to employ tactics similar to his own and attack the rebels under the cover of darkness. 'He naturally assumed that Judah would not expect a Seleucid attack at night,' suggest Herzog and Gichon, 'as the Seleucids were unaccustomed to night fighting. Accordingly, Gorgias moved up into the hills at the head of 5000 infantry and 1000 cavalry troops.'

Armed with crucial intelligence as to his enemy's plan of battle, Judah responded accordingly. He ordered his troops to leave their own campfires burning, plainly visible to the Seleucids, and slipped away with his entire force, except for a small rearguard of 200 men.

EMMAUS

Gorgias attacked the vacated Jewish camp and took the bait, believing that the rearguard, withdrawing up the valley towards Jerusalem, was the entire army of Judah. As they pursued the rearguard, the Seleucids were set upon by small bands of rebels, who harassed them relentlessly in the darkness. By this time, Judah had again divided his force, sending 1500 soldiers to the north to join the battle when they observed him striking the enemy's camp at Emmaus with 3000 men.

At this point, however, Judah's plan went somewhat awry. He moved against the Seleucid camp but found a tremendous force of 18,000 deployed and ready to do battle. However, he quickly adapted to the tactical situation facing him. The enemy phalanx was directed towards the south, while his own force was on its western flank and the northern force beyond the camp. Judah divided his 3000 troops into three equal units, one taking on the

The Seleucid commanders were confident that they could join with reinforcements from the south and from Jerusalem, extend their influence throughout the region and end the revolt. Either by invitation of the commanders or through the word of travellers, slave traders became aware of the coming battle:

When the traders of the region heard what was said to them, they took silver and gold in immense amounts, and fetters, and went to the camp to get the Israelites for slaves. And forces from Syria and the land of the Philistines joined with them. (I Maccabees 3: 41)

JUDAS GIRDS FOR BATTLE

Meanwhile, Judas took action, assembling his force at Mizpah, northeast of Jerusalem and within striking distance of the enemy

King Antiochus IV Epiphanes, determined to exact vengeance for the costly Jewish uprising against his Seleucid Empire, enters Jerusalem. In this rendering, the monarch appears to be slaughtering innocent citizens along the route.

Seleucid cavalry and two others penetrating the phalanx where it was most vulnerable. Meanwhile, like shock troops, the northern force hit the Emmaus camp from that direction.

Judah had now literally divided and conquered. The Seleucid troops in the camp were not on alert, believing that Gorgias had carried the fight against the Jewish rebels into the hills. They were seized with panic. Judah had fractured the phalanx. Gorgias was too distant to remedy the situation quickly.

The Seleucid phalanx disintegrated, and its soldiers fled towards the camp, contributing to the jumble of confused troops and slave traders who had been taken by surprise:

The Gentiles were crushed and fled into the plain, and all those in the rear fell by the sword.

They pursued them to Gazara, and to the plains of Idumea, and to Azotus and Jamnia; and 3000 of them fell. (I Maccabees 4: 14–16.)

The Book of I Maccabees continues, telling that Judah maintained tight control of his forces, urging them to complete the rout of the Seleucids before halting to gather plunder.

While the force under Gorgias continued to pose a threat, it appears that Judah need not have worried. When Gorgias and what was left of his 6000 troops came within sight of their now flaming camp, they, too, fled in panic toward the Mediterranean coast.

THE TEMPLE REDEDICATED

For the third time, Judas Maccabeus had led an army of Jewish rebels to victory against the oppression of the Seleucid

EMMAUS

This map illustrates the campaigns waged by Judah Maccabee from 167–164 BC. When the Seleucid governor, Apollonius, first invaded Judah from the north (1), the Maccabean army retreated into the mountains around Gophna, from where they ambushed the advancing Seleucid army. However, a second Seleucid army under General Seron advanced down the coastal road and headed inland (2), where they were ambushed and defeated in 165 BC at Beth-Horon. A third Seleucid Army, under generals Nicanor and Gorgias, marched on Gezer (3) and met the Maccabean army at Emmaus, where they were again defeated by Judah the Maccabee's superior tactics. A fourth Seleucid army under Lysias approaches from the south (4), but was again beaten at Beth-Zur in 164 BC.

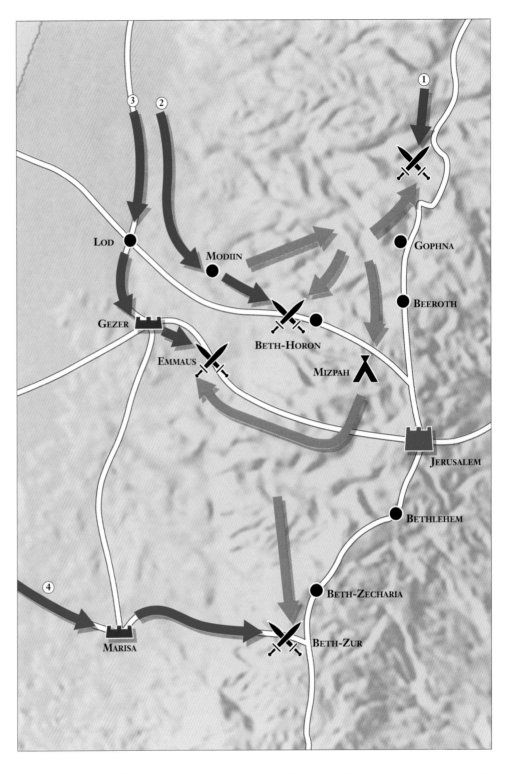

Opposite: In this medieval illustration, Bacchides and his army of 20,000 infantry and 2000 cavalry meet Judas Maccabeus and the Jewish rebels at Elasa. Judas was killed in the battle, and his army fled the field.

regime. As a result of the victory at Emmaus, the army grew considerably. A year later, at Beth-Zur, Lysias himself met Judah and the rebels on the field of battle. The result was another defeat.

Following the victory at Beth-Zur, the Jewish army entered Jerusalem in triumph. Judah ordered that the Temple be cleansed and restored to its former holy state. According to Jewish tradition, only a single day's oil was available to fuel the ceremonial light, but miraculously it continued to burn for eight days. In modern times, the Jews remember this event as Hannukah, the Festival of Lights.

The great period of revolt, unrest and armed conflict, however, did not come to an end. Judah was later killed during the Battle of Elasa, when much of his army fled the field and he continued to resist against overwhelming odds. The freedom of the Jewish people to worship as they chose would not ultimately be secured for some time.

BETH-ZUR
164 BC

WOULD HELLENISTIC MILITARY EXPERTISE BE ENOUGH TO OVERCOME THE FURY OF RESURGENT HEBREW NATIONALISM UNDER NEW LEADERSHIP? THE FATES OF A RELIGION AND AN EMPIRE HUNG IN THE BALANCE AS AN IMPERIAL VICEROY MOVED TO QUELL AN UNEXPECTEDLY SUCCESSFUL REVOLT.

WHY DID IT HAPPEN?

WHO Lysias, a general of the shaken Seleucid Empire, faces Judas 'The Hammer' Maccabeus and his followers.

WHAT With equipment captured from a shattered Seleucid army, Judas Maccabeus and 10,000 determined followers awaited the advance of 20,000 infantry and 4000 cavalry on the road to Jerusalem.

WHERE A narrow area in between surrounding hills, separated by gullies and ravines, provided Maccabeus with the perfect place for a large-scale ambush while the advancing Seleucids were still in column.

WHEN 164 BC.

WHY The last bastion of Seleucid control was the Acra fortress looming over the Temple in Jerusalem. With it would fall Antiochus IV's claim to rule Palestine.

OUTCOME Lysias had the force and the ability to overcome the rebels in a set-piece battle. Judas Maccabeus, however, outwitted Lysias tactically, clearing the way for the Jewish reconquest of Jerusalem and the rededication of the Temple.

Alexander the Great had conquered and ruled as none before – and many of his generals who came to rule segments of his empire nurtured similar ambitions, which they passed on to their descendants. Antiochus III, 'the Great', had come very close to succeeding where so many since Alexander had failed, weakening Egypt and conquering most of Asia Minor. However, he came to a halt in Europe after a disastrous collision with Roman legions at Magnesia in 190 BC and the Rhodian fleet off Side in 191 BC.

His son, Antiochus IV Epiphanes ('God Manifest'), who had been held hostage in Rome, was returned by his Roman overlords to rule and reinvigorate the shaken Seleucid Empire. The empire still had money, which could be used to buy mercenaries, whom Antiochus equipped in the Roman manner and sent off to attempt, once again, to conquer Egypt. A Roman legate then ordered him back to Syria, so a humiliated and frustrated Antiochus set about strengthening his empire before it collapsed altogether.

THE BURDEN OF A DREAM

Since Alexander, the Ptolemies in Egypt had ruled the land of Israel, and on the whole had been content to tax the volatile region from a safe distance, preserving the

God and his father urge Judas ben Matthias onward in this depiction of the champion of Jewish nationalism's inspiration for his struggle to preserve his faith and people against a nearly universal Hellenistic rule and culture. From a coloured wood engraving by Julius Schnorr von Carolsfeld (1794-1874); II Maccabees 15: 15-16.

trade routes to Asia and going so far as to make gifts for the decoration of the Temple in Jerusalem. Antiochus III, who had captured the region in 199 BC, paid for temple sacrifices on his own behalf.

Antiochus IV did not appreciate the wisdom of his father's policies and, as always, the strategic significance of the land of Israel drew more attention than its size or the population would seem to warrant. Antiochus wanted a clear road to Egypt. Sectarian disagreements kept Jerusalem in a state of semi-instability, and the obstinate refusal of the Jewish people to accept Greek culture and institutions provoked his anger and acts of repression, helping to establish his reputation as Epiphanes 'the Insane'.

Antiochus IV's efforts to eradicate Jewish culture led to massacres in Jerusalem and the plundering and desecration of the Temple. A new fortress, the Acra, now loomed over the temple, and a garrison was permanently stationed in the occupied city to enforce abhorrent cultural practices – the Hellenized norms of the rest of the Empire – on the Jewish people.

THE RISE OF MACCABEUS

Antiochus's determination to force the Jews to conform to his wishes caused anger, unrest and murder until, finally, a new Jewish leader emerged. Judas ben Matthias was a man of traditional faith, strong qualities of leadership and impressive military ability. There is some debate over the precise meaning of the epithet 'Maccabeus' awarded to him, but there is no doubt that it signifies force and decisiveness.

In 167 BC, Antiochus sent an army under the command of Apollonius, governor of the city of Samaria, to crush Maccabeus and the thousands who had rallied to him in the hills. Neither Apollonius nor his army survived the encounter, one in which Maccabeus quickly established his trademark tactics: superb use of the terrain by his light, irregular troops; and striking, deliberately, at the enemy commander to neutralize him and thus deprive his forces of leadership. According to the Bible, Maccabeus took the slain Apollonius's sword and used it in further battles.

Two more armies and two more generals failed under similar circumstances at Beth-horon the following year, and at Emmaus in 165 BC. With every successful encounter, the rebellion increased in numbers and acquired more equipment, much of it taken from the slain or fleeing enemy. By 165 BC, rebel pressure on the garrison and city of Jerusalem had become so intense that a new general and a new army were despatched to relieve the beleaguered bastion.

IMPERIAL RESPONSE

The new general was no provincial governor in charge of a small, local force. Antiochus IV had made Lysias viceroy over all territories from the Euphrates to the Egyptian border, and given him the authority to confiscate the rebels' property and distribute it among those still loyal to the Seleucid Empire. Lysias's ultimate objective was the same as ever it was when suppressing Jewish revolt: Jerusalem. With access to the capital secured and the Temple in Gentile hands, Maccabeus's credibility as a leader would, perhaps, be fatally damaged while the pacification of the area would be well in hand.

Lysias's strategy requires no great analysis, but the seriousness with which he sought to implement it, and the powers he had to do so, made him the most formidable Seleucid leader Maccabeus had to face.

Modern estimates put the size of Lysias's army at 20,000 infantry and 4000 cavalry – about the same size as the force defeated at Emmaus. Lysias, however, had learned from the mistakes of those who had gone before him, and was careful to avoid the mountain defiles where the rebels could ambush and kill foraging parties or

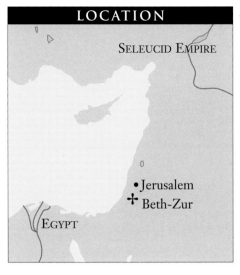

LOCATION

SELEUCID EMPIRE

Jerusalem
✝ Beth-Zur

EGYPT

Since capital is cause, the shrewdest of the Seleucid generals, the viceroy Lysias, made directly for Jerusalem and its Temple. The narrow mountain roads offered Maccabeus one too many opportunity for a successful ambush.

SELEUCID HOPLITE
Caught between worlds, the equipment of this Seleucid hoplite shows the result of Antiochus III's defeat and his son's fascination with the Roman military technique that had defeated the Hellenistic phalanx. The traditional small shield of the phalangite has been replaced by a circular imitation of the Roman scutum, *but its use is hindered by the continued adherence to the long Macedonian sarissa that had won an empire for Alexander. Falling between two stools, the soldiers of the Seleucid Empire would be in a tactically as well as figuratively uncomfortable position when Maccabeus's dedicated followers crowded close upon them from ambush.*

BETH-ZUR

The Word and Will of God go forth to Matthias, the Jewish priest who struck down a Seleucid officer, compelling the sacrifice and consumption of a pig. His son Judas would prove a determined, intelligent successor and a general whose sense of tactics and terrain bolstered the rebellion his father had started through a decade of intense warfare (from a nineteenth-century French lithograph).

THE OPPOSED FORCES

SELEUCIDS (estimated)
Infantry:	20,000
Cavalry:	4000
Total:	**24,000**

MACCABEANS (estimated)
Infantry:	10,000
Cavalry scouts:	unknown
Total:	**10,000**

Opposite: The athletic nudity of this Hellenistic sculpture meant anything but beauty to the devout Jews (Hasidim). Antiochus IV sought to force them out of their faith and into his gymnasia. Deep-seated disgust at public nudity, normal to exercising Greeks, swelled the ranks of the Maccabean army.

scouts. He knew, too, to avoid the steep hillsides that would exhaust charging men in armour and leave them exposed to arrows and slingshot, with no hope of retaliation. Lysias's force followed the coastal road down from Syria, only turning inland through friendly territory to reach the city of Marisa, which was still subject to Seleucid rule, to pick up fresh supplies before the final approach to Jerusalem from the south.

There was, however, still one bottleneck in the way: a narrow area with gullies and defiles on either side, where troops could hide and where a large force would have difficulty deploying into a proper combat formation. Meanwhile, near an old border fortification at Beth-Zur, Maccabeus gathered his forces and planned his tactics.

ALEXANDER'S SYSTEM

The ideal military system of all the Hellenistic kingdoms was that created by Alexander the Great. Over time, however, Alexander's model had been adapted to suit the demands of a fast-changing world. Moreover, no one in the second century BC had experienced the original model first-hand. Alexander's massive phalanx of long pikes and superbly trained Macedonian nationals was long gone.

So, too, were the large cavalry formations that had guarded the conqueror's flanks and, on more than one occasion, actually won battles by outflanking the enemy's line or exploiting weaknesses where gaps had developed.

What Lysias had at his disposal were mercenaries, bought wherever the Seleucid Empire could find them, and native levies

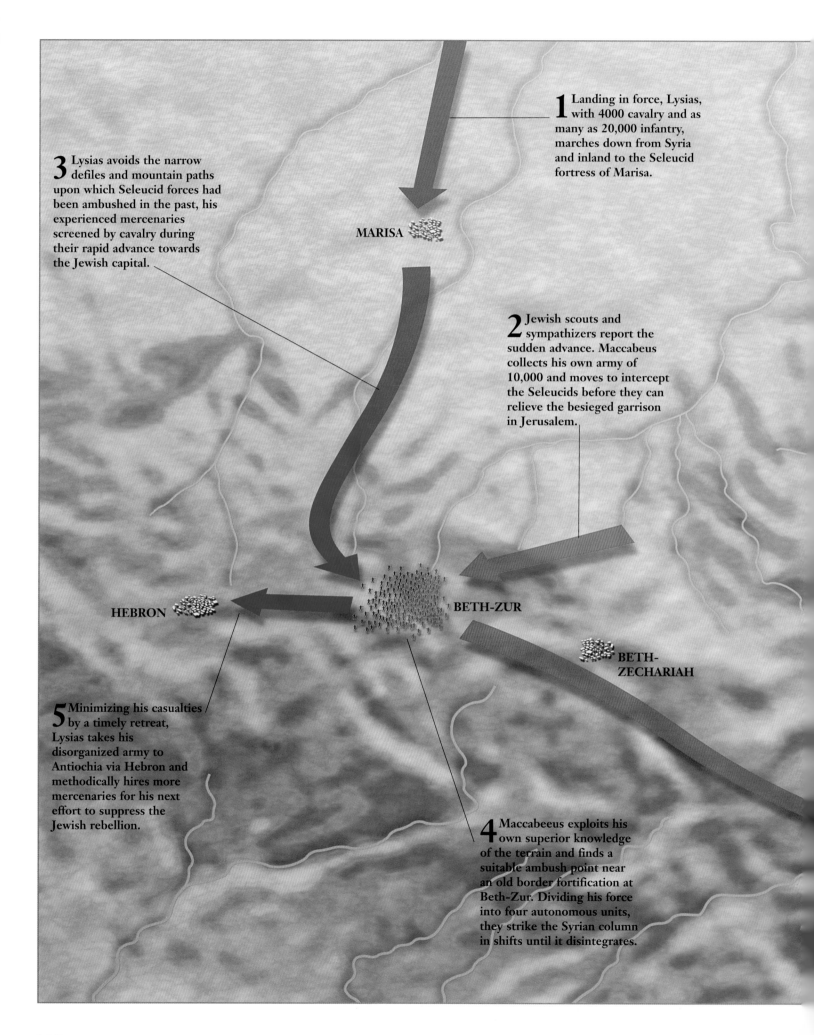

1 Landing in force, Lysias, with 4000 cavalry and as many as 20,000 infantry, marches down from Syria and inland to the Seleucid fortress of Marisa.

3 Lysias avoids the narrow defiles and mountain paths upon which Seleucid forces had been ambushed in the past, his experienced mercenaries screened by cavalry during their rapid advance towards the Jewish capital.

MARISA

2 Jewish scouts and sympathizers report the sudden advance. Maccabeus collects his own army of 10,000 and moves to intercept the Seleucids before they can relieve the besieged garrison in Jerusalem.

HEBRON

BETH-ZUR

BETH-ZECHARIAH

5 Minimizing his casualties by a timely retreat, Lysias takes his disorganized army to Antiochia via Hebron and methodically hires more mercenaries for his next effort to suppress the Jewish rebellion.

4 Maccabeeus exploits his own superior knowledge of the terrain and finds a suitable ambush point near an old border fortification at Beth-Zur. Dividing his force into four autonomous units, they strike the Syrian column in shifts until it disintegrates.

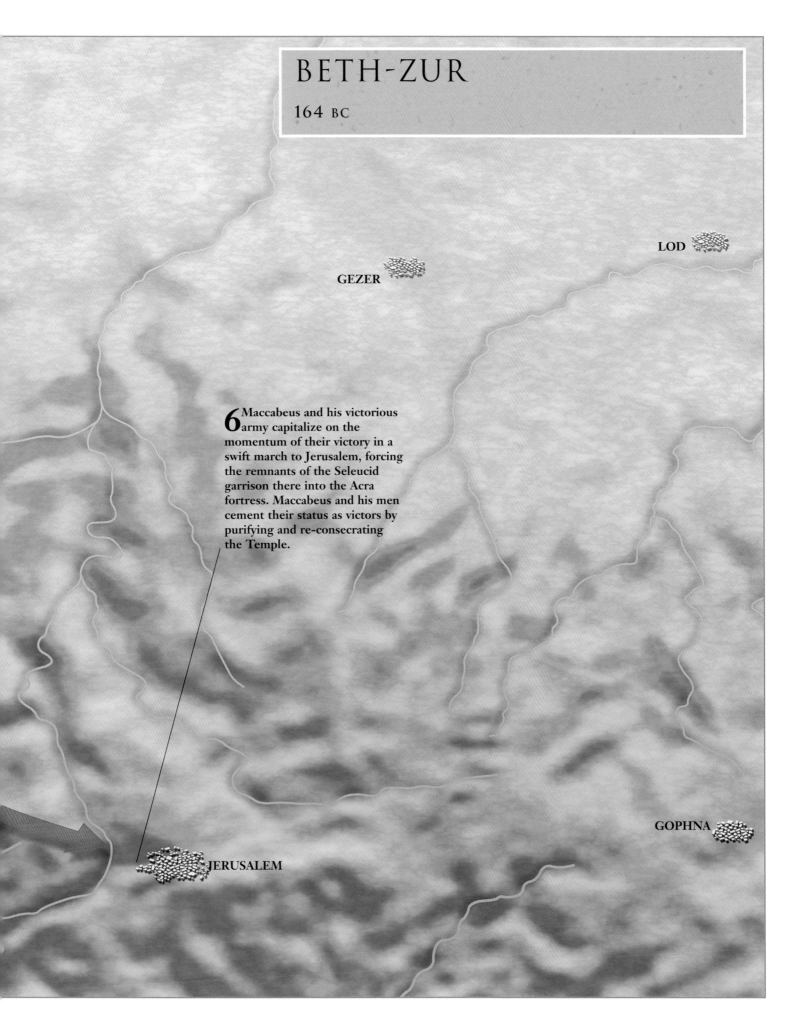

BETH-ZUR

164 BC

LOD

GEZER

6Maccabeus and his victorious army capitalize on the momentum of their victory in a swift march to Jerusalem, forcing the remnants of the Seleucid garrison there into the Acra fortress. Maccabeus and his men cement their status as victors by purifying and re-consecrating the Temple.

GOPHNA

JERUSALEM

BETH-ZUR

The best and brightest – and richest – of the Seleucid Empire's youth, the prestige arm since the days of Alexander, would carry a shortened sarissa *and armour unadulterated by Roman practice. These cavalrymen worked on a tried and tested formula for exploiting a gap in an enemy's line and butchering fleeing survivors.*

who were either useless from lack of military experience or intensely depleted by the unending cycle of wars waged in attempts to resurrect Alexander's dream. While Lysias had been preparing his army, the rebels were also able to consolidate and train their own forces, and to secure resources from a growing number of liberated territories. Though the pressing need to relieve the garrison of the Acra would have been a constant spur to action, Lysias was well aware that haste in preparation for battle is inevitably reflected in failures on the battlefield itself.

The Seleucid phalanx employed by Antiochus III against the Romans at Magnesia had corrected many of the defects in Alexander's original model. A chequered series of isolated rectangles of pikemen linked together by shield-wielding formations of lighter troops allowed for greater flexibility. The prevalence of such *thureophoroi* (a type of infantry soldier carrying a large oval shield) and armoured *chalkaspides* (phalanx pikemen) reflect the replacement of Alexander's Macedonian nationals with locally recruited *condottieri* (mercenaries).

Dead mercenaries, however, could collect neither pay nor booty. Their very presence as armoured troops weakened the power of the phalanx considerably because regular soldiers knew that these troops would collapse under the stresses of battle, leaving gaps in the main formations for more lightly equipped Roman legionaries – or Jewish irregulars – to exploit. With fewer cavalry to guard its sides or drive a disrupted army, the military machine that had destroyed the Persian Empire was suddenly much more vulnerable

Lysias and his forces had another handicap to overcome, one that has not received its due in other accounts of the battle. The Seleucid army of the time was trying to adapt to Antiochus's decision to emulate Roman equipment and tactics, given how successful both had been against his own father's army. Until Antiochus III faced the Romans, he had prevailed against all opposition on land.

Unfortunately, Antiochus IV's soldiers were unfamiliar with the Roman-style shields and swords that they had been given, and no amount of training over a mere decade could hope to equal the skill of the Roman army, or its professionalism that would soon make the Romans the masters of the Mediterranean World.

It is also fairly certain that elephants, one of the more celebrated elements of later Hellenistic warfare, did not appear in this battle. They presented logistical difficulties in the line of battle, and at this point Lysias thought he could do without them. Likewise, the celebrated catapults of Hellenistic antiquity would not make an appearance at Beth-Zur. The longer-ranged artillery of the time was heavy and cumbersome to bring into battery, and in any sort of sudden battle it would go unused, and therefore be ineffective, at the onset. On the battlefield, lighter weapons would be less useful than the same number of men employed as archers or slingers, and with Jerusalem still under Seleucid control, Lysias felt no need to burden his advance with a siege train.

A DISCIPLINED ARMY

Judas Maccabeus had fewer resources but many enormous advantages that would, in the end, prove decisive. First of all, he and his men had a thorough and invaluable

knowledge of their native terrain. No party of scouts on a swift reconnaissance could hope to match the Israelites' decades of familiarity with the paths, caves, springs and gullies surrounding their capital. Reconnaissance of the approaching army was, therefore, much easier for the Jews than for the Seleucid forces. The sullen fellow at the well might be no more than a disgruntled local farmer; or he might, at the first opportunity, be off to the hillside to provide Maccabeus with a full report of what to expect, and when.

There was also the matter of experience, an area in which Lysias's professional mercenaries might well have been expected to have a major advantage. However, with four Seleucid armies routed and scattered so far in the revolt, it is questionable how many of even the most experienced veterans desired to fight impoverished opponents, who were motivated by deep religious faith to fight to the bitter end, in a territory that had already been thoroughly looted in Antiochus's earlier repressions.

By the time Lysias and his army drew near to Beth-Zur, the core of Maccabeus's army had been in the field and under his

Scratch, but useful, mounted scouts such as these would be no match for their Seleucid counterparts, but tremendously good in shadowing the approaching army and reporting its movements back to Maccabeus. Their lack of formal equipment besides a spear would have made it easy for them to melt back into the civilian population from which Maccabeus drew them.

BETH-ZUR

Knights in deed if not in reality, Judas Maccabeus and his four brothers visit God's justice upon their Seleucid enemies in this sixteenth-century woodcut illustration of their struggle to preserve their faith.

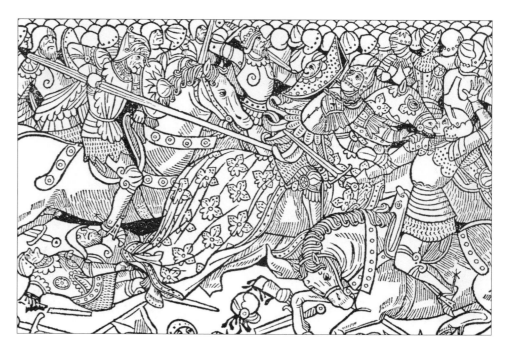

The torments of the damned manifest themselves upon the person of Antiochus I – 'the Mad', as even his own people knew him. The Seleucid king's efforts to suppress the faith and people of Judeah drew upon him more torments than the worms shown devouring his flesh in this Renaissance woodcut.

command for a minimum of two years. Such was the discipline of his troops that he had repeatedly been able to divide his forces and yet co-ordinate their attacks. At Emmaus the year before, he had been able to halt the pursuit and plunder of the retreating Seleucids, and return his troops to good order with the spoils of battle glittering before them.

In their long months in the field, the rebels had put to flight several armies of the kind they now faced and seized great amounts of armour and other equipment, right down to the enemy commander's own sword.

Discipline, religious faith and belief in their leader gave the rebels a strong edge in this and other battles. Judas Maccabeus

would exploit these factors, and the terrain of his native soil, to the utmost.

THE BATTLE

As a commander, Maccabeus was intelligent enough to avoid the cardinal sin of predictability. In a previous battle, he had attacked the encamped Seleucid army, so there would be no repetition of that tactic at Beth-Zur.

The earliest historical sources say the Jewish army comprised 10,000 infantry, but make no mention of cavalry. It is not known how many troops Maccabeus himself had under his hand, though the number would have been dictated by the topography at the time of the battle.

Maccaebeus divided his forces and positioned them in different areas, ready for a multi-stage ambush, concealed not far from Lysias's bivouac. They would catch the Seleucids at their sleepiest and most disorganized, at the start of the march at daybreak. As sound travelled easily in the defiles of the narrowing canyon around the road, the noise of the first attack under Maccabeus's personal command would be signal enough for the others to commence their attack.

Soldiers of any era are accustomed to resist an enemy directly in front of them with established formations and tactics, leaving their backs and sides to be protected by their comrades. Maccabeus's initial attack at the head of the column would have stopped the march of Lysias's army immediately, throwing its smooth movement into disorder, from the van to the rear. The Hellenistic phalanx needed time and room to deploy, and the sudden ferocity of the Jewish attack granted neither luxury to the Seleucid column.

Tetradrachm of Antiochus IV Epiphanes (175-163 BC), Seleucidan king of Syria who, by his imposition of Greek law and customs in Judea, caused the Macabeean Revolt (167 BC). From the Israel Museum (IDAM), Jerusalem.

Sources indicate that the Seleucid army collapsed rapidly as the Jewish units attacked individually, increasing the disorder of the onset. One of the most basic of human instincts is to retreat to the last known place of safety – in this case, the Seleucid camp, which Maccabeus had left unmolested during the night. As the routed soldiers rushed in panic back to camp – or, more precisely, to what little of it had not yet been packed in preparation for the march – it would have been impossible to establish a defensive line there.

Moreover, although the Roman practice of fortifying even the daily camp along the march was greatly admired in the Hellenistic world, there are no records to suggest that Antiochus IV had adopted this useful practice.

It says something about Lysias's abilities as a commander, and indeed about the professionalism of his army, that his casualties were, according to the oldest accounts, as low as 5000. Soldiers running without their arms and armour at least have the advantage of speed over armoured soldiers pursuing them on foot. Without cavalry or sufficient numbers to corral the scattering Seleucids, it was a considerable achievement for Maccabeus to inflict such a loss on the retreating enemy.

AFTERMATH

Lysias regrouped his forces at the Seleucid base of Antiochia and began hiring more mercenaries in readiness for the next effort to supplant the rebellion. What remained of the Seleucid garrison within the Acra could only watch, over the following weeks, as Maccabeus and his followers removed all foreign traces from the temple and renewed the ancient rituals of their faith.

BETH-ZUR

173

BETH-ZECHARIAH
162 BC

ONLY A SINGLE FORTRESS REMAINED TO THE SELEUCID OVERLORDS, ONE THAT OVERLOOKED THE VERY TEMPLE OF JERUSALEM ITSELF. WITH THE CONFIDENCE BORN OF MULTIPLE VICTORIES, JUDAS MACCABEUS FOUND HIS HOPES AND ARMY CRUSHED BENEATH THE FEET OF BEHEMOTHS.

WHY DID IT HAPPEN?

WHO Judas Maccabeus and his rebels had defeated the Seleucid General Lysias two years previously, but Lysias was more than ready for a second encounter.

WHAT To succeed in his ultimate goal of restoring Israel as an independent power, Judas Maccabeus knew that he would have to defeat Lysias in a pitched battle.

WHERE The citadel at Beth-Zur, Jerusalem's last external defence.

WHEN 162 BC, following the death of King Antiochus IV (175–164 BC).

WHY Either Israel would defend its capital or fail as a nation – and Judas Maccabeus had sufficient faith in his own skills and his army to risk a fight to the finish.

OUTCOME One of the most feared weapons in the Hellenistic arsenal – elephants – broke the Jewish army and almost completely destroyed a resurgent Israel.

There comes a time in any new nation's history when it must hold territory and defeat an attacker in open, decisive battle. In the American Revolution, George Washington understood that basic fact of national existence well enough to risk open battle repeatedly throughout the disasters of New York, Brandywine and Germantown in Pennsylvania, and on and on until he achieved the decisive victories of Saratoga and Yorktown.

Centuries earlier, Judas Maccabeus, father of his country, had been forced to take a similar stand. On five occasions by ambush, night attack and stealth, Maccabeus had faced, fought and beaten the armies of the Seleucid Empire, reducing its presence in Jerusalem to an isolated garrison on a hill overlooking the Temple

central to the Jewish faith and the Israelites' national existence. General Lysias, a viceroy of the Seleucid Empire, had retreated two years previously from Maccabeus's ambush at Beth-Zur. On that occasion, the Jewish rebels had the forces to repel the Seleucid invaders, but it would take a battle of annihilation, or at least a crushing defeat, to force such a powerful empire to abandon its desire to reclaim Israel for its king.

A CLAIM TO EXISTENCE

For the moment, time was on the side of Maccabeus and his followers. Antiochus IV had died after an abortive wealth-gathering campaign among the cities of ancient Persia, which, like Israel, had been growing restive under Greco-Macedonian control. Lysias had returned to the imperial capital

Armoured combat in close formation was a tradition for the Greeks going back three centuries, as illustrated on this Athenian vase from the fifth century BC. If the formation's flanks could be protected, the Greek or Hellenistic phalanx formed a threat no opposing general or army could take lightly.

SELEUCID ELEPHANT

On his second try for the Jewish capital, Lysias brought along the ultimate manifestation of the war elephant in the Mediterranean world. Heavy barding protected the animal's flanks and body from arrows and thrown spears, while a wooden turret on the elephant's back shielded archers and javelin men while they returned fire and marked the movements of the foe. It was ready for the battleline or house-to-house combat, and rare was the horse or infantryman who could watch such a juggernaut bearing down upon him without trepidation. One such man there was in the Maccabean army.

of Antioch to restore order following the king's death and to declare the son left in his own care the new ruler of the Empire – Antiochus V Eupator.

Maccabeus, meanwhile, busied himself fortifying the hill town overlooking the site of his victory at Beth-Zur and constructing artillery and other apparatus to reduce the Seleucid garrison of the Acra. The more firmly the rebels asserted their claim to Jerusalem and nationhood, however, the greater their obligation to maintain control of the ancient capital. Lysias's next attack would have the same objective as the last one: the taking of Jerusalem. This time, though, he could be certain of facing an even more determined defence.

A MASSIVE ADVANCE

Lysias was an intelligent general, known to honour his enemies. It is reasonable to imagine that he would have been willing to abandon the costly effort to subdue a deeply entrenched rebellion had matters not required him to do otherwise. As kingmaker of the Seleucid Empire, however, he knew that Israel had to be pacified, finally and decisively. To keep his protégé, Antiochus V, on the throne, Lysias had to crush the revolt utterly. Maccabeus, for his part, knew that he had to reduce the Acra and hold Jerusalem. These conflicting imperatives of the two opposing leaders made a massive set-piece battle inevitable .

Maccabeus would fight with all his resources to protect the restored Temple and to maintain the ongoing siege of the outpost. A good number of troops and substantial amounts of equipment were also dedicated to maintaining the new bastion at Beth-Zur. With the Jews nailed to two strategic spots, Lysias took full advantage of his imperial resources to strike with all the force he could muster.

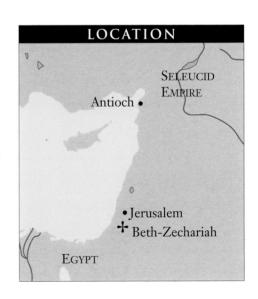

LOCATION

SELEUCID EMPIRE

Antioch

Jerusalem
Beth-Zechariah

EGYPT

At the last rampart before the fortifications of Jerusalem itself, Judas Maccabeus and his army sought victory in a set-piece battle with the approaching Seleucid column. The fortified town of Beth-Zechariah would be the victor's prize.

BETH-ZECHARIAH

Ambush in the narrows had worked two years before for Maccabeus at the battle of Beth-Zur, but the wary Lysias had flankers and scouts at the ready as his army emerged and found the Jewish forces drawn up on the hillside in front of the outpost at Beth-Zecharia (from a nineteenth-century illustration).

THE OPPOSED FORCES

SELEUCIDS (estimated)
Infantry:	34,000
Cavalry:	16,000
Elephants:	32
Total:	**50,032**

MACCABEANS (estimated)
Infantry:	40,000
Cavalry:	unknown
Total:	**40,000**

On this march, Lysias would be accompanied by a siege train of artillery and breaching gear to assail the walls of Beth-Zur and the formidable defences of Jerusalem, as rebuilt by Maccabeus and his followers. With territory to be defended, however, the rebels would stand their ground in the face of the coming onslaught. Given time, though, they knew that torsion catapults capable of throwing 27kg (60lb) stone could breach any defence. And, unlike at Bet-Zur, Lysias had another special force to call upon – his elephants.

THE EARTH-SHAKING BEAST

In the year 168 BC, Antiochus IV had held a month-long pageant of pomp and propaganda, perhaps meant to convince himself, as much as his rivals and subjects, that the Seleucid Empire was still a force to be reckoned with. Among the units displayed was a corps of 42 elephants pulling chariots or decked out in full battle array, a unit the Romans had expressly forbidden to his father after the Seleucid defeat at Magnesia in 191 BC.

The elephants were a legacy of Alexander the Great, although the conqueror had never, in fact, deployed them. His successors, however, were well aware of the enormous difficulty Alexander's army had faced in trying to overcome the elephants thrown against the

phalanx by the Indian Rajah Porus at the Hydaspes River in 326 BC. Having themselves to face such phalanxes in battle, all of Alexander's successors avidly sought elephants of their own.

So it was that 32 elephants, probably Indian, imported through Persia or bred in the service of the Seleucids, accompanied Lysias on his march. The animals had experience in combat, a function of their

long Seleucid employment in wars against Egypt and Rome. Even Rajah Porus's elephant corps had not been sufficiently war-seasoned to withstand Alexander's phalanx and cavalry, and had, in the end, panicked and stampeded through the Indian lines at Hydaspes.

Elephants and mahouts (elephant drivers) used to battle would be far less likely to get out of control. However, there

were two additional methods of keeping the beasts in check. Each Carthaginian mahout carried a hammer and a chisel, and had orders to use them to sever his animal's spinal cord if it became a liability in battle. Also, among the stores in Lysias's siege train was 'the blood of grapes and mulberries', strong drink to be given to the elephants directly before the battle, because intoxicated elephants are noted for their

'As terrible as an army with banners,' the spectacle of the advancing Seleucid army matched the danger it presented to the Jewish line, waiting for the first time in the revolt in a defensive formation. Neither the attack of the night before nor the terrain was sufficient to disrupt the awesome power of the force brought by Lysias against the rebels. From a woodcut by Gustave Doré.

177

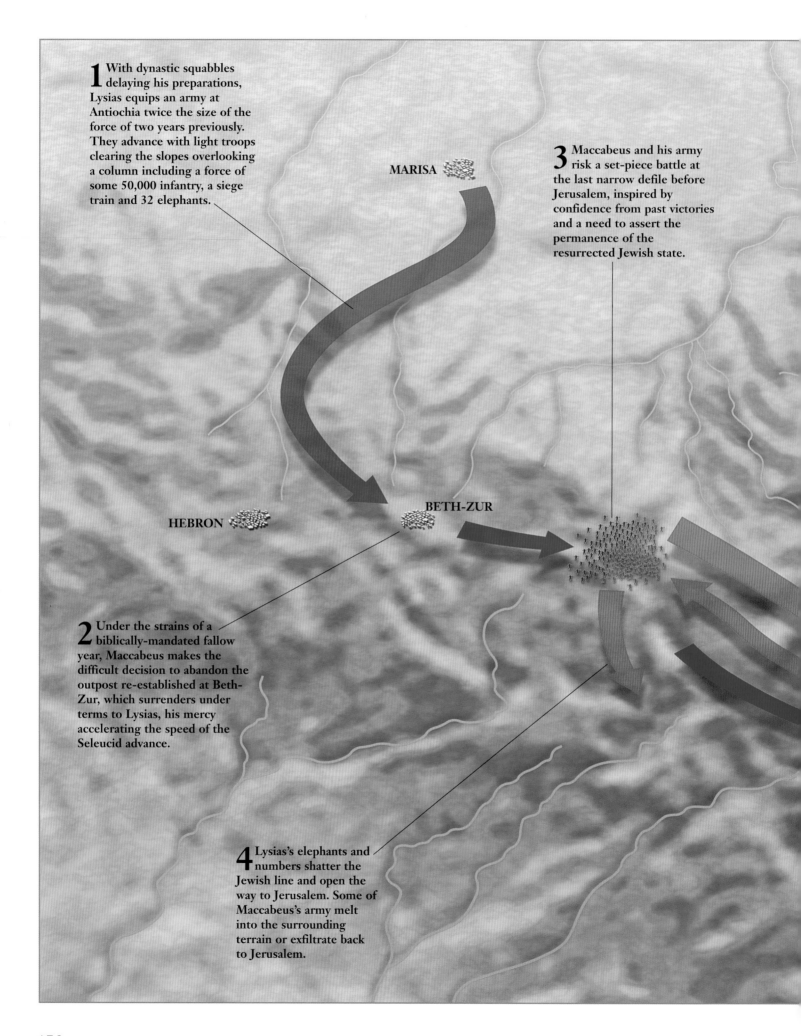

1 With dynastic squabbles delaying his preparations, Lysias equips an army at Antiochia twice the size of the force of two years previously. They advance with light troops clearing the slopes overlooking a column including a force of some 50,000 infantry, a siege train and 32 elephants.

MARISA

3 Maccabeus and his army risk a set-piece battle at the last narrow defile before Jerusalem, inspired by confidence from past victories and a need to assert the permanence of the resurrected Jewish state.

HEBRON

BETH-ZUR

2 Under the strains of a biblically-mandated fallow year, Maccabeus makes the difficult decision to abandon the outpost re-established at Beth-Zur, which surrenders under terms to Lysias, his mercy accelerating the speed of the Seleucid advance.

4 Lysias's elephants and numbers shatter the Jewish line and open the way to Jerusalem. Some of Maccabeus's army melt into the surrounding terrain or exfiltrate back to Jerusalem.

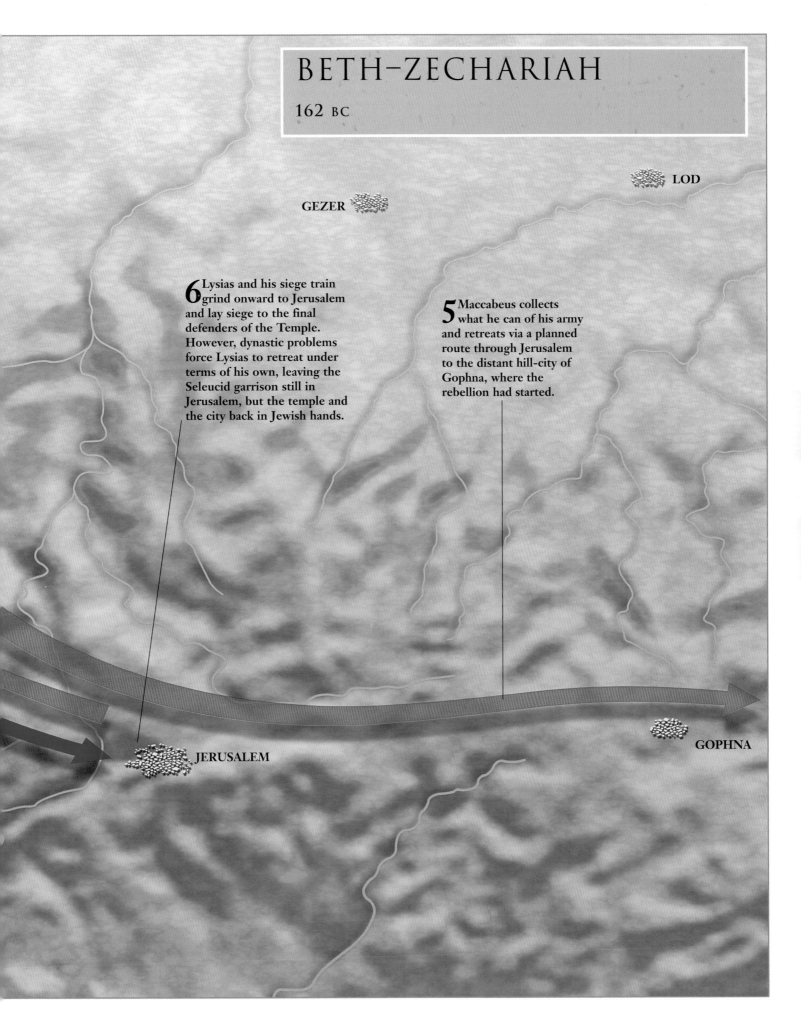

BETH–ZECHARIAH

162 BC

GEZER

LOD

6 Lysias and his siege train grind onward to Jerusalem and lay siege to the final defenders of the Temple. However, dynastic problems force Lysias to retreat under terms of his own, leaving the Seleucid garrison still in Jerusalem, but the temple and the city back in Jewish hands.

5 Maccabeus collects what he can of his army and retreats via a planned route through Jerusalem to the distant hill-city of Gophna, where the rebellion had started.

JERUSALEM

GOPHNA

BETH-ZECHARIAH

Multiple javelins and a light shield were the marks of the skirmishers Lysias put out on the flanks of his army and his elephants to protect his formations from yet another disastrous ambush. On this occasion, Maccabeus chose to meet the enemy in a pitched, open battle – and lost.

exceptional savagery. Ptolemy IV of Egypt had planned to use drunken elephants to slaughter Jews in the Alexandrian hippodrome. At Beth-Zachariah, it would be Jews in the field.

ARMOURED FIGHTING VEHICLES

Elephants in ancient warfare are often equated with modern armoured fighting vehicles (AFVs). This view is neither entirely correct nor incorrect in understanding their deployment, at least on this occasion. The tank in battle carries missile fire into the ranks of the enemy, moves rapidly and demolishes obstacles. Lysias equipped his elephant corps to do all three.

On the back of each animal rose a stout wooden *howdah* (an ornate carriage), held firmly in place by a stable harness. Stationed within each *howdah* were, typically, one or two archers and a pikeman, the latter to jab away any attacker the animal itself did not despatch with its trunk or forelegs. An elephant could kill even an armoured soldier by raising him with its trunk and crushing him against its forehead; or in the same way it kills a tiger in the wild – by throwing his victim before its fore-knees and kneeling on him. Goring with the tusks was another option, and there are depictions showing elephants with metal tips on the ends, to make the attack all the more vicious and, inevitably, lethal.

At a fast walk, an elephant can reach a pace of 22km/h (14mph) – about equal to the speed of a man running in armour. Lysias's elephants wore the heaviest of armour, which strengthens the comparison with modern AFVs. Josephus refers to the 'breastplates' (thoraxes) worn by the animals, while biblical references seem to indicate that there were 'trappings' about the animals, presumably to protect their feet and vulnerable hamstrings.

Horses unaccustomed to elephants have been known to shy and bolt from the strangeness of the sight and smell of the massive pachyderms. With

Macedonian and Roman cavalry, this resulted in more than one military disaster. Although Maccabeus and his rebels had no cavalry to speak of, the elephants could also perform another task: the removal of heavy obstacles. And, in fact, there are descriptions of elephants smashing walls and infantry strong points during house-

to-house fighting in both Beth-Sura and Jerusalem.

The tactics employed by Lysias as he moved to engage Maccabeus and his forces prompt another modern analogy. Modern cavalry commanders have learned from bitter experience to surround their tanks with infantry: the tanks supplement the firepower of the infantry and eradicate enemy choke points, while the infantry protect the tank from close-in assault.

Lysias apparently understood this principle, for all accounts mention that he parcelled the elephants out between the sub-units of the phalanx, each with a large number of standard infantry surrounding it,

Under a rush of Seleucid horsemen, Judas Maccabeus perishes, too proud to retreat some four years after his tactical withdrawal at Beth-Zechariah. As he had succeeded his father, Judas's surviving brothers would take up in succession the leadership of the revolt, to ultimate success.

181

The belly of the beast was fatal to both Eleazar and the elephant he stabbed in a desperate effort to throw the Seleucid army into confusion by downing what he thought was the elephant carrying Lysias or the young Antiochus V. The dying animal fell upon Maccabeus's younger brother and crushed him, but the Seleucid command were elsewhere – and victorious.

and a smaller unit of more heavily armoured soldiers immediately next to the beast. Cavalry units stood on hand to protect the elephants and to exploit any disruption the animals caused in the Jewish line. None of Lysias's preparations, however, would be enough to allow his elephants to escape the battle unscathed.

BACKS TO THE WALLS

All accounts of the battle are also agreed that Lysias's force consisted of more than heavy weapons and the elephant core. As his huge column of some 50,000 men moved up

towards Beth-Zur, lighter troops appeared on the heights overlooking the central valley, where Maccabeus had ambushed him two years previously.

A test of a great commander's prowess is his ability to make difficult decisions quickly. Lysias appreciated the value of military showmanship, and all accounts record the fear spreading throughout the ranks of the Maccabean army as Lysias's monstrous column, and its accompanying monsters, drew ever closer.

In the face of the advance he had planned to withstand, Maccabeus made the difficult decision to retreat, some 10km (6 miles) northwards, up the valley to the even narrower defile of Beth-Zechariah. At that place, he hoped, there would not be room for the weight of the elephants and their support forces to bear down upon his army, which would be fighting defensively for the first time. By retreating, he could gain time for further preparation and deny Lysias a familiar battlefield, but in so doing he had to sacrifice the position and garrison of Beth-Zur, which Lysias systematically and scientifically reduced. In this, he was aided by Jewish religious practice.

Very early in the revolt the Maccabean forces learned to fight on the Sabbath after their piety had proved fatal in the course of the fighting. The year of Lysias's onslaught, however, was the one in seven when Mosaic Law commanded that the fields be left fallow. As a result, food in both Beth-Zur and Jerusalem was in short supply. Lysias used this to his advantage and, moreover, was wise enough to appreciate the value of mercy in allowing an enemy to capitulate. The garrison of Beth-Zur surrendered quickly under terms.

Onwards once more ground the Seleucid column. The elephants, which had led the advance, fell out of line and into column as they and the balance of the Seleucid host moved slowly up towards the higher ground at Beth-Zechariah, where Maccabeus and his army waited. Jerusalem itself lay only about 11km (7 miles) further up the valley.

The situation was clearly desperate – so desperate, in fact, that Maccabeus's younger brother Eleazar was driven to make a rash decision. The lead elephant's trappings were particularly splendid, and it was not altogether irrational to hope that Lysias or even the young Antiochus V might be perched with the howdah at the very van. Though there was no hope of the slain elephant's body blocking the advance of the others, Eleazar undoubtedly remembered the success of Maccabeus's 'decapitation strike' at Apollonius five years before. The slain Seleucid general's sword was glittering in his brother's scabbard to remind him.

So, Eleazar broke out of the line and moved quickly enough to get under the advancing elephant's belly, the one place where the surrounding infantry and the animal itself would have difficulty getting at him. The wound Eleazar inflicted upon the elephant was fatal to them both, for the dying animal fell upon its slayer. Undying glory was the only benefit of Eleazar's ploy, however, for Lysias had not been so foolish as to put his king and cause in a position of such obvious danger.

ORDERLY RETREAT

The Jews held for a while – long enough, the accounts say, to inflict 600 casualties upon their attackers. Then they broke, and it was after the collapse of his line that another of Judas Maccabeus's great qualities became manifest. The army that had maintained order in victory found order enough in retreat for a controlled withdrawal into the fortification.

Maccabeus had left himself an escape route in the event that the pitched battle he himself had sought should go against him. The battle was lost, but while the army endured, so could the war – even at the cost of the capital and the Temple. Leadership displays itself to best advantage in adversity.

Instead of retreating to Jerusalem, Maccabeus led his army through the city and left as many of his forces as he could in the rebuilt fortifications. He then led the balance of his troops another 24km (15 miles) further north to the hill town of Gophna, the cradle of his revolt. He was clearly getting ready to start over, not to capitulate.

Lysias brought up his column and invested Jerusalem, unlimbering his formidable siege train once more as he conquered the lower city. The fortifications of the Temple Mount held out with dwindling supplies while Lysias relieved his own garrison in the Acra fortress. Cannily, he allowed rite and sacrifice within the Temple itself to proceed during the siege, thus dampening a major flame of the rebellion.

Lysias's wisdom and honour during the campaign brought him one final reward. News came from the north that Lysias's rival Philip was *en route* to seize the imperial capital at Antioch. Terms were offered and accepted, and the Seleucid army withdrew back to Syria.

It was only after the deaths of Lysias and Antiochus V later that year – at the hands of a successful pretender, Demetrius – that the persecutions and rebellion of the Jews resumed once more.

This photograph shows a part of the harbour wall in Seleucia Pieria, with Mount Casius behind. The port was built by Seleucus I Nicator in 300 BC. It lay near the mouth of the Orontes River, and functioned as the commercial and naval seaport of Antioch. Seleucia was of great strategic importance in the struggle between the Seleucids and the Ptolemies: it changed hands several times until 219 BC, when the Seleucid Antiochus III ('the Great') captured it.

JERUSALEM
63 BC

DISPUTES AMONG JEWISH FACTIONS WERE COMMON. IN 64 BC, THE JEWISH PRINCES ARISTOBULUS AND HYRCANUS WERE IN CONFLICT, AND THIS LED TO DISASTER WHEN THE ROMANS UNDER POMPEY DECIDED TO BECOME INVOLVED.

WHY DID IT HAPPEN?

WHO A Roman army under Gnaeus Pompeius Magnus (Pompey) (106–48 BC) versus Jewish forces loyal to Aristobulus (104–103 BC).

WHAT Pompey's forces gradually wore down the defences around the Temple and then launched a successful assault.

WHERE The city of Jerusalem in Judea.

WHEN 63 BC.

WHY Pompey had wide-ranging powers to end a threat to Rome, and decided that there were sufficient grounds for intervention in Jerusalem.

OUTCOME Pompey's forces were successful and captured the Temple. He then installed a High Priest of his own choosing.

The career of Gnaeus Pompeius Magnus, better known as Pompey, was an extremely successful one. Like many Roman politicians, his political fortunes were largely based on successes as a military commander, and he was quite willing to embark upon a campaign with the intention of furthering his career.

Pompey was a supporter of Lucius Cornelius Sulla (c.138–78 BC), who at that time was Roman Dictator: absolute ruler of all things Roman. Pompey had supported Sulla in his power struggles and been rewarded accordingly. Among other prizes he was given the hand in marriage of Sulla's stepdaughter, Aemilia Scaura (c.100–82 BC), which required that both Aemilia and Pompey divorce their own spouses.

Pompey went on to campaign in Sulla's name, and with great success, in Sicily and in North Africa (81–82 BC). Despite some

rifts in the relationship with Sulla, and increasing fear of the up-and-coming young general among the higher leadership in Rome, Pompey was indispensable. Sulla was still trying to suppress the supporters of Gaius Marius (157–86 BC), against whom he had fought for many years. After others had failed, Pompey was sent to Hispania to finish the job. It took six years, but not only did he pacify the province he also created the basis of a stable province.

Pompey had, in fact, asked to be sent to Hispania on at least one occasion, but he was too young to hold the rank of Proconsul, which was required to command the army he would need. Those higher up in the hierarchy of Rome were reluctant to bend the rules for several reasons, few of them to do with respect for the law or precedent. If Pompey were to become a Proconsul at such a young age, what would

A classical depiction of the election of Gnaeus Pompeius Magnus to the rank of Consul. The triumphant procession indicates the popularity of the decision even though Pompey was rather young for the post.

he want next? He was not the sort to be satisfied until he had gone as far as possible, and the implications of that worried his superiors. However, the Marian forces in Hispania had to be put down, and it seemed that Pompey thought he could succeed where others had failed.

Events proved him correct. He benefited from treachery in the enemy ranks, when a less able subordinate murdered the skilled Marian general and took over his forces. Pompey was able to defeat his enemies, and showed considerable skill in cementing Roman control over the province.

Having completed the pacification of Hispania, Pompey returned to Italy just in time to crush a rebel army that was fleeing from defeat at the hands of Marcus Licinius Crassus (c.115–53 BC). Pompey was able to claim the glory for having successfully put down the slaves' revolt inspired by Spartacus, which cemented his own reputation even further and annoyed Crassus no end.

With this record of military success, Pompey was a logical choice for the task of eliminating pirate activity based out of Cilicia. He was given a great deal of latitude in order to complete the task, along with autonomous command of a considerable force for the period of three years. It is possible that packing him off to the frontiers with a prestigious but lengthy job to do was seen as a useful way of getting rid of this ambitious young man.

In the event, it took Pompey only three months to pacify Cilicia and scatter the surviving pirates. With a military force at his disposal for the remainder of the three-year command, Pompey set about finding something to do with it. In true Roman tradition, he set about conquering new lands and adding them to those already controlled by Rome.

First, Pompey headed north across what is today Turkey and annexed the province of Pontus in the name of Rome. He then turned east and conquered several Armenian tribes in a drive that took him most of the way to the Caspian Sea by the end of 65 BC. With some time remaining to him, Pompey then marched south into Syria and annexed it as a Roman province.

This put Pompey's force in a position to intervene in a Jewish conflict that had developed. The death of the Jewish queen, Alexandra-Salome (139–67 BC), left two princes vying for power. Aristobulus, supported by the Sadducees, controlled the Temple of Jerusalem but was more or less besieged within it by Hyrcanus (high priest from 76–40 BC), who enjoyed the support of the Pharisees as well as foreign allies including an Arabian Sheik from Petra.

POMPEY AND JEWISH POLITICS

The two Jewish princes asked for Roman mediation in their dispute, along with a third group that did not want a king at all but preferred instead to establish a theocratic republic. Pompey was at that

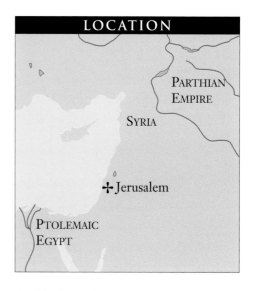

LOCATION

Israel lay far from Rome, at the outer edge of the Empire. After a successful campaign to the north, Pompey moved southwards and exploited local politics to his advantage.

JERUSALEM, 63 BC

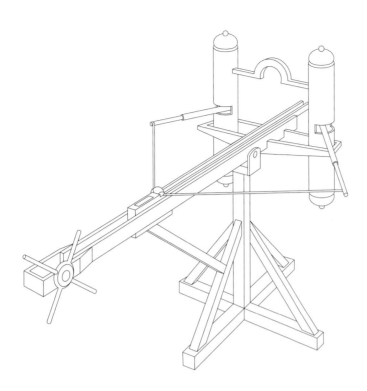

The cheiroballistra, *which first appeared in the first century* AD. *This bolt-shooting weapon had a sturdier frame, but the greatest innovation was that its head was now constructed almost completely from metal. The springs were encased in bronze cylinders to protect them against weather and enemy fire, which gave the machine a longer life. It was a supremely accurate piece of artillery, and was aimed by the use of a sight-arch in between the two springs. Cheiroballistra were mounted in siege towers to keep the defenders heads down as the siege engines were pushed ever closer to the walls.*

THE OPPOSED FORCES

ROMANS
   Unknown number of regular
   infantry

JEWS
   Unknown number of townspeople

time involved in a minor campaign against local tribes, but saw an opportunity to profit from the situation.

Bribery being a common tool of state at the time, there was nothing unusual about the huge amount of silver sent by Aristobulus to Marcus Aemilius Scaurus (c.163–89 BC), Pompey's representative in Syria. In return for this donation, he forced Hyrcanus's Arabian allies to abandon their alliance and return home to Petra. Aristobulus sent an even larger bribe to Pompey upon his arrival in the region, winning his favour, for the time being at least.

Pompey heard the delegations at Damascus, and insisted that the two princes came in person to meet with him. In this way, he established a level of dominance over them. Pompey did not rule on the dispute immediately, however. He decided to deal with the Nabatean tribes first.

Despite having successfully bribed the Romans, Aristobulus hedged his bets and walled himself up in the fortress of Alexandrium. Pompey was displeased and ordered him to depart, forcing Aristobulus to surrender the fortress. He instead returned to Jerusalem, with Pompey headed for the same destination, via Jericho.

Whether or not he was still confident of Roman friendship remains unclear, but in

any case Aristobulus sent messages to Pompey, accusing Aemilius of extorting money rather than being offered it as a legitimate bribe. Pompey investigated personally and upon his arrival in Jerusalem decided to side with Hyrcanus. It is not known whether money changed hands over this matter, but given the politics of the time, this is entirely possible.

Aristobulus was arrested. However, his followers still held the Temple and the dispute continued. Pompey, deciding that more than mediation was required, brought a portion of his forces to Jerusalem. They were able to move freely with the support of Hyrcanus's faction and were soon in a position to surround the Temple Mount.

PREPARATIONS

Hyrcanus and his new Roman allies were in control of the lower town of Jerusalem and the surrounding countryside, but the Sadducees were firmly fortified in the Temple and its immediate environs. They had destroyed the bridge between the city and the Temple, making access difficult. An attack from the south or east was more or less out of the question due to deep and steep-sided valleys. Pompey would have to assault from the north, and in typically methodical Roman fashion he set about preparing for the attack.

The Romans were tremendously well organized and set about the reduction of the fortress with characteristic logic. Siege engines were brought up to cover the engineering works that would be required, and kept up a steady hail of stones and javelins that wore down the defenders and, more importantly, prevented them from interfering effectively with the assault preparations.

Under cover of this bombardment, legionaries set about the construction of a ramp that would allow their siege towers to be pushed right up to the defenders' walls. This was a common tactic in sieges of the period and represented a huge investment

Opposite: A stature of Pompeius Magnus. The title Magnus ('the great') was probably bestowed by Sulla as an ironic insult, though later Pompey fully merited it.

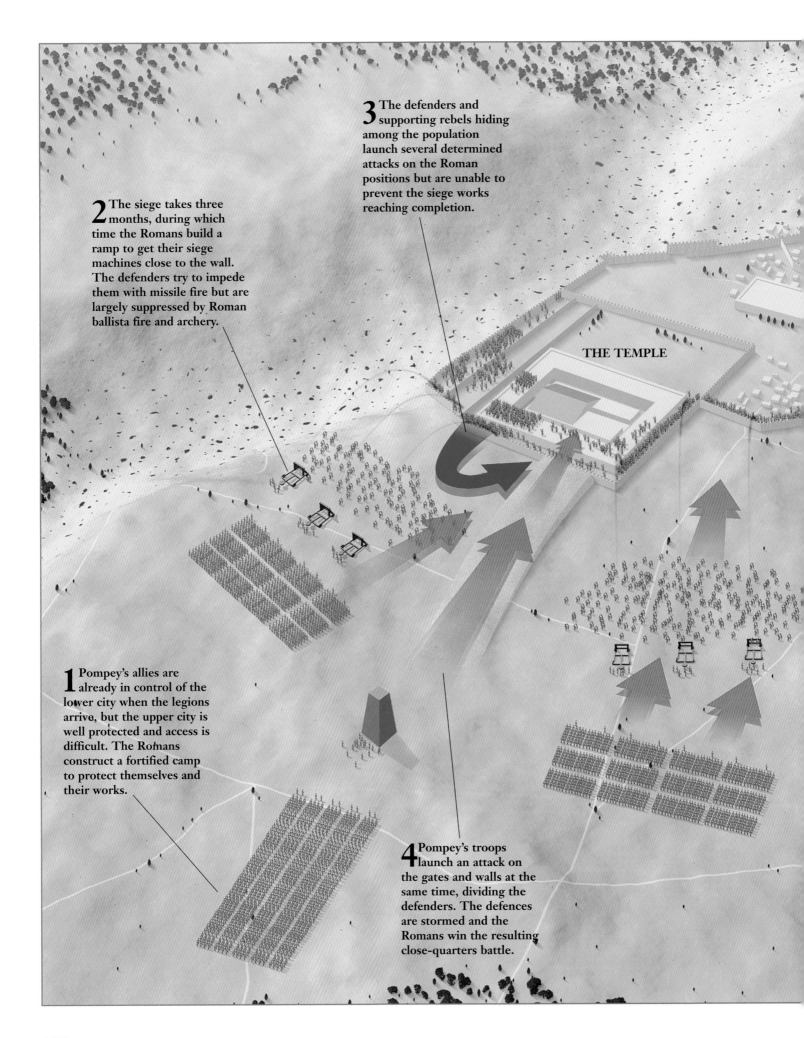

3 The defenders and supporting rebels hiding among the population launch several determined attacks on the Roman positions but are unable to prevent the siege works reaching completion.

2 The siege takes three months, during which time the Romans build a ramp to get their siege machines close to the wall. The defenders try to impede them with missile fire but are largely suppressed by Roman ballista fire and archery.

THE TEMPLE

1 Pompey's allies are already in control of the lower city when the legions arrive, but the upper city is well protected and access is difficult. The Romans construct a fortified camp to protect themselves and their works.

4 Pompey's troops launch an attack on the gates and walls at the same time, dividing the defenders. The defences are stormed and the Romans win the resulting close-quarters battle.

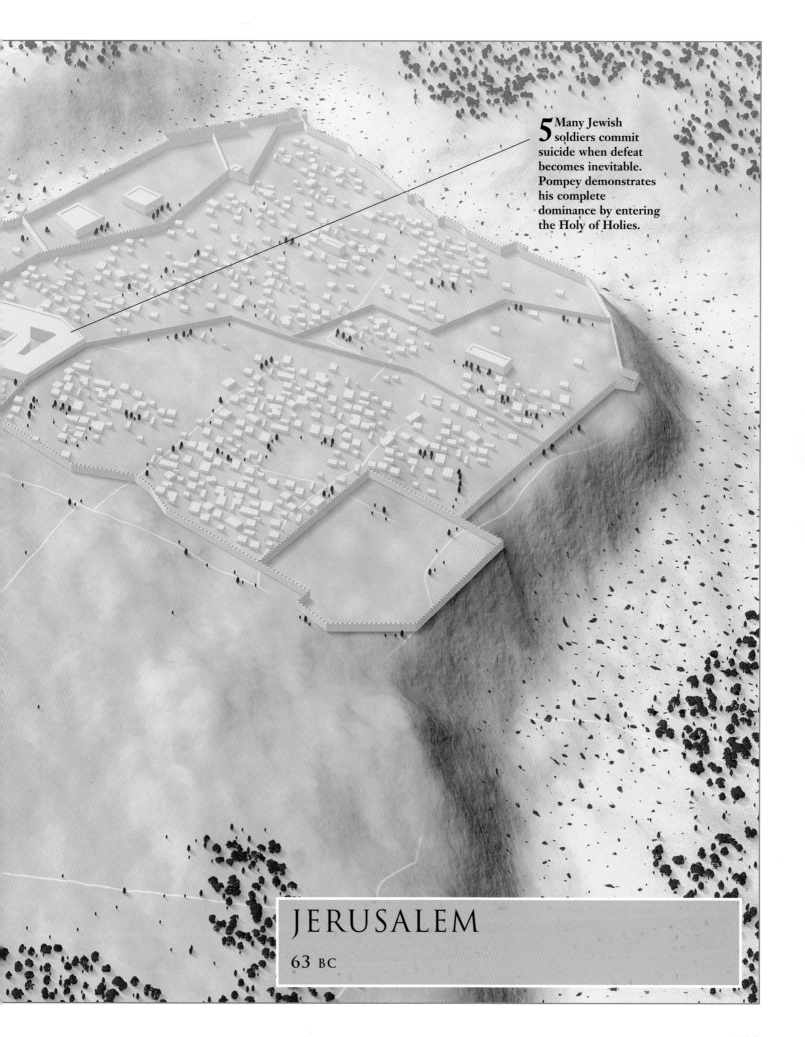

5 Many Jewish soldiers commit suicide when defeat becomes inevitable. Pompey demonstrates his complete dominance by entering the Holy of Holies.

JERUSALEM

63 BC

The remains of the original altar of the Temple at Jerusalem. Pompey found scrolls and altars in the Holy of Holies, but no statues or images of God. To a Roman, that seemed very strange.

JERUSALEM, 63 BC

in time and manpower. However, once it was finished, the ramp and towers would give easy access to the walls. If it could be completed, the assault was more or less guaranteed to succeed.

The ramp was a significant field-engineering work, and had to be constructed in the face of opposition from the defenders. Roman legionaries, however, were well used to fortification work. On the march, they would build a fortified camp every night, so spadework was neither foreign nor beneath their dignity. The work was led by experienced officers and skilled pioneers, and conducted efficiently by disciplined soldiers.

THE SIEGE

Protected by their artillery and body armour, the Romans built up a ramp of

earth, rubble and whatever materials they had available. The Jews fought back with missile weapons and came out to attack the workers from time to time, although they were extremely reluctant to fight on the Sabbath.

Details of the defending force are hard to come by, but it is likely that there was a small core of trained soldiers loyal to Aristobulus backed up by a larger number of irregulars. These would have included civilian volunteers, temple guards and religious fanatics who rallied to the cause of defending their holy place from the foreign invaders.

The siege went on for three months. There are few records of what was happening outside the Temple area, but it is likely that a significant portion of the city's population was offended by the

JERUSALEM, 63 BC

Romans' presence around the Temple Mount. Inspired by the Sadducees and the political influence of Aristobulus, raids on the besieging Romans were likely. However, Pompey's forces were highly skilled at providing for their own security, and the well-equipped, tough and experienced legionaries would have had little difficulty fending off raids by bands of armed irregulars, no matter how fanatical or determined they might have been.

THE ROMAN ASSAULT

The siege continued, unbroken, until Pompey was sure that his preparations were complete. With the defenders showing no signs of wanting to surrender, the attack was ordered for a Sabbath day.

Some sources claim that the Jews were not defending the walls on the day of the assault, but it seems unlikely that there was no one at all on duty while the Romans readied themselves for the attack. Records of the actual storming are hard to come by, but the pattern is familiar from other Roman operations.

Covered by intense shooting by their artillery and auxiliary missile troops, the assault columns made their way forwards. The gates were attacked with rams brought from Tyre, while infantrymen charged up the ramp and onto the wall. Attacking at multiple points split the defenders and made it difficult to reinforce a threatened area.

Above: The Testudo *(Tortoise) formation had its limitations (it could be slow and unwieldy to manoeuvre), but it afforded excellent protection from missile fire during an approach or when preparing for an assault.*

Many ancient armies favoured spears or other unwieldy weapons, which were useful in massed formations but not so effective in the close-quarters scramble of an assault. Not so the Roman legionaries. Some threw their *pila* as they advanced to the wall, but at the moment of contact it was their short swords that were the decisive weapons. The gladius was light and handy, capable of cutting or stabbing; an ideal weapon for a wall assault.

The *scutum*, the legionary's shield, protected him from missiles and blows as he advanced to the assault, but it was more than that. Long training taught legionaries

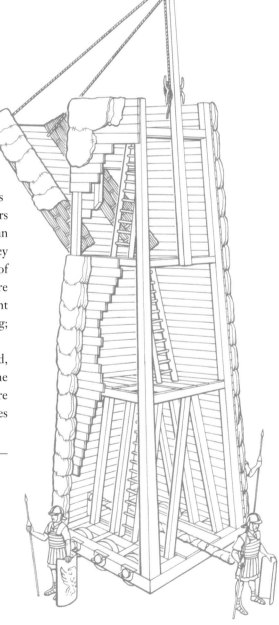

Right: A Roman siege tower complete with ram and assault ramp. The small wheels could not move well over rough ground, so a 'ramp' or 'dam' was built to allow the towers access to their target. The Romans began to use siege towers from 200 BC onwards, initially based on Hellenistic designs of the period. Roman pragmatism added such details as the battering ram. The boarding ramp could be either lowered by ropes and pulleys or manually pushed forward by the assaulting troops.

JERUSALEM, 63 BC

This Neo-Classical depiction of the storming of Jerusalem superimposes a number of inaccuracies. One example is the swords; they are more akin to a broadsword than the Roman gladius.

to use their shields as a mobile obstacle, reducing the odds against any given man by presenting what amounted to a wall to the assailant on his right while the legionary attacked those to his left with his sword. The shield could also be used to crash into an enemy, forcing him back against his fellows and hampering his movements. A defender who found himself pinned against the man behind could quickly be despatched with the thrust of a sword.

The legionaries were also better armoured than their opponents, and they had other advantages too. They were disciplined and confident of victory, having come from a successful campaign to the north. The Romans were also well led, by commanders who were prepared to engage with the enemy and showed a fine example. The first man over the wall was Faustus Cornelius Sulla (78–47 BC), son of the Dictator himself.

The assault was bloody and more or less one sided. When defeat became obvious, many Jewish defenders committed suicide rather than see their Temple defiled by the Romans. Some accounts claim as many as 12,000 Jewish casualties in the fighting, including many priests. Whether this is accurate or not, the Temple was soon in the hands of Pompey and his troops.

Pompey entered the Holy of Holies with his officers, which was a grave insult to the Jews. However, out of respect for the sanctity of the Temple, he ordered that nothing be removed or damaged. Pompey tended to take the long view, to ensure that today's conquest become a stable Roman province in years to come. He may well have thought it necessary to demonstrate his power by entering the Temple – showing that his hands were not tied by somebody else's beliefs – but at the same time he showed a willingness to respect the Jewish faith and leave their holy place unviolated, if they did not force him to do otherwise.

AFTERMATH

Judea became a Roman possession and tribute requirements were imposed. Several cities were either made independent or transferred to the province of Syria. Hyrcanus was named 'Ethnarch' (National Leader) of Judea, while Aristobulus and his children were taken as prisoners to Rome, where they were forced to take part in Pompey's triumphal entry to the city. Many of the prisoners taken in Judea were, however, eventually freed and given homes in Rome. Marcus Aemilius Scaurus continued to campaign in the region, waging war on the Arabian Sheik, Aretas,

who had supported Hyrcanus. He allowed himself to be bribed with another vast amount of silver and was killed soon after.

Meanwhile, Pompey returned to Rome by way of a pacification campaign in Crete. He had gone far beyond his original objectives, adding greatly to Rome's possessions. No longer did the Jews have an independent kingdom. Now they were just another vassal state of Rome, and would remain so for many years.

Spartacus and his fellow slaves take on the might of the Roman legions, 70 BC. Following his successful campaign in Judea, Pompey had a stroke of good luck, arriving back in Italy in time to defeat what remained of Spartacus' slave revolt and steal the credit for winning the Third Servile War from Crassus.

JERUSALEM
AD 70

ALTHOUGH IT STARTED WELL FOR THE REBELS, THE JEWISH REVOLT THAT BEGAN IN AD 66 ENDED IN CATASTROPHIC DEFEAT AT THE HANDS OF TITUS FLAVIUS. THE JEWS SUFFERED MASSIVE CASUALTIES, AND ROMAN REPRISALS WERE SAVAGE.

WHY DID IT HAPPEN?

WHO A Roman army numbering around 35,000 under Titus Flavius – soon to become Emperor Vespasian (AD 69–79) – opposed by at least 24,000 rebel Jews.

WHAT Jerusalem was besieged for much of the war and finally taken by storm.

WHERE The city of Jerusalem in Judea.

WHEN AD 70.

WHY Outraged by practices allowed by the Romans, the Jews rebelled against their conquerors.

OUTCOME The Jews were utterly defeated.

Judea had been a Roman province for many years when rebellion broke out in AD 66. As in any occupied territory, there had been some unrest over the years, but incidents tended to be localized and easily dealt with. However, the Jews were a deeply religious people and not inclined to tolerate affronts to their faith, of which there had been several in the years since Pompey (106–48 BC) took control of the region for Rome.

Pompey's intrusion into the Holy of Holies was perhaps the first such offence, and was very serious as far as the Jews were concerned. When, around AD 6, the Romans began insisting upon appointing the High Priest, the Jews were further offended. However, Rome was a practised overlord and had many ways to discourage or put down opposition.

Tension was partially relieved by the Roman practice of allowing the Jews to follow their own religion, rather than imposing the official cult of the Empire upon them. However, the benefits of such pragmatism were partially undone in AD 39, when Emperor Caligula (AD 12–41) declared himself to be a god and insisted that statues of himself be erected in all temples within the Empire. Deeply

The ruins of Herod's palace, giving some idea of its grand scope. Allowing the Jews to keep their own king was one of a number of measures intended to reduce tension in the province.

offended, the Jews decided to resist the command.

Still, the province did not quite boil over into open rebellion. Taking up arms against Rome was always punished savagely, and fear of the consequences helped prevent disaffection from becoming insurrection. The Romans were also able to defuse several volatile situations. For example, a Roman soldier who was part of a force assigned to punish local villagers for not helping the authorities deal with brigands, destroyed religious documents while uttering blasphemies. The local population were outraged, and the governor agreed with them that the soldier had gone too far in attacking their God. He was publicly beheaded in front of the angry mob, which pacified them for a time.

On other occasions, incidents were allowed to pass, but anger among the Jews gradually grew until a large segment of the population was in favour of an uprising. Matters were made worse when the Procurator (Roman ruler) of Judea was accused, probably with reason, of stealing money from the Temple treasury in Jerusalem. As anti-Roman sentiment increased, the Zealot movement gained popularity. The Zealots were radicals who believed that any means were justified in order for Judea to achieve independence from Rome – both spiritually and politically.

Preparations for insurrection were made and a number of incidents occurred, but the Romans were able to keep a lid on the situation for a time. It was not until AD 66 that the rebellion began in earnest. It began with a refusal by the High Priest to offer up prayers and sacrifices to the Roman Emperor. This was in protest at seeing Greeks sacrificing birds right in front of the synagogue and the refusal of the Roman garrison to do anything about it. Soon after, the incident escalated and a Roman garrison was attacked.

THE REVOLT

The Jewish King of Judea at the time was Agrippa II, who was very pro-Roman. Fearing for his safety, he fled to Galilee and sought sanctuary with the Romans. Fighting spread throughout the province and the Jews were initially successful. The

rebels destroyed the debt archives as soon as possible, increasing their support among the poorer classes who benefited most from this rather dramatic writing-off of their debts. Rebels have used measures of this sort for most of recorded history, for the simple reason that they work.

The standard Roman response to an uprising was to act fast and decisively, so Gaius Cestius Gallus (d. AD 67), the Roman leader in Syria, marched immediately to put down the rebellion. The tactic had worked well in the past, for Caesar among others, but not this time.

Gallus's force was built around the 12th Legion, with detachments from three others plus regular auxiliaries. To this, he

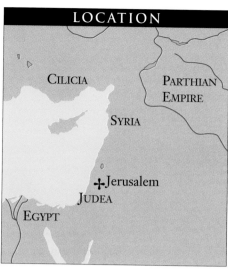

Judea never really rested easy as a province of the Roman Empire. Unrest and open rebellion flared up many times despite Roman conciliation and harsh measures, in approximately equal proportions.

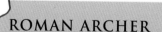

ROMAN ARCHER

It was shock action, delivered with gladius and pilum, that overthrew the enemy, and the heavily armoured legionary was the backbone of the Roman army. But for all that, the attack went better against an enemy softened up by a hail of missiles. The Romans knew how to get the best advantage from missile support, and used slingers and archers as well as siege artillery as a supporting arm. Archers could be extremely effective, especially in an assault against a defended position. This auxiliary archer has a coat of scale mail and a metal helmet to protect him from both enemy arrows and in case he must fight hand-to-hand.

195

JERUSALEM, AD 70

Emperor Caligula ruled for less than four years but did untold damage in that time. His insistence that his statue be placed in synagogues and worshipped as a god enraged the Jews.

invincible was one reason why small numbers of legionaries and auxilia were able to hold down large areas. Now that the Jews knew their foes could be beaten in battle, and ambushed in the streets or attacked in their garrisons, morale among the rebels increased accordingly.

ROMAN RESPONSES

Emperor Nero (AD 37–68) knew that the revolt could not be allowed to gather momentum. Unchecked, it might spread to other provinces. He thus fell back on another principle of Roman governance – to rebel against Rome meant to fight all of the Empire. Rebels might defeat local garrison forces, but this would trigger a full-scale intervention that could have only one ending. This was another way Rome discouraged rebellion: any success would be short-lived, and leading an insurrection was a death sentence.

The commander assigned to put down the rebellion in Judea was Titus Flavius Vespasianus, soon to become Emperor Vespasian. He was given an army of 60,000 men, including two legions and supporting auxiliary forces, and set off with great vigour to deal with the problem before matters got any worse.

The rebellion was at that time more or less divided into two main segments, in the north and south of the province. The north was quickly overrun. In some areas, the population put up a vigorous fight. Other towns surrendered without offering resistance, and within two years the insurrection had been put down in the northern half of the province.

INTERNAL PROBLEMS

All was not well in Rome at that time. Emperor Nero had run into major political troubles and lost the support of the senate and even his own Praetorian Guard. In despair, he ordered a slave to kill him, leaving the Empire without a

added a large number of levies, and set out without properly training his force. To his surprise, Gallus encountered strong resistance and suffered a number of minor setbacks before laying siege to Jerusalem.

Jerusalem was heavily fortified and occupied by a large number of well-armed rebels. Many of them had access to arms taken from the massacred garrison, and it was obvious that Gallus could not take the city with the troops he had available. He began to fall back and was harried constantly until he reached the pass of Beth-horon. There, his army came under heavy attack. Almost 6000 Roman soldiers were killed and the 12th legion lost its eagle.

This was a serious setback for Rome, denting its prestige in the region. The general belief that Roman troops were

THE OPPOSED FORCES

ROMANS (estimated)
Mostly infantry
Total: **30–40,000**

ISREALITES (estimated)
Irregular infantry
Total: **23–24,000**

Opposite: A stone relief showing soldiers of the Praetorian Guard. Originally an elite fighting force, the Praetorians gradually became corrupt and more concerned with getting rich from bribes than training for war.

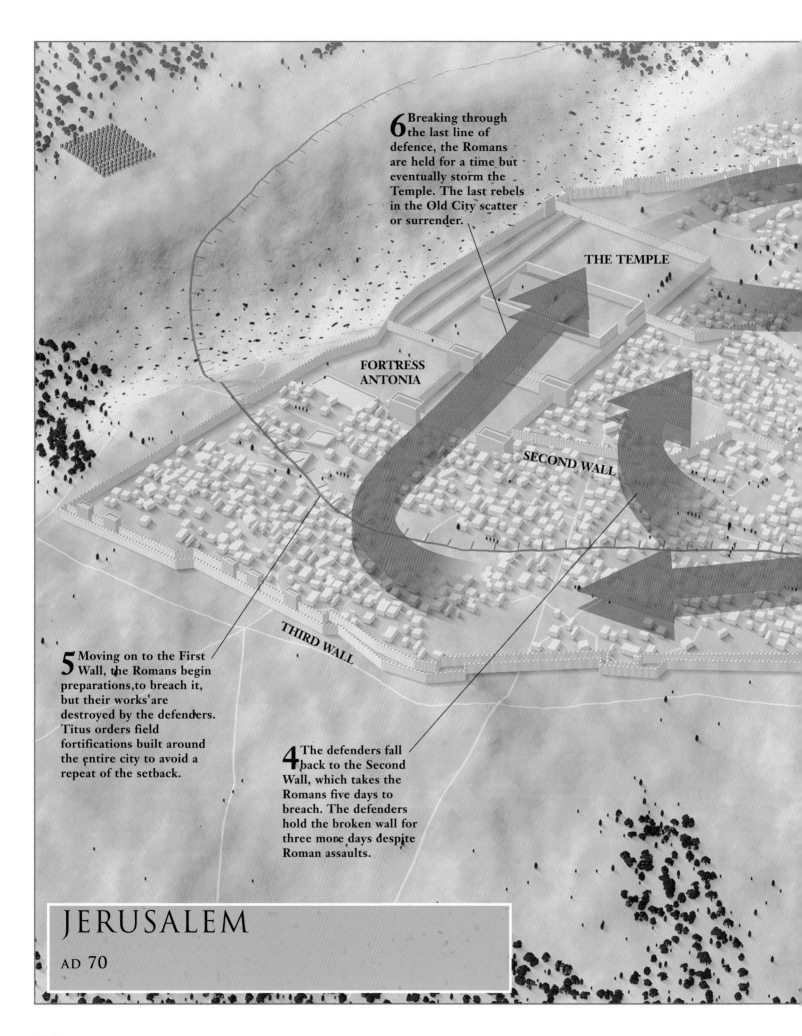

6 Breaking through the last line of defence, the Romans are held for a time but eventually storm the Temple. The last rebels in the Old City scatter or surrender.

THE TEMPLE

FORTRESS ANTONIA

SECOND WALL

THIRD WALL

5 Moving on to the First Wall, the Romans begin preparations to breach it, but their works are destroyed by the defenders. Titus orders field fortifications built around the entire city to avoid a repeat of the setback.

4 The defenders fall back to the Second Wall, which takes the Romans five days to breach. The defenders hold the broken wall for three more days despite Roman assaults.

JERUSALEM

AD 70

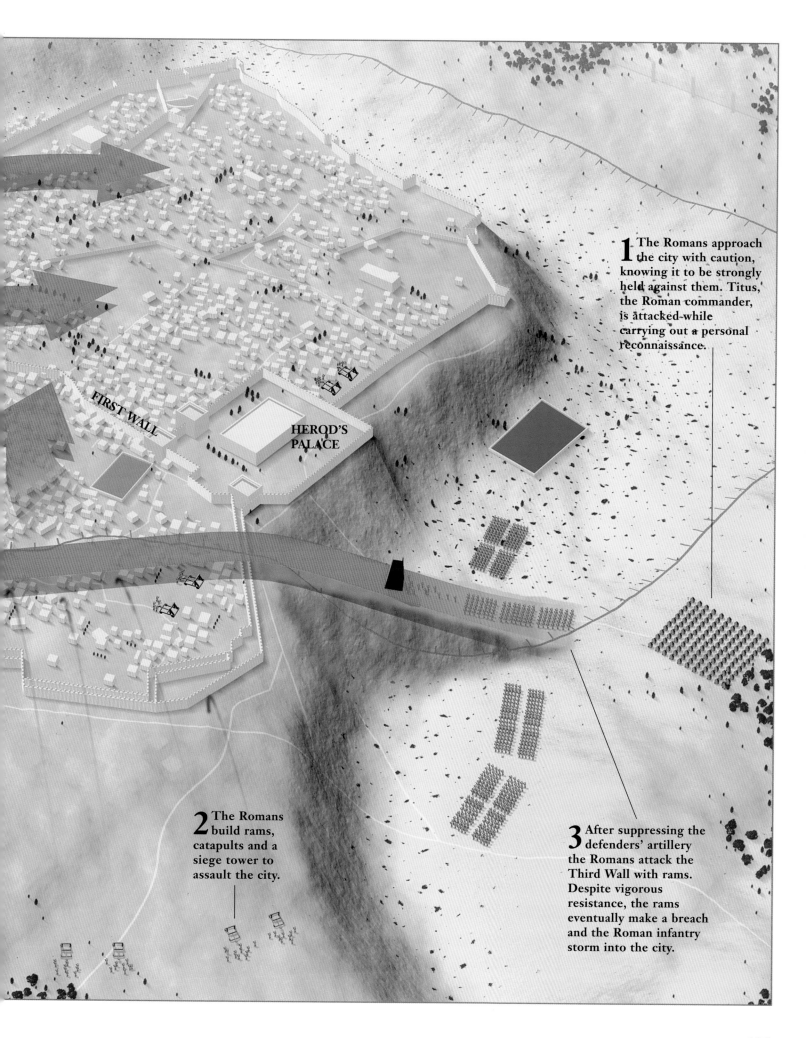

1 The Romans approach the city with caution, knowing it to be strongly held against them. Titus, the Roman commander, is attacked while carrying out a personal reconnaissance.

FIRST WALL

HEROD'S PALACE

2 The Romans build rams, catapults and a siege tower to assault the city.

3 After suppressing the defenders' artillery the Romans attack the Third Wall with rams. Despite vigorous resistance, the rams eventually make a breach and the Roman infantry storm into the city.

The tombs of Absalom and Zahariah in the Kidron Valley, Jerusalem. To the Jews, the occupation was just about bearable unless their holy places were threatened.

Roman soldiers move a wooden palisade into position. Essentially a mobile wall that gave cover from arrows, the palisade protected archers, miners or siege machines.

leader, as he had no heir. What followed became known as the Year of Four Emperors, as first one and then another contender emerged to seize the throne, only to be deposed and replaced.

The first two successors, Galba (AD 68–69) and Otho (AD 69), bribed their way to power and lasted a mere few months. The next was Vitellius (AD 69), Governor of Germania Inferior. He used force of arms in his bid for the throne. Vitellius came to Italy with the Rhine legions at his back and defeated the forces of Otho, who then committed suicide.

Vitellius reigned for just eight months before his forces were defeated by another military challenger, Vespasian, who had come from Judea to defeat Vitellius and storm Rome, thus establishing himself as emperor. One factor thought to have contributed to Vespasian's victory was a rumour heard by his legionaries to the effect that Vitellius intended to relocate them

to the dangerous Rhine frontier while sending his own supporters to the (normally) more convivial surroundings of the eastern Empire.

Vespasian turned out to be a strong and good Emperor, but the distraction caused by the civil war of AD 68–69 allowed the Jewish revolt to survive longer than it might otherwise have done.

Meanwhile, the Jews had their own internal troubles. The Zealots and other radical factions fought among themselves and murdered anyone they considered insufficiently rabid in their hatred of Rome. Fellow Jews killed every one of the leaders of the southern insurrection, along with anyone who seemed to be considering surrender. At times, the internal conflicts among the Jewish rebels amounted to civil war.

THE ROMANS AT JERUSALEM
By AD 70, there were three main factions in Jerusalem. Two were Zealot groups, the other loyal to the rebel leader Simon bar Giora. Their squabbles hampered the campaign against the Romans and resulted in the destruction of supplies. A measure of

cooperation was forced when the Roman army arrived at Jerusalem.

The Roman field commander was now Titus Flavius, who at 27 was somewhat young by the standards of Roman legates. He owed his position largely to the fact that Vespasian was his father, but he was both a skilled leader and a good fighter in personal combat. Titus had served with distinction early in the campaign, but the taking of Jerusalem was a greater challenge than any he had previously faced.

Titus had under his hand four legions plus supporting forces – more than his father had commanded in the early stages of the Judea campaign. Among these was the 12th Legion, which had been badly defeated earlier and was keen to redeem its reputation.

Titus's legions were below strength because of the campaign – disease, combat and the need to detach troops for security duty had all taken their toll – but they had support in the form of detachments from two inexperienced legions stationed in Egypt, as well as troops from Syria, in addition to auxiliaries and forces sent by friendly local rulers.

Titus commanded 30,000–40,000 troops, but Jerusalem was strongly held and well fortified. It was going to be a tough battle.

THE FORTRESS

Jerusalem was built on high ground, with two hills forming natural strong points. The Temple itself, surrounded by good, strong walls, was a formidable fortress. The defenders had worked to strengthen the city's defences – when they were not fighting among themselves – and were ready to defend it fanatically.

The Roman historian Tacitus states that there were 600,000 people in the city. The Jewish writer Josephus claims an even larger figure: as many as a million occupants. These figures seem very high, but Jerusalem was a large and populous city and a significant portion of its population took up arms to repel the Romans. However, Simon bar Giora's followers and the Zealots provided the main Jewish fighting forces: perhaps 23,000–24,000 men in total. They were well equipped, experienced and also highly motivated.

The city had grown up over many years, and its defences grew with it. Above the Kidron Valley lay the Upper and Lower halves of the old city. Herod's Palace and its towers dominated the area. Separating the old city from the new was the First Wall, which joined to the fortress-within-a-fortress that was the Great Temple. The Second Wall enclosed part of the New City, and all of it lay within the First Wall, which was the most recent, and weakest, of the city's defences.

THE INITIAL CLASHES

Titus's army approached its objective cautiously, with Titus undertaking a personal reconnaissance that was nearly his undoing, when his party came under attack from defenders who had sallied out of the city. Titus was not armoured for war and was cut off from most of his bodyguards. Titus responded with a reckless charge through his enemies and was able to escape the trap despite a hail of arrows launched in his direction.

The Roman force then set about establishing itself in position for a siege and eventual assault. There was much work to be done: a secure camp was necessary before any offensive operations could be carried

Believers on the Temple platform in Jerusalem at Passover. Seen here from the inside of the Temple, the tower known as Castle (or Fortress) Antonia was a powerful fortification that was eventually undermined and brought down by rams.

out. However, while the legions were thus engaged, a large force sallied out of the east side of the city and attacked them.

The attack was determined and very aggressive, and caught the Romans unawares. Some units fell back in disorder and others openly fled. Amid the chaos, Titus was able to rally some of his troops to form a shaky fighting line before leading his cavalry into the enemy flank. This broke the attack and sent the rebels back across the Kidron Valley, allowing the Romans to reorganize themselves.

When the fighting died down somewhat, Titus ordered part of his force to return to the work of establishing camp. The Jews had been waiting for this and so launched another vigorous attack. For a second time, the Romans were thrown back in disorder. Titus gathered to him every

Roman he could find and led a series of counterattacks in which he personally fought like a common trooper. Finally, the attack was beaten off and the Romans gained control of the situation.

Even though the siege was established, the defenders had no intention of being defeated easily. They tried various stratagems, including successfully luring a group of Roman soldiers close to the walls by offering to surrender. Many of the Romans were cut down in a hail of missiles. Titus was furious about the incident but was dissuaded from executing the survivors by entreaties from their comrades.

THE SIEGE

Titus decided that he would enter the city through the Third Wall. This would be a lengthy process, but one familiar to the

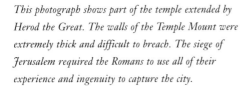

This photograph shows part of the temple extended by Herod the Great. The walls of the Temple Mount were extremely thick and difficult to breach. The siege of Jerusalem required the Romans to use all of their experience and ingenuity to capture the city.

veterans among the Roman troops. Covered by missile fire, the troops cleared ground around the wall and gathered timber, under constant fire from light siege engines – scorpions and *ballistae* – that the rebels had captured from the Roman garrison. The Romans, of course, replied with counter-battery fire from their own engines.

The Romans did not have it all their own way, but they gradually won the artillery duel even though the rebels quickly became skilled with their weapons. It was not, however, possible to breach the walls with artillery, so the more usual method of employing rams was undertaken.

Deploying rams necessitated the creation of three ramps up to the walls, a common undertaking in sieges of the period. Constructing the ramps was a costly business, but once they were complete, breaching the wall was a simple matter. The rules of war adhered to by the Romans indicated that until a ram struck the first blow against a city's wall, it was possible to surrender on decent terms, so the arrival of the engines at the wall was a decisive point in the siege.

Protected by the fire of artillery and archers, the rams began their work, to the dismay of the city's occupants. The defenders did what they could, shooting at the crews and sallying out to try to burn the engines. One attack would have succeeded but for the determined resistance of the inexperienced Egyptian legionaries.

THE STORMING OF JERUSALEM

After 15 days, a breach was created. Many of the defenders decided that the Third Wall was lost and fell back to the Second, but enough remained to put up some resistance as the storming parties entered the breach. A short fight resulted in a rout for the defenders, and the Romans were able to establish themselves in the city.

The Second Wall was defended with the same determination – and more desperation – than the Third. Groups sallied out from the wall to harass the attackers, and skirmishing in the streets of the new city became commonplace. The

rams were brought forward nonetheless, and after five days a breach was opened.

Titus advanced into the breach with a handpicked force of about 1000 men who, after initial light resistance, were heavily attacked. The Romans were repulsed and forced to fight through the streets to make their escape. The breach was held for another three days before being stormed a second time. Titus ordered the breach widened and garrisoned, and granted his troops a period of rest before the final assault. A parade was held and the troops were paid – always good for morale.

THE FIRST WALL

The First Wall was a strong fortification and determinedly held. Storming it was going to be a hard task, and Titus knew it. The key to the position was the Great Temple and, in particular, a tower built in its corner, known as the Fortress of Antonia. More siege ramps were built against this tower, and despite both counterattacks and missile fire, they were ready after 17 days.

However, the Jews had been busy during this time and had, in fact, dug mines under the siege ramps. No sooner were they completed than they were demolished by the deliberate collapse of the mine tunnels. This was followed by an attempt to storm the Roman camp, suggesting that the rebels still had plenty of fight in them.

The Romans were dismayed at this turn of events – so much so that some actually

Roman soldiers man a ballista. *Light siege weapons of this type could shoot fairly rapidly and suppress the defenders while larger engines worked to bring down a wall.*

At the siege of Jotapata (AD 67) in northern Israel, the Romans used a battering ram similar to the one illustrated here. Legionaries swung the ram using ropes, while a hide-covered canopy provided protection. Archers and catapults provided covering fire. Once the wall was breached, other legionaries stormed through the gap to take the city.

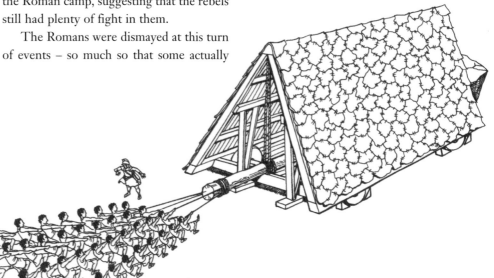

When Pompey stormed Jerusalem in 67 BC, he left the Temple intact. Not so this time; the Romans pillaged and destroyed the temple, killing many civilians who happened to be in the way (from a detail of a painting by Francesco Hayez, 1867).

joined the rebels inside the First Wall. Titus considered various options and decided to continue with the assault. His father needed a victory here to help consolidate his power, and Titus was determined to provide one. However, he resolved to proceed cautiously.

The siege work resumed, but now the Roman troops built their own fortification, a wall of circumvallation around the whole city. It was a major undertaking, but one that the Romans knew well how to complete. In only three days, they had thrown a ring of fortifications around the city, and completing it gave a sense of achievement that helped restore morale.

There were practical benefits to the wall, too. Food was getting short in the city, and the defences made it even harder for parties to slip out to forage. Work then began on another set of siege ramps. This took 21 days and was completed despite an attempt to sally out and destroy the works. It was repulsed and the rams began their work at last. The rams weakened the formidable Fortress of Antonia tower, and with its foundations undermined by the Zealots' own tunnels, it duly collapsed.

Although the breach created was wide, it was barricaded with a makeshift wall that proved to be a major obstacle. After an initial attempt at storming failed, a party of pickets succeeded in gaining the wall – apparently on their own initiative – during the night. One of this intrepid band was a trumpeter, and on hearing his call from the enemy position, Titus threw together a scratch assault force and attacked. A rather chaotic fight took place in the Temple Court, but the Romans made no further gains. A second assault was a little more successful, and the rubble of the tower was cleared to make access easier.

Now Titus formed an elite storming force of about 1000 men, which attacked during the night with initial success. However, the resistance quickly firmed up, leading to a life-and-death struggle that lasted the whole day. Several more days of combat were necessary before the Temple Court was secured.

THE TEMPLE FALLS

Titus did not want to destroy the Great Temple, but the stubborn defence by the rebels made damage inevitable. A period of bitter fighting ensued, in which the Jews were able to launch raids against the Roman camp. Some of them were fairly successful, but most were beaten off. Meantime, the Romans slowly ground their way through the temple, with even the cavalry fighting dismounted in support of the infantry.

Finally, the rebels held only the Inner Court, and this too was stormed. At some point in the close-quarters fighting, the Temple caught fire. Sections had already been burned, but this time the conflagration was general. Some efforts were made to fight the fire, but as the rebels were driven out, the victors were more interested in plunder than civil defence. Large numbers of civilians were also killed in the final storming of the Temple.

THE FINAL ASSAULT

Now, the only part of the city still in Jewish hands was the Old City, which the Romans had access to via the wrecked Temple. Refusing to negotiate, Titus ordered an assault and began building ramps once again. By the time they were ready, the defenders were starving and demoralized.

The final assault was something of an anti-climax, with most of the defenders scattering before the Romans could reach them. Several important Jewish leaders were captured and the rebellion more or less came to an end.

Titus paraded his troops and showered them with honours, then toured the region, holding various ceremonies and putting the seal on the re-conquest of Judea. Finally, he returned to Italy. Given recent history, there were some who anticipated that he might try to seize the throne. Instead, Titus and his father Vespasian conducted a joint Triumph in celebration of their victory in Judea. The high point of the event was the formal execution, by strangulation, of Simon bar Giora.

Titus commanded the Praetorian Guard and acted as a hatchet man for his father until, in due course, he became Emperor. His reign was short, but he was a just Emperor who was succeeded by his brother Domitian.

Roman troops advance into the Temple platform up a wide ramp built over a section of the outer wall. The remains of the Fortress of Antonia tower can be seen to the left of the ramp.

MASADA
AD 73–74

THE TALE OF MASADA HAS INSPIRED JEWS FOR NEARLY TWO THOUSAND YEARS. ALTHOUGH BEATEN IN THE FIELD, THE ZEALOTS REMAINED DEFIANT TO THE VERY END. VASTLY OUTNUMBERED, THEY TOOK REFUGE IN THEIR FORTRESS AND DEFENDED IT UNTIL DEFEAT WAS INEVITABLE. EVEN THEN, THEY TOOK THEIR OWN LIVES RATHER THAN SUBMIT TO ROME.

WHY DID IT HAPPEN?

WHO Around 1000 Jews (including non-combatants) led by Eleazar ben Ya'ir, opposed by around 7000 Roman troops from the 10th Legion and attached forces, under Lucius Flavius Silva, Procurator of Judea (AD 73–81).

WHAT Masada was virtually impregnable and well supplied, so the Romans undertook elaborate works of siege engineering to gain entry.

WHERE The fortress of Masada, on the Dead Sea coast in Israel.

WHEN AD 73–74.

WHY After the Jewish revolt of AD 66–72 was largely put down, the remaining Zealots were gradually mopped up. Those besieged at Masada represented their last significant force.

OUTCOME After lengthy preparations, the Romans were ready to storm the fortress. The defenders committed suicide rather than be taken.

Although the Jewish revolt of AD 66 was initially successful, it was quelled fairly quickly in the north. Roman politics and the struggle for the throne of the Empire distracted attention for a while, but by AD 70 the insurrection was effectively over. With the storming of Jerusalem and the fall of the Great Temple, only small pockets of resistance remained. However, these were extremely determined.

Foremost among the rebels were the Zealots, who were determined to use any and all means to resist Rome and free the Jewish people from occupation. Although the spiritual heart of the nation had been taken and many of their leaders were dead,

the Zealots and other factions hostile to Rome still held out in some places.

Minor pockets of resistance existed here and there, but these were easy enough for the experienced Roman troops to mop up. Even the fortresses of Herodium and Machaerus were quickly reduced. Here and there, small bands of Zealots still made a nuisance of themselves but the occupation was re-established and the province once more firmly under control.

Yet, even while the bureaucrats were calculating the back taxes that had not been collected during the rebellion, one fortress still held out against the Romans. This was Masada, a fortification built on a formidable

First built in the second century BC, the fortress of Machaerus was rebuilt and restored by King Herod the Great. It fell quickly to the Romans during the mopping-up operations after the capture of Jerusalem in AD 70.

natural obstacle near the Dead Sea coast. Masada had been captured by the Zealots early in the rebellion and was now their final refuge. Almost a thousand people were within the fortifications, though many of them were women and children.

Some accounts suggest that the defenders of Masada were Sicarii, a splinter group of Zealots whom even other Zealots considered extreme. The fanaticism of the defenders seems to uphold this view. Certainly, those holding the fortress would not submit, even though their cause was entirely lost. The rebellion had been crushed and the rest of Judea was under Roman control once more, yet the handful of fanatics based at Masada continued to carry out harassing raids in the surrounding countryside.

Although Rome had achieved near-total victory and had, to all intents and purposes, put down the rebellion, this was not enough for the Emperor. Total victory was needed, perhaps as an indication to other potential rebels that opposition to Rome would be crushed utterly. Thus Masada must be wrested back from the Zealots.

The task fell to Lucius Flavius Silva, newly appointed Procurator of Judea. Although the forces ranged against him were not great, the fortress itself was virtually impossible to take. Built by Herod the Great a century before, Masada (which simply means 'fortress' in Hebrew) was intended as a royal stronghold. Herod was not a popular king, having been appointed by the Roman invaders. He felt that the time might come when he needed an unconquerable refuge.

THE FORTRESS OF MASADA

Masada stood atop a natural rock outcrop some 50m (164ft) above sea level. This put it 450m (1476ft) above the Dead Sea, the lowest area of land on Earth, to the east. To the west, the drop was 100m (328ft), and there was no easy approach from any direction. Only three paths led to the top of the plateau, and these were difficult even for those climbing unopposed.

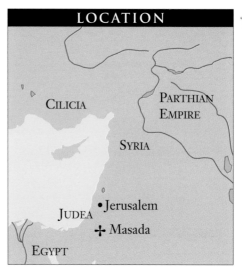

The fortress of Masada held out even after the rebellion had been put down elsewhere. As a final refuge, it was as unassailable as the convictions of the fanatics that held it.

ROMAN LEGIONARIES

The primary weapon of the legionary was his deadly sword, used from behind the protection of his shield. Enemies were softened up before a charge, or their charges were broken up, by massed volleys of pila, *or javelins. The* pilum *was a 'fire' weapon used to weaken the enemy so that the 'shock' effect of the legionary assault could more easily shatter his formations and drive him from the field. The combination of fire and shock has been a fundamental concept in successful tactics for centuries, and the Romans had it down to an art.*

MASADA

This aerial view gives an idea of just how formidable the site of Masada was even before the fortress was built atop it. With its own water supply, Masada could hold out for a long time.

These impressive natural defences were augmented by the construction of a wall around the edge of the plateau, almost 1500m (4921ft) long and 4m (13ft) wide. A heavily fortified gate guarded the top of each of the paths and elsewhere there were towers.

Within the walls were homes for the population and the palace built for Herod the Great. All buildings had thick walls constructed with blocks of stone faced with plaster, mainly to keep out the heat. More importantly, the fortress had its own water supply. Rock cisterns were cut into the mountaintop and filled during the winter rains. They were large enough to last a very long time, and the storehouses contained provisions for a similar period.

The Zealots took Masada early in the revolt, probably by stealth and surprise; they could not otherwise have gained control of such a potent fortress. As the last stronghold against Rome, it was a symbol that the rebellion was not quite defeated. To take it, the Romans would not have the advantage of surprise, and they thus faced a daunting task.

THE ROMANS RETURN

Flavius Silva had under his command the 10th Legion plus its attached auxiliary units – a total of about 7000 soldiers. These were experienced troops who had fought throughout the long Judean revolt. During the siege of Jerusalem, the legion became noted for the skilled use of its siege engines. And once that city was stormed, the 10th Legion went on to capture Herodium and Machaerus.

Opposite: A spectacular view from the North Palace at Masada. The fortress was built by King Herod the Great, who worried that some day his people might turn on him, and spared no expense in preparing his bolt-hole.

MASADA

AD 73–74

4 While Roman artillery keeps the defenders' heads down, the ram inside the siege tower destroys part of the western wall.

2 The Romans build a series of eight camps and a wall connecting them, in an attempt to starve the defenders out.

3 The Romans now decide to take Masada by assault. A ramp of wood, sand and stone is built for the wood and metal siege tower to be pushed up.

5 The defenders build an inner wall, but that too is breached. In despair, all but a handful commit suicide.

1 This fortress had been captured by stealth by the Jews in AD 66. Its location and fortifications made it seem impregnable.

MASADA

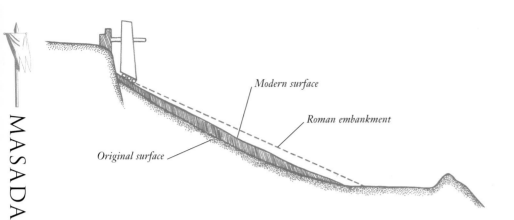

Modern surface

Roman embankment

Original surface

The Romans constructed their siege embankment on an existing geological spur that sloped up to the fortress. Experts have suggested that up to 20m (60ft) would have had to be added to create a surface raised enough and smooth enough for the Romans to move their siege towers up to the fortress's wall.

Arriving at the base of the plateau of Masada, Lucius Flavius Silva called upon the defenders to surrender. They refused to do so, which meant that the fortress would have to be taken. Neither deception nor stealth was possible, and a sudden assault impracticable. Masada would have to be taken by methodical siege operations.

This suited the Romans. They were experienced at this sort of thing, and though

Masada was even more formidable than Jerusalem, they had no doubts that they could succeed.

With the rest of the country more or less pacified, there were no threats to the Roman supply lines or any chance of relief for the defenders. Surrender was not much of an option, given that the Romans would certainly crucify them all as a warning to others, and nor could they escape. All that was left was proud defiance.

ROMAN PREPARATIONS

The Romans had time on their side and could afford to do everything properly. The first task was to make themselves secure. To this end, the usual fortified camp was augmented by the construction of a wall of circumvallation. This was a lengthy undertaking, and some sources claim that large numbers of Jewish slaves were used to assist with the work. Eventually, it was completed, and at this point any attempt by

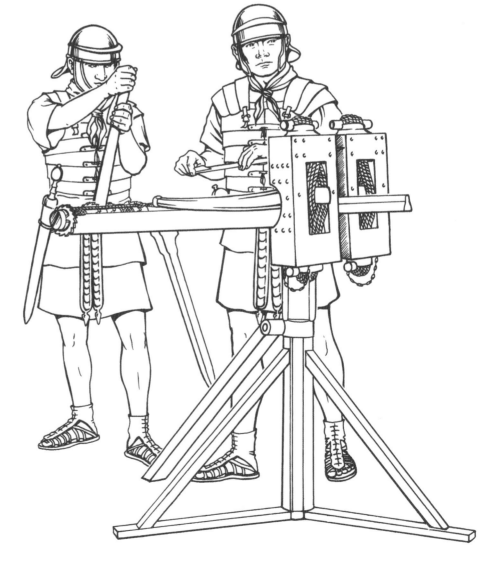

Mobile siege weapons such as this catapult were used as powerful anti-personnel weapons. They could be set up to cover a section of the defences from longer range than archery, and would defeat most protection.

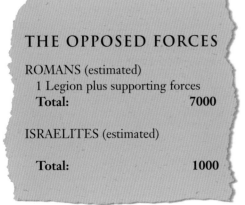

THE OPPOSED FORCES

ROMANS (estimated)
1 Legion plus supporting forces
Total: 7000

ISRAELITES (estimated)

Total: 1000

the defenders to escape or to sally out and attack the besieging army would be no more than an exercise in futility.

Next, the Romans faced another challenge. Masada lay on the edge of the Judean Desert, so how would they obtain supplies for a lengthy siege? Plentiful slaves and a successful pacification of the countryside proved to be the answer, leaving the Romans needing only to figure out a way to break a fortress located 100m (328ft) above their heads. They set about this task just as they had done at Jerusalem, albeit on a larger scale.

THE SIEGE WORKS

The key to taking Masada was the construction of a gigantic siege ramp. This was built on a foundation of crushed rocks with packed earth atop it. It was 100m (328ft) high at its highest point, and represented a stupendous undertaking. The ramp was begun in the autumn of AD 73 and completed the following spring.

Some sources claim that Jewish slaves were used in the construction of the ramp, and that the defenders were reluctant to kill them. However, it is more likely that the legionaries themselves built the ramp. They were used to siege work and perhaps unwilling to trust their lives to a ramp constructed by those who hated them. Certainly, the average Roman soldier was fit and no stranger to spade work. Construction would be faster and more efficient with such men doing the work.

The ramp permitted a siege tower to be pushed up to the walls. This engine was small compared to the giant ramp, but was itself no mean feat of engineering. At 30m (98ft) high, it contained a massive battering ram as well as fighting positions for troops to protect it. Once it reached the wall, creating a breach did not take long.

As the ram did its work, it was covered by missile fire from the legion's siege engines. These were not heavy enough to breach the wall but were quite capable of sweeping away the defenders from its top, allowing the ram to do its work unmolested.

THE LAST STAND

The Zealots did what they could to prevent the Romans gaining entry to the fortress.

With plenty of time to see which wall would be attacked, they set about constructing a second line of defence inside the fortress. This consisted of a wall improvised from heavy wooden beams over which earth was piled.

When at last the Romans gained entry through the breach they had made, they were faced with this final obstacle, which was defended by men who had absolutely nothing left to lose and nowhere to run. The only written account of the action

Blocks from a ruined stone column at Masada. Not only were the outer walls a formidable obstacle, most of the internal architecture was very solidly built, too.

MASADA

MASADA

Opposite: The remains of a Roman camp at Masada. Security of the legion's supplies and resting personnel was of paramount importance, especially during a siege operation.

makes no mention of fighting within the fortress, but it is obvious from the measures taken to remove it that the improvised inner wall was a considerable obstacle.

Flavius decided that the wall must be removed if Masada were to be taken, and ordered his men to burn it. This was something of a risky undertaking since the fire might easily have spread to the Roman siege engines, although by then their work was done.

The heavy wooden beams cannot have burned easily, and it is very unlikely that the defenders did not attempt to interfere with the operation, but eventually the task was completed and the makeshift wall was well ablaze. For a time, it seemed that the fire would indeed consume the siege machines, but the wind shifted and the defenders' work was consumed instead. The legionaries fell back to allow the flames to do their work.

A FINAL ACT OF DEFIANCE

Eleazar ben Ya'ir addressed his followers for the last time. It was obvious that they were doomed. Soon, the fortress would be stormed and everyone in it put to the sword. Alternatively, if they were captured, they would be crucified or otherwise done to death in a gruesome manner to demonstrate the futility of challenging Rome. The Zealots were not prepared to give victory to the Romans in this manner, nor to allow such a fate to fall upon their wives and children, who sheltered within the fortress.

There was only one alternative: a suicide pact. Drawing lots, they selected ten of their number to kill all the rest, and one of the ten to kill the others. With that done, the last man alive in Masada would slay himself rather than submit to Rome. They chose this method since their religion frowned upon suicide; this way, only one of the Zealots actually killed himself.

Before the mass suicide was enacted, Eleazar ben Ya'ir also gave orders for as much of the fortress as possible to be set on fire, with the exception of the storehouses. He wanted the Romans to see that the place was still well provisioned and that hunger had not defeated the defenders. This done, the final act of defiance was carried out.

When the first Roman soldiers cleared the remains of the inner wall, they were confronted with the results. Apart from two women and five children who had hidden away, there were no survivors left in Masada. There was no final assault, no surrender and not much of a victory. True, the last of the rebels had been destroyed and there could be no more raids out of Masada against the occupying forces, but neither was there great glory to be had here.

AFTERMATH

The fall of Masada was the final end of the Jewish Revolt, though rebellious sentiment still existed among the Jews. The province of Judea was sufficiently troubled that the Emperor made reference to the 'interminable tendency of the Jews to revolution', and severe measures were taken at times to prevent further insurrection.

The Romans are known to have built ballistae *large enough to shoot stones weighing 26kg (80lb). According to the chronicler Josephus, such a machine was used at the siege of Jotapata in* AD 67. *Similar siege weapons may have been used at Masada.*

These were not always successful. The province of Judea revolted again in AD 132–135, and once more the Roman 10th Legion was involved in putting down the rebellion. Jerusalem was stormed a second time, and once more a last fortress held out (this time it was Betar) after the rebellion was more or less crushed. A second legion was assigned to the province to help keep order. This unusually heavy concentration of troops indicates just how hard the Romans found it to keep their Jewish subjects down.

Masada was and remains a symbol of the Jewish spirit of defiance. Indeed, nearly two thousand years later, Israeli soldiers take an oath that 'Masada shall never fall again'. The Roman Empire is long gone, but the spirit of those who opposed it to the death lingers on.

BIBLIOGRAPHY

Ben-Sasson, Hayim. *A History of the Jewish People*. Cambridge, Massachusetts: Harvard University Press, 1985.

Bright, John. *A History of Israel*. London: SCM Press Ltd, 1960.

Carey, Brian Todd. *Warfare in the Ancient World*. Barnsley, UK: Pen and Sword, 2006.

Carmen, John. *Ancient Warfare*. London: Sutton Publishing, 2004.

Carson, David C. *Maccabee*. Parker, Colorado: Outskirts Press, 2007.

Edersheim, Alfred. *Bible History: Old Testament*. Peabody, Massachusetts: Hendrickson Publishers, 1995.

Free, Joseph P. and Howard F. Vos. *Archaeology and Bible History*. Grand Rapids, Michigan: Zondervan, 1992.

Fuller, J.F.C. *The Generalship of Alexander the Great*. New York: Da Capo Press, 1960.

Gabriel, Richard A. *The Military History of Ancient Israel*. Westport, Connecticut: Praeger, 2003.

Gichon, Mordechai and Chaim Herzog. *Battles of the Bible*. New York: Barnes & Noble, 2006.

Gilbert, Martin. *Atlas of the Arab-Israeli Conflict*. Oxford: Oxford University Press, 1993.

Goldsworthy, Adrian. *In the Name of Rome*. London: Wiedenfield & Nicholson, 2003.

Goodman, Martin. *Rome and Jerusalem*. London: Penguin Books Ltd, 2007.

Graetz, Heinrich. *History of the Jews* (Volume I). Philadelphia: The Jewish Publication Society of America, 1891.

Grant, Michael. *The History of Ancient Israel*. New York: Scribner, 1984.

Hackett, John, ed. *Warfare in the Ancient World*. New York: Facts on File, 1989.

Healy, Mark. *The Ancient Assyrians*. Oxford: Osprey, 1991.

Keller, Werner. *The Bible as History*. New York: William Morrow and Company, Inc., 1981.

Kern, Paul. *Ancient Siege Warfare*. Bloomington: Indiana University Press, 1999.

Kossoff, David. *The Voices Of Masada*. London: Valentine Mitchell & Co Ltd, 1973.

Longstreth, Edward. Decisive *Battles of the Bible*. Philadelphia: Lippincott, 1962.

Price, Jonathan J. *Jerusalem under Siege*. Leiden: Brill, 1992.

Price, Randall. *The Stones Cry Out: How Archaeology Reveals the Truth of the Bible*. Eugene, Oregon: Harvest House Publishers, 1997.

Saggs, H.W.F. *The Might that was Assyria*. London: Sidgwick and Jackson, 1984.

Schomp, Virginia. *Ancient Mesopotamia: the Sumerians, Babylonians, and Assyrians*. London: Franklin Watts, 2005.

Shaw, Ian. *Oxford History of Ancient Egypt*. New York: Oxford University Press, 2004.

Ussishkin, David. *The Conquest of Lachish by Sennacherib*. Tel Aviv: Tel Aviv University Press, 1982.

Yadin, Yigael. *The Art of Warfare in Biblical Lands* (two volumes). New York: McGraw Hill, 1963.

INDEX

Page numbers in *italics* refer to illustrations; those in **bold** type refer to information displays with maps, illustrations and text. Abbreviations are as follows: (B) – battle; (S) – siege.

PICTURE AND ILLUSTRATION CREDITS

All maps and black-and-white line artworks produced by **JB Illustrations**.

AKG-Images: 7 (Erich Lessing), 9 (Erich Lessing), 18 (Erich Lessing), 28 (Herve Champollion), 30/1, 37, 48, 62 (Erich Lessing), 74 (Erich Lessing), 87, 100 (Erich Lessing), 102t (Erich Lessing), 102b (Erich Lessing), 107 (Erich Lessing), 111b (Erich Lessing), 118l (Erich Lessing), 120/1 (Gerard Degeorge), 132, 142 (Peter Connolly), 149r (Peter Connolly), 158/9, 164, 173 (Erich Lessing), 176/7, 183 (Erich Lessing), 190 (Erich Lessing), 194 (Erich Lessing), 201 (Peter Connolly), 202 (Erich Lessing), 204 (Cameraphoto), 205 (Peter Connolly), 209 (Robert O'Dea), 214 (Erich Lessing)

Amber Books: 6, 17b, 18

Ancient Art & Architecture Collection: 128t (Ronald Sheridan), 130 (Ronald Sheridan)

Bridgeman Art Library: 27 (Pierpont Morgan Library), 44b, 80/1 (Bible Society), 83 (Look and Learn), 125 (The British Museum)

Corbis: 10 (Fred de Noyelle), 13 (Ruggero Vanni), 14/5 (Richard T. Nowitz), 15 (Bettmann), 34 (Gianni Dagli Orti), 38 (William Holman Hunt), 40 (Shai Ginott), 41 (Richard T. Nowitz), 46 (Philip de Bay), 53 (Bettmann), 56 (Richard T. Nowitz), 63 (Ali Meyer), 64 (Felix Bonfils), 72 (Francis G. Mayer), 73 (Arte & Immagini srl), 77 (Richard T. Nowitz), 81 (Gianni Dagli Orti), 86 (David Rubinger), 92/3 (Philip de Bay), 101 (Charles & Josette Lenars), 104 (Charles & Josette Lenars), 111t (Charles & Josette Lenars), 114/5 (Gianni Dagli Orti), 122 (Vanni Archive), 128b (Bettmann), 129 (Ruggero Vanni), 131 (Christie's Images), 134 (Bettmann), 138t (Philip de Bay), 139 (Adam Woolfitt), 140 (Hanan Isachar), 145b (Krause, Johansen), 150t (Alfredo Dagli Orti), 166 (Michael Nicholson), 167 (Araldo de Luca), 172t (Bettmann), 172b (Philip de Bay), 187 (Bettmann), 196 (Burstein Collection), 206 (Harvey Lloyd), 208 (Richard T. Nowitz), 213 (Charles Lenars)

De Agostini: 150b, 151, 174

Getty Images: 12 (Hulton Archive), 45 (Imagno), 67 (Hulton Archive), 91 (Hulton Archive), 94 (Hulton Archive), 103 (Imagno), 121 (Hulton Archive), 200t (Alistair Duncan)

Heritage Image Partnership: 21 (The Print Collector), 35 (CM Dixon), 44t (The Print Collector), 92 (The Print Collector), 118r (The British Museum), 152 (The Print Collector), 163 (The Print Collector)

Mary Evans Picture Library: 24, 24/5, 26, 36, 52, 57, 60t, 66/7, 82, 84, 106, 135, 141, 154, 160, 161, 176, 180/1, 182, 184, 192, 193

Photos12: 16 (Oronoz), 54 (Oronoz), 70 (Oronoz), 71 (Oronoz), 96/7 (Oronoz), 197 (ARJ)